Spiritual, But Not Religious

Spiritual, But Not Religious

Understanding Unchurched America

Robert C. Fuller

OXFORD

UNIVERSITY PRESS

2001

OXFORD
UNIVERSITY PRESS

Oxford   New York
Athens   Auckland   Bangkok   Bogotá   Buenos Aires
Cape Town   Chennai   Dar es Salaam   Delhi   Florence
Hong Kong   Istanbul   Karachi   Kolkata   Kuala Lumpur
Madrid   Melbourne   Mexico City   Mumbai   Nairobi
Paris   São Paulo   Shanghai   Singapore   Taipei
Tokyo   Toronto   Warsaw

and associated companies in
Berlin   Ibadan

Library of Congress Cataloging-in-Publication Data
Fuller, Robert C., 1952–
Spiritual, but not religious : understanding unchurched
America / Robert C. Fuller.
p.   cm.
Includes bibliographical references and index.
ISBN 0–19–514680–8
1. Non church-affiliated people—United States.
2. Spirituality—United States.
3. United States—Religion.
I. Title.
BR526.F58 2001
200ʹ.973—dc21   2001032149

Book design and typesetting by
Glen R.J. Mules, New Rochelle, NY

1 3 5 7 9 8 6 4 2
Printed in the United States of America
on acid-free paper

Contents

Spiritual, But Not Religious

Unchurched Spirituality
An Introduction

The United States is arguably the most religious nation on earth. Public opinion polls indicate that more than 90 percent of all Americans believe in some kind of Higher Power. Sixty-two percent belong to a church or synagogue.[1] Most of us tend to think about religion almost exclusively in terms of these religious organizations. Yet this is hardly the whole picture. Almost 40 percent of Americans have no connection with organized religion. Despite their unchurched status, however, most nonetheless claim to be strongly religious or spiritual on a personal level. Any attempt to understand contemporary American spirituality must therefore look well beyond the boundaries of the nation's churches.

The purpose of this book is to explore the history and present status of unchurched religion in the United States. This is not an easy task. It is one thing to acknowledge the existence of unchurched religion. To define, categorize, and understand it is considerably more difficult. We can with some precision determine how many people regularly attend church and how many almost never do. But many individuals fall somewhere in between. To complicate matters, some church attenders are very liberal in their beliefs and find themselves attracted to a wide variety of unorthodox ideas and practices. Meanwhile, many who don't attend church continue to draw on their religious backgrounds when they find themselves praying or when they construct stories about their own personal spiritual journeys. One sociological study documented how freely Americans combine traditional and nontraditional elements in their personal spiritual practice.[2] Among those interviewed in this study was a thirty-eight-year-old teacher who was raised Roman Catholic but now attends Mass only a few times a year. Despite her spotty church attendance, she considers herself a deeply spiritual person. She daily sets aside at least an hour for meditation. She has a home altar that symbolizes her personal spiritual beliefs. On this altar are eighteen candles, an amulet attached to a photo of her grandmother, amethyst crystals used in healing meditations, oriental incense, a Tibetan prayer bell, a representation of the Virgin of Guadalupe, and some other traditional Catholic items. This one woman's eclectic approach to personal spirituality conveys how difficult it is to define or categorize unchurched spirituality. Although we know that between 38 to 40 percent of the adult population in the United States have no formal religious affiliation, we have much to learn about the role of unchurched religion in Americans' personal spiritual lives.

Three Types of Unchurched Americans

We must begin by recognizing that the unchurched aren't all alike.[3] Some aren't religious at all. About one in every seven Americans is completely indifferent to religion. We often call these people "secular humanists" because they reject supernatural understandings of the world and instead rely solely on reason and common sense. There have doubtless been nonbelievers in every era of human history. Yet there is reason to believe that the social and intellectual forces shaping modern life have combined to make religion increasingly less relevant to the lives of many educated people. One such force has been the ascendency of science as a way of understanding our world. Scientific education makes it difficult for some people to believe in the supernatural or accept the "blind faith" that religion often requires.

Many of us have also been introduced to the results of modern biblical scholarship that illuminates the human authorship of the Bible
(as opposed to accepting it as divinely revealed). And, too, most educated people are aware of the role that cultural conditioning plays in
shaping our beliefs and attitudes. These modern intellectual forces
have prompted many to become skeptical of religious doctrines that
claim absolute truth. This secularization process is clearly evident in
Western Europe where most educated persons consider themselves
secular and less than 10 percent of the population regularly attend
church. Far fewer Americans are this secular. Survey results vary depending on just how this category is described and how comfortable
respondents feel about voicing their dissatisfaction with religion to a
stranger. It is probably safe to assume that somewhere between 8 and
15 percent of the total population can be considered wholly nonreligious.[4] Because these people consider themselves neither religious
nor spiritual, they are outside the scope of this book.

A second group of unchurched Americans consists of those whose
relationships with organized religion are ambiguous. This group
would include both those who belong to a church but rarely attend
and those who often attend church but choose not to join. About 10
percent of the population attend church more than six times per year
but are not members of any church. Some of them may refrain from
joining a religious organization even though they believe in its basic
teachings. Indeed, it is possible that some unchurched persons are actually more religious than many of those who do belong to churches.
They may, for example, be put off by what they see as the hypocrisy of
many church members or be too upset over a particular church pol-
icy (or clergy member) to feel like affiliating. Still others may have
moved to a different part of the country and have not made the kind
of friendships that would make church membership comfortable for
them. Of course, others in this group may be only marginally religious, attending only on special holidays. Then there are those who
sustain nominal membership in a church but attend less than six
times per year. Although they are usually counted among the
churched, many don't really believe the churches' teachings. They
might be motivated to continue such marginal connection with a
church due to their family background, out of concern with social
standing, or simply because they are timid about making a final break
from religion.[5] Perhaps half of those with ambiguous relationships to

organized religion should actually be considered as belonging to the next group, which will be the focus of this book.

There is a third group of unchurched people. Up to 21 percent of all Americans are unaffiliated with a church, but should nonetheless be considered religious in some broad sense of the term. The largest group of the unchurched, then, is concerned with spiritual issues but choose to pursue them outside the context of a formal religious organization. These Americans can be described as "spiritual, but not religious." To be sure, those in this category are not uniformly interested in personal spirituality. Some are strongly influenced by modern secular thought and have only mild spiritual impulses. Others, however, are deeply interested in pursuing spiritual growth. Wade Clark Roof has estimated that somewhere between 9 and 19 percent of the total adult population in the United States are "highly active seekers, or people for whom spiritual and metaphysical concerns are a driving force."[6] These seekers, although unchurched, are much more concerned with spiritual development than the vast majority of churchgoers. They view their lives as spiritual journeys, hoping to make new discoveries and gain new insights on an almost daily basis. Religion isn't a fixed thing for them. They fully expect to change their religious beliefs regularly. Importantly, the terms they adopt in their effort to understand such things as the nature of God, the essence of the human soul, and the practices that promote spiritual growth are almost all drawn from spiritual philosophies outside of our dominant religious institutions.

It has become increasingly common for such people to describe themselves as "spiritual" rather than "religious." They feel a tension between their personal spirituality and membership in a conventional religious organization. Most of them value curiosity, intellectual freedom, and an experimental approach to religion. They often find established religious institutions stifling. Many go so far as to view organized religion as the major enemy of authentic spirituality. Genuine spirituality, they believe, has to do with personal efforts to achieve greater harmony with the sacred. For them spirituality has to do with private reflection and private experience—not public ritual. Those who are "spiritual, but not religious" tend to agree with psychologist Abraham Maslow's belief that there is a potential antagonism between the private realm of religious experience and the public realm of formal religious practices. Maslow warned of the threat to vital spirituality "when people lose or forget the subjectively religious experience, and redefine religion as a set of habits, behaviors, dogmas, forms ... at the extreme [this causes spirituality to become] entirely legalistic and bureaucratic, conventional, empty, and in the true meaning of the word, antireligious."[7] This idea became widespread during the last few decades of the twentieth century. One survey showed that as much as 54 percent of the population has come to believe "that churches and synagogues have lost the real spiritual part of religion." One out of every three adults interviewed in this survey endorsed the still more radical conclusion that "people have God within them, so churches aren't really necessary."[8]

What It Means to be Spiritual, But Not Religious

A large number of Americans identify themselves as "spiritual, but not religious." It is likely that perhaps one in every five persons (roughly half of all the unchurched) could describe themselves in this way.[9] This phrase probably means different things to different people. The confusion stems from the fact that the words "spiritual" and "religious" are really synonyms. Both connote belief in a Higher Power of some kind. Both also imply a desire to connect, or enter into a more intense relationship, with this Higher Power. And, finally, both connote interest in rituals, practices, and daily moral behaviors that foster such a connection or relationship.

Before the twentieth century the terms religious and spiritual were used more or less interchangeably. But a number of modern intellectual and cultural forces have accentuated differences between the "private" and "public" spheres of life. The increasing prestige of the sciences, the insights of modern biblical scholarship, and greater awareness of cultural relativism all made it more difficult for educated Americans to sustain unqualified loyalty to traditional religious institutions. Many began to associate genuine faith with the "private" realm of personal experience rather than the "public" realm of institutions, creeds, and rituals. The word *spiritual* gradually came to be associated with the private realm of thought and experience while the word *religious* came to be connected with the public realm of membership in religious institutions, participation in formal rituals, and adherence to official denominational doctrines.

A group of social scientists studied 346 people representing a wide range of religious backgrounds in an attempt to clarify what is implied when individuals describe themselves as "spiritual, but not religious." Religiousness, they found, was associated with higher levels of church attendance and commitment to orthodox beliefs.[10] Spirituality, in contrast, was associated with higher levels of interest in mysticism, experimentation with unorthodox beliefs and practices, and negative feelings toward both clergy and churches. Most respondents in their study tried to integrate elements of religiousness and spirituality. Yet 19 percent of their sample constituted a separate category best described as "spiritual, not religious." Compared with those who connected interest in private spirituality with membership in a public religious group, the "spiritual, but not religious" group was

> less likely to evaluate religiousness positively, less likely to engage in traditional forms of worship such as church attendance and prayer, less likely to engage in group experiences related to spiritual growth, more likely to be agnostic, more likely to characterize religiousness and spirituality as different and nonoverlapping concepts, more likely to hold nontraditional "new age" beliefs, and more likely to have had mystical experiences.[11]

Those who see themselves as "spiritual, but not religious" reject traditional organized religion as the sole—or even the most valuable—means of furthering their spiritual growth. Many have had negative experiences with churches or church leaders. For example, they may have perceived church leaders as more concerned with building an organization than promoting spirituality, as hypocritical, or as narrow-minded. Some may have experienced various forms of emotional or even sexual abuse. Forsaking formal religious organizations, these people have instead embraced an individualized spirituality that includes picking and choosing from a wide range of alternative religious philosophies. They typically view spirituality as a journey intimately linked with the pursuit of personal growth or development. A woman who joined a meditation center after going through a divorce and experiencing low self-esteem offers an excellent example. All she originally sought was a way to lose weight and get her life back on track. The Eastern religious philosophy that accompanied the meditation exercises was of little or no interest to her. Yet she received so many benefits from this initial exposure to alternative spiritual practice that she began experimenting with other systems including vegetarianism, mandalas, incense, breathing practices, and crystals. When interviewed nine years later by sociologist Meredith McGuire, this woman reported that she was still "just beginning to grow" and she was continuing to shop around for new spiritual insights. McGuire found that many spiritual seekers use the "journey" image to describe a weekend workshop or retreat—the modern equivalents of religious pilgrimages. The fact that most seekers dabble or experiment rather than making once-and-forever commitments is in McGuire's opinion "particularly apt for late modern societies with their high degrees of pluralism, mobility and temporally limited social ties, communications, and voluntarism."[12]

Finally, we also know a few things about today's unchurched seekers as a group.[13] They are more likely than other Americans to have a college education, to belong to a white-collar profession, to be liberal in their political views, to have parents who attended church less frequently, and to be more independent in the sense of having weaker social relationships. Quantitative data about how those who are "spiritual, but not religious" differ socially and economically from their churched counterparts is helpful. But it is difficult to move to a more qualitative understanding. We don't fully understand how unchurched Americans assemble various bits and pieces of spiritual philosophy into a meaningful whole. We are even further from understanding how to compare the overall spirituality of unchurched persons with that of those who belong to religious institutions.

Putting Unchurched Spirituality in Historical and Cultural Contexts

An important first step toward understanding unchurched spirituality is to realize that it has its own traditions and recurring themes. Surprisingly, few scholars or journalists have been interested in providing a broad overview of America's nonecclesial religious history. There have, however, been some excellent studies of a closely related topic—popular religion.[14] Indeed, a great deal of the religiosity I link with America's unchurched spiritual traditions can surely be subsumed under this heading. But the category of popular religion is far broader than what I mean by unchurched spirituality. Popular religion comprises religious beliefs and practices that, while not officially sanctioned by church authorities, are nonetheless part of everyday piety. Examples of popular religion include athletes praying on the playing field, the use of artifacts associated with Catholic saints to obtain prosperity, or traditions connected with family celebrations of Hannukah or Christmas. Most kinds of popular religiosity are in some way connected with formal religious institutions and are thought of by laypersons as acts of piety consistent with these traditions. In contrast, unchurched spirituality consists of beliefs and practices that originate wholly outside our dominant religious institutions. It is a distinct category and needs to be distinguished from "unofficial" beliefs and practices that laypersons nonetheless associate with the practice of organized religion.

It is also important to distinguish unchurched spirituality from secular interests. It is not sufficient for beliefs or practices to function *like* a religion for us to consider them spiritual. Many secular activities meet some of the social and psychological needs often associated with religion (providing a sense of meaning, fostering inner satisfaction, building community). Some people find that membership in a bowling league or service organization provides a total sense of meaning, identity, and purpose. Although such secular activities may function like religion, they lack a distinctively spiritual quality. The psychologist William James developed helpful criteria for distinguishing between a spiritual and a secular orientation to life. In James's view, spirituality consists of attitudes, ideas, lifestyles, and specific practices based upon a conviction (1) that the visible world is part of a more spiritual universe from which it draws its chief significance, and (2) that union or harmonious relation with this "spiritual more" is our true end.[15]

These criteria help us eliminate many secular interests and activities that can become all-absorbing yet lack any concern with a larger reality. More important, these criteria can help us identify beliefs and actions that are distinctively spiritual, even when they have no overt connection with organized religion. Spirituality exists wherever we struggle with the issue of how our lives fit into the greater cosmic scheme of things. This is true even when our questions never give way to specific answers or give rise to specific practices such as prayer or meditation. We encounter spiritual issues every time we wonder where the universe comes from, why we are here, or what happens when we die. We also become spiritual when we become moved by values such as beauty, love, or creativity that seem to reveal a meaning or power beyond our visible world. An idea or practice is "spiritual" when it reveals our personal desire to establish a felt-relationship with the deepest meanings or powers governing life.

Spirituality, then, pertains to silent reflection or coffeehouse conversations as much as it does to what transpires during a formal worship service. People find spiritual inspiration not just in sermons, but also in books and seminars about humanity's creative potentials. A great deal of modern spirituality exists outside religious institutions, and even church members now self-consciously supplement their church's teachings by "consuming" books, articles, or lectures that are decidedly nontheological. Indeed, recent research indicates that a sizable percentage of church members have little loyalty to their churches' theological traditions.[16] Put differently, many church members have a great deal in common with those who are "spiritual, but not religious." As Charles Lippy observes,

> While many persons will become involved with a formal religious institution at least while they are rearing children, most assume that no single group captures the whole of religious truth; hence they are more likely to have a practical rather than affective relation to a denomination or similar body. They will remain part of the group while it functions to give some semblance of meaning, provides an experience of community, or offers opportunities for social contact. But they will not retain long-term loyalty once the group ceases to function in these ways.[17]

A major thesis of this book is that unchurched spirituality is gradually reshaping the personal faith of many who belong to mainstream religious organizations. Consider, for example, the fact that 55 percent of all church members privately subscribe to some belief pertaining to the occult (e.g., astrology, reincarnation, fortune-telling, or trance channeling).[18] Church members are also among the millions who avidly read such spiritual bestsellers as *The Road Less Traveled*, *The Celestine Prophecy*, and the *Seven Spiritual Laws of Success* and strive to integrate concepts from these unchurched sources into their overall worldview. Church members differ from the unchurched, however, in that they must deal with the cognitive dissonance created by their "dual allegiance." Most do so by compartmentalizing their "churched" and "unchurched" beliefs into separate categories. They might define their formal religious faith as dealing with issues concerning the afterlife while defining their other spiritual beliefs as dealing with issues that arise in everyday life, such as reducing stress, keeping healthy, or sustaining optimistic attitudes. And thus, even though they continue to be members of a biblically based religious community, their lives are enriched by unchurched spiritual philosophies.

It is important to keep in mind that church members also occasionally avail themselves of unchurched spiritual thought and practices. This book will focus, however, on the roughly 20 percent of Americans who develop a vital spirituality exclusively on the basis of nonecclesial beliefs and practices. Those who are "spiritual, but not religious" differ from their churched counterparts in two important ways. First, they have usually become dissatisfied with institutional religion even before their exposure to unchurched spirituality. Such prior dissatisfaction makes unchurched spirituality more likely to become a sole, rather than supplemental, form of religious understanding. Second, those drawn to unchurched spirituality show a greater interest in personal religious experience. Unchurched forms of spirituality often have a pronounced mystical dimension, which meets the important spiritual need of having a felt-sense of the sacred. Many Americans are dissatisfied with our materialistic culture and yearn for an existentially significant spiritual path. To the extent that unchurched forms of spirituality are able to generate an aura of mystical excitement, they are to this same extent likely to be embraced as attractive alternatives to existing religious institutions.

The history of unchurched spirituality in America is as long and textured as that of the nation's denominational churches. In fact, those who today might describe themselves as "spiritual, but not religious" are heirs of a historical and philosophical lineage that goes back as far as the colonial era. Colonial Americans were especially eclectic when it came to their beliefs about the supernatural. While less than one in five belonged to a church, most subscribed to a potpourri of unchurched religious beliefs including astrology, numerology, magic, and witchcraft. By the Revolutionary War this supernatural curiosity was often combined with the free-thinking rationalism advocated by intellectuals such as Thomas Paine, Benjamin Franklin, and Thomas Jefferson. And, by the early nineteenth century, groups such as the Universalists and Freemasons sewed new seeds of religious unrest. The result was an outcropping of several new metaphysical philosophies. Swedenborgianism, Transcendentalism, and mesmerism caught the attention of middle-class Americans whose intellectual progressivism and mystical hunger made them impatient with the seemingly encrusted piety of established churches.

By the late nineteenth century conditions were ripe for the full flowering of metaphysical religion in America. First spiritualism, then the New Thought or Mind Cure movement, and finally Theosophy refined the occult-leaning vocabularies of the century's earlier metaphysical "isms." These new metaphysical movements created an enduring tradition in unchurched American spirituality. Perhaps their most important legacy was introducing middle-class clientele to a wide range of "exotic philosophies" including Eastern religions, Native American traditions, and pagan teachings. Only a small minority of Americans have been interested in studying these exotic teachings in their own right. Instead, most have approached these novel systems with an agenda already defined by the nation's unchurched spiritual traditions. The same, too, might be said of middle-class interest in alternative medicines and popular psychologies extolling the powers of the hidden self.

Other scholars have produced in-depth studies of the various movements and philosophies that will be covered in this book. Nowhere have I tried to add new information about these groups. What I have attempted to show is how these diverse spiritual interests are linked as part of a larger historical tradition. My goal is to illuminate the common themes that constitute a "tradition" of unchurched spirituality in America. All evidence suggests that this tradition will have a continuing influence on American religious life. For this reason I am also interested in assessing the overall role of unchurched spirituality in American culture. It is, I think, appropriate to ask whether these unchurched spiritual traditions are capable of promoting a balanced spirituality. Most of the world's highly regarded spiritual traditions have tried to strengthen both our capacity for receptivity (i.e., contemplative awareness of our innerconnection with a wider spiritual universe) and our capacity for agency (i.e., moral action that makes us effective agents of wholeness-making in the surrounding world). Unchurched spiritual systems have an uneven record in promoting these dual spiritual concerns. They are, after all, frequently transmitted by persons who lack the training and theological sophistication that many church leaders bring to these same tasks. And, too, their lack of a strong institutional base makes it difficult for them to help people sustain their spiritual enthusiasm or to connect persons together into a cohesive community. But we must also recognize that there are millions of Americans for whom churched religion is no longer a viable option. These persons find themselves so emotionally or intellectually disenfranchised from institutional religion that they are not choosing between conventional and alternative spirituality. They are instead choosing between alternative spiritual philosophies or going without any spiritual outlook whatsoever. A good many of those who find themselves "spiritual, but not religious" have fought their way to a set of beliefs and practices that enables them to reject a purely materialistic view of life. To this extent, our unchurched traditions have enabled a sizable percentage of Americans to achieve as mature a spiritual orientation to life as can be reasonably expected in our contemporary world.

1

The Emergence of Unchurched Traditions

Most histories of the United States depict the nation's earliest colonists as very religious people. This might be true, but not in the traditional sense. Relatively few were churchgoers. In the late 1600s, less than one-third of all adults belonged to a church. This percentage actually declined over the next hundred years. By the time of the Revolutionary War only about 15 percent belonged to any church.[1] In his famous chronicle of life in the American colonies, the Frenchman Hector St. John de Crevecoeur observed that "religious indifference is imperceptibly disseminated from one end of the continent to another, which is at present one of the strongest characteristics of the American people."[2] It seems that the majority of colonists were uninterested in belonging to churches or committing themselves to particular theological creeds.

This is not to say that colonial Americans were unreligious. Most early Americans, for example, engaged in a wide array of magical and occult practices. Astrology, divination, and witchcraft permeated everyday life in the colonies.[3] These occult systems filled the same kinds of needs that Christianity did. That is, they provided beliefs concerning superhuman powers as well as techniques for gaining the support, protection, and aid of these powers. One historian, Jon Butler, argues that "magic and Christianity in colonial America were not generically different entities but were subsets of the same phenomenon—religion. They posited a resort to superhuman powers and they offered techniques for invoking those powers to control human events."[4]

Divination, fortune-telling, astrology, witchcraft, and even folk medicine competed with the Christian churches as sources of the colonists' understanding of the supernatural powers that affected their destiny. Divination was perhaps the most widespread of these unchurched attempts to understand and manipulate supernatural power. One of the most common tools of divination, the divining rod, was used throughout the colonies for detecting sources of underground water or locating lost treasure. Explanations of how the divining rod worked were vague. Some theories attributed its powers to the existence of natural sympathies between wood and water, others focused on mystical powers somehow present in the rod, and still others believed that the rod was but a conduit for the ritual magic originating in the individual practitioner. Fortune-telling was also relied on as a means of gaining supernatural insight into the powers affecting one's life. Fortune-tellers utilized a variety of techniques, but all worked on the assumption that certain individuals have especially developed connections with the supernatural realm from which they derived their prognosticating powers. Astrology, too, was pervasive throughout the colonies. Horoscopes and astrological charts were printed in many of the colonial era's best-selling almanacs, giving wide popular currency to these occult systems for planning one's commercial, agricultural, and romantic affairs.[5]

Witchcraft took many forms during the colonial period. Virtually every colonist believed that certain individuals could harness supernatural power through the use of charms, conjures, and spells. Witches were not so much a distinct category of occult practitioners, but rather one of many varieties of "cunning persons" who drew on supernatural power in an effort to affect specific worldly activities. The infamous witchcraft trials at Andover and Salem rivet attention on colonial fear of witchcraft. The truth is, however, that almost all colonists believed that astrology, divination, and sorcery were all occasionally effective means of either predicting or controlling their fates. And thus although few Americans would ever have labeled themselves as witches, a majority nonetheless subscribed to the basic belief system underlying the practice of witchcraft.[6]

Colonial healing practices were also rife with supernatural elements. European immigrants brought with them a host of beliefs concerning the supernatural cause of many illnesses. It was common for persons to resort to conjurers or witches who prepared charms that were deemed capable of fending off malevolent supernatural influence. Even the era's herb doctors typically believed that their medicines unleashed magical powers and thus understood healing more in terms of supernatural intervention than botanical science. The "powow" healing system utilized by Pennsylvania Germans was typical in this regard. The powow system borrowed loosely from Christianity, popular magic, and even Native-American understandings of supernatural influence. Powow healing books encouraged colonists to understand themselves as living at a precarious juncture between the natural and supernatural realms and offered strategies for fending off injurious influences. African Americans also took an eclectic approach to healing that utilized herbal remedies, potions, charms, amulets, and sundry other occult techniques.[7]

Interest in magic and the occult was as prevalent among the upper classes as it was among the common folk. The library inventories that survive from seventeenth- and eighteenth-century colonial estates indicate that it was common for the most affluent members of society to own books describing occult practices.[8] Typical of the works appearing in these inventories were medical books written by the era's astrologer-physicians. Many colonists also avidly collected works dealing with astrology, alchemy, Hermeticism, Rociscrucianism, and a variety of decidedly heterodox mystical philosophies. Historical records thus indicate that colonial Americans had access to a wide range of occult books and that a sufficient core of the era's intellectuals were quite conversant with even the most esoteric occult systems. It is difficult to know just what role these individuals had in laying the foundations for the metaphysical systems that would gain popularity in the eighteenth and nineteenth centuries. What is certain is that, from the outset, Americans have had a persistent interest in religious ideas that fall well outside the parameters of Bible-centered theology.

Occult and magical practices appealed to the early colonists for many reasons. Most were probably hoping to find a cure for sickness, injury, or other bodily afflictions. A good many others were hoping to locate a reliable water supply, find lost treasure, or receive guidance about weather-related issues such as appropriate times for planting and harvesting. We need to be cautious, however, about interpreting the significance of these practical motives turning to magical practices. Many historians make too great a distinction between magic and religion. Following the scholarship of Bronislaw Malinowski, they tend to view magic as mundane, practical, and concerned with manipulating supernatural forces for highly utilitarian reasons. In contrast, religion—particularly Christianity—is thought of as transcendent, philosophical, and dealing with broad issues of universal order and meaning.[9] Thus, one well-known study of magic and religion in early American history assumes that religion is supplicative while magic is manipulative.[10] It is common for scholars to assume that religion postulates the existence of a transcendent supernatural authority and seeks to influence this authority through prayer and devotional ritual. This sets up a clean separation between religion and magic. In this view religion is a realm in which humans remain ultimately impotent and at the mercy of a supernatural authority who may or may not be moved to act on their behalf. Magic, on the other hand, is thought to reflect the idea that human beings can learn to harness supernatural power for their own use. Magic thus centers upon empowering human beings and enhancing their ability to control the world around them.

Unfortunately, such hard-and-fast distinctions do not hold up when we look at American religious history. Many Christian churchgoers were motivated by such practical issues, too. They hoped to secure an afterlife, be reunited with loved ones, ward off supernatural influence, or align themselves with God's providential powers. To procure these desired ends they made use of "religious" techniques such as petitionary prayers, sacraments, and faith in Bible miracles. All of these, of course, are fraught with magical elements. And, on the other side, many who dabbled in magic and the occult were highly interested in philosophical and metaphysical issues. They sought a cosmology or worldview that might help them understand broad issues of universal order and meaning. As historian Jon Butler cautions, "If we want to understand the full range of religious expression in Western culture generally and early America specifically, it is imperative that we stop calling only the Christian or Judeo-Christian tradition 'religious' and that we begin looking seriously at the place of magic and the occult arts in religious history."[11]

Churched and unchurched religiosity have factored about equally in Americans' understandings of the supernatural since the nation's beginnings. The exact relationship between the two varied person by person. It seems that, on the whole, most people saw magic and Christianity as distinct, but complementary.[12] Most were aware that Christian clergy urged them to stay clear of unbiblical beliefs about the supernatural. Yet in order to meet their spiritual needs, the laity sometimes turned to magic and sometimes to Christian ritual. They didn't share the clergy's concern for theological consistency, but switched back and forth between magical and Christian beliefs without any sense of guilt or intellectual inconsistency.

This "spiritual eclecticism" must have exasperated the clergy. Their Puritan theology posited a wide gulf between a majestic deity and His finite creation. It was thought impossible for mortal humans to bridge that gulf and gain access to any "higher" spiritual powers. It followed that apparent supernatural events must either be delusions or the work of the devil. What colonial clergy failed to see was that their insistence on the remoteness of God rendered Christianity largely irrelevant to everyday spiritual concerns. An aloof, judgmental God failed to mesh with colonists' desire to fashion a vital spirituality.

Christian theology thus inadvertently helped create a consumer market for unchurched religious practices. Most colonists who turned to magical beliefs and practices had no intention of denying the special divinity of Jesus or the Bible's value as a guide to eternal salvation. They were merely supplementing their biblical beliefs with other ideas seemingly more relevant to their wider interests and concerns. Magical and occult practices during the colonial period rarely gave rise to full-blown metaphysical perspectives that challenged Christian theology. It was, as historian Richard Godbeer shows, "the very informality of magical tradition [that] made it easier for layfolk to accommodate magical and religious strategies. Because folk magic rested upon nothing more than a series of implicit assumptions, people could avoid possibly unsettling comparisons with Puritan doctrine and thus adhere to both, switching from one to the other as deemed approporiate."[13]

The "implicit assumptions" underlying magic and occult beliefs in colonial times weakened as the Revolutionary Era drew closer. Following the infamous witchcraft trials, Puritan ministers became even more insistent that humans don't have the ability to gain access to the supernatural. The growth of experimental science and the dawning of the Enlightenment, or Age of Reason, posed an even greater challenge to magical practices. The Enlightenment spawned a bold faith in the lawfulness of nature and in the power of human reason to discover the precise working of these natural laws. It was thought that reason and the scientific method would unleash humanity's potential for unlimited progress. Reliance on supernatural assistance was no longer thought to be necessary. Nor for that matter was it thought possible. The era's most educated citizens reasoned their way to a position of skepticism regarding the supernatural—magical and religious alike.

Enlightenment Rationality and Religious Eclecticism

The Age of Reason reached its zenith in the decades surrounding the American Revolution. First in Europe, then in North America, there were astonishing advances in mathematics and the natural sciences. These breakthroughs in scientific knowledge stimulated a new confidence in the power of human reason to comprehend the universe. Each new discovery weakened theology's claim that the universe mirrored the will of a distant, inscrutable God and was therefore essentially unknowable. Instead, the universe was now seen as an intricate machine whose lawful rules of operation would soon be disclosed through scientific inquiry. It appeared that humanity stood on the threshold of unlimited intellectual and technological progress.

The Enlightenment depicted a universe that is intelligible, harmonious, and thoroughly rational. It sought the lawful principles underlying every facet of existence in order to further the movement of history toward a utopian order. Enlightenment principles prompted many intellectuals to rebel against Christian orthodoxy. The boldest thinkers of the day confidently proclaimed that the "essentials" of true religion are those truths that can be known by human reason without the aid of any special revelation. In place of the theism and supernaturalism associated with biblical religion they championed what came to be known as "deism." According to deism, God is best understood as the Grand Architect or rational designer of the universe. Deism insisted that God, having imparted a rational design to His creation, does not intervene in the lawful operations of the universe. Deists were repudiating the traditional biblical view of a personal God who miraculously intervenes in worldly events or sends special revelations. For deists, the true worship of God has nothing to do with prayer, ritual, or doctrine. It was thought instead that we best serve God by diligently living according to the dictates of reason, striving to understand the scientific principles that underlie nature, and behaving in reasonable, moral ways. What was noteworthy and even shocking about deism was its implicit denial of the Bible's claim to revealed truth, the validity of biblical claims concerning miracles, and the special divinity of Jesus. But what earned the deistic faith of the Enlightenment an enthusiastic following was not what it denied so much as what it affirmed. The Age of Reason instilled confidence in every person's potential for greater understanding, hope for the continued moral progress of the human race, and an inspiring vision that we are all sons and daughters of a rational, progressive deity.

Although the Enlightenment began in Europe, it spread rapidly among American intellectuals. Thomas Paine, Ethan Allen, John Adams, Benjamin Franklin, and Thomas Jefferson were all among those whose attitudes toward religion bore the stamp of Enlightenment rationality. In contrast to Paine and Allen who verged on atheism, Adams, Franklin, and Jefferson were more typical of the era's quest for a "reasonable religion." Franklin, for example, "never doubted ... the existence of the Deity; that he made the world, and govern'd it by his Providence; that the most acceptable service of God was the doing of good to man; that our souls are immortal; and that all crime will be punished, and virtues rewarded, either here or hereafter. These I esteem'd the essentials of every religion."[14] Thomas Jefferson was more outspoken than Franklin in his opposition to what he considered the irrational nature of institutional religion. Jefferson railed against all theological concepts, particularly those based on an appeal to some alleged revelation. Claims to revealed truth were for him nothing but "charlatanry of the mind."[15] Jefferson even went so far as to use his scissors to cut apart a copy of the New Testament until every last reference to miracles or supernatural occurrences had been removed. What remained were the simple ethical teachings of Jesus that, in Jefferson's opinion, were the only parts of the New Testament that were fit to be read by a rational person.[16] It should be noted that Jefferson's antipathy toward credal religion by no means inclined him to atheism. Instead, Jefferson identified religion with an acute sense of God's invisible presence within nature. True spirituality, he thought, was the capacity "to perceive and feel a conviction of design, consummate skill, and indefinite power in every atom [of the universe]."[17] It seems, then, that intellectual difficulty with Christian theology by no means prevented eighteenth-century American intellectuals from adopting a spiritual orientation to life.

The Enlightenment furnished intellectual criteria for identifying the "essentials" of religion. It was considered reasonable for a religious outlook to focus on such essentially humanistic concepts as morality, free will, and the ideal of this-worldly progress. The implication was that much of what we have come to associate with religion is nonessential. Ritual, beliefs concerning human sinfulness, and preoccupation with the afterlife were all deemed examples of what is backward and even harmful in the way of religion. Even beliefs about the nature of God could be assessed according to the principles of Enlightenment rationality. Thus, for example, it could be considered reasonable to think of God in such impersonal terms as Divine Architect, Mind, or Principle. Images of God as a personal being who craves admiration, worship, and obedience could be summarily dismissed as inconsistent with the goal of enhancing human agency. Picking and choosing among competing religious ideas was not only possible, it was a necessary step toward full intellectual integrity.

Another important impetus toward "rational religion" and "religious eclecticism" was the influence of the Freemasons. The origin of Freemasonry is not entirely clear. It probably arose out of periodic gatherings of the stonemasons who built churches and cathedrals in England.[18] What was first an association concerned with the work and moral development of stonemasons eventually developed an interest in ancient wisdom, particularly as promulgated in contemporary esoteric philosophies such as Rosicrucianism. The tools of masonry (the square and compass) became symbols for building moral and spiritual character. The ritual and symbolism of the craft tradition were embellished in ways that distinguished among grades or degrees of advancement in Masonic teachings. By the early eighteenth century, the movement began to organize into "lodges," which were responsible for recruiting, initiating, and educating new members. Soon the movement spread to France, Scotland, and colonial North America. By 1776, there were over forty lodges in the colonies. The influence of Freemasonry on early American religious and intellectual history can hardly be overestimated as evidenced by the fact that fifty-two of the fifty-six signers of the Declaration of Independence were Masons.

By the time Freemasonry became popular in colonial America it was thoroughly infected with Enlightenment views. Symbol-laden ceremonies were used both to initiate new members and to mark their progress through successive levels of acquiring Enlightenment beliefs. Historian Catherine Albanese explains that "the square and compass, tools of building, became emblems of building a perfect human character. Here the square stood for earth, while the compass suggested the sky. The message being taught was clear: out of nature, humans fashioned their character, and by using nature well, they could become perfect human beings."[19]

Freemasonry had its esoteric side. To begin with, Freemasons only initiated select individuals and they conducted all their ceremonies in secret. They also expected new members to embrace abstract intellectual ideals garnered not only from Enlightenment philosophy, but also from magical and occult traditions that flourished in the colonial era. Masonry was also steeped in deism. Masons viewed God in impersonal terms, as the Grand Architect of the natural order. They neither approved nor condemned Christianity, but rather viewed it as one manifestation in a long series of historical religions—a series that would culminate in the emergence of a universal faith. Their purpose was to unite persons in "that religion in which all men agree." Masonry helped its members work through their former allegiance to a specific denominational faith to a more tolerant, ecumenical outlook. Edmond Mazet has noted that the way Masonry deals "with differences of religions suggests an underlying belief in a transcendental truth of which the various religions would be different expressions in different historical and cultural contexts."[20]

All who joined the Freemasons were indoctrinated into the basic principles of "rational religion." They were given careful instructions concerning the basic beliefs on which, supposedly, all religions agree: belief in a creator God, the existence of an immortal soul, and the importance of expressing spiritual conviction through moral living and charity. At the very least these deistic concepts worked against blind faith in various denominational theologies. Masonry encouraged its members to build an eclectic, consciously chosen religious outlook. Many who joined were no doubt primarily interested in the convivial, social side of Masonry. For them it was more another men's club than a lodge for the dissemination of ancient, esoteric spiritual wisdom. But for others Masonry was an introduction to a wholly new form of spiritual thinking that blended Enlightenment rationality with a mystical appreciation of the hidden mysteries of our universe. The higher degrees of Masonic teaching initiated members into such esoteric matters as cabalistic Judaism, alchemy, Rosicrucianism, and Vedanta metaphysics. Although they often denied that they were a religious organization, nonetheless the expressed goal of the Masons was the initiation of members into a process of spiritual growth and experimentation.

Freemasonry was not the only organization that attracted those wishing to venture into uncharted spiritual territories. Two liberal Protestant denominations, the Unitarians and the Universalists, also fostered religious experimentalism. The Unitarian movement spread through American culture along the very lines opened up by Enlightenment rationality. Unitarians acknowledged that the Bible was in some sense the inspired Word of God, but they insisted that it was written by men, in the language of men, with the limitations of a humanly written document. The Bible should not, therefore, be taken as inerrant. It demanded the same kind of intellectual scrutiny as any other book. Unitarians also denied the special divinity of Jesus. With the passage of time, American Unitarianism adopted virtually every feature of deism. Rationality and moral conduct replaced theological doctrines as the core elements of their faith. For this reason Unitarians were routinely at the forefront of almost every progressive intellectual and social cause. Although Unitarianism appealed primarily to affluent, urban New Englanders, it attracted a wide range of individuals who yearned for a progressive spirituality that encouraged free thinking.

The Universalists were also at variance with American Protestantism. Universalists held that a loving God would not consign His creatures to eternal damnation. Rejecting evangelical Christianity's doctrine that only a select few were destined for salvation, they preached universal salvation. The concept of universal salvation necessarily fostered liberal and experimental approaches to spiritual living. If we have salvation regardless of our specific beliefs or practices, then we are free to follow our personal spiritual inclinations rather than conform to institutional norms. For this reason Universalists tended to draw the era's "free spirits." Though typically drawn from a less affluent, more rural background than their Unitarian counterparts, the Universalists also became magnets for the era's most progressive religious ideas.

Deists, Freemasons, Unitarians, and Universalists were thus among the first to think their way into the status of religious nonconformists. They honored the principle of free, rational inquiry in the matter of religious belief. And, in so doing, they laid the foundations for the first flowering of metaphysical religion.

| The Great Metaphysical Awakening

Historians have long debated the role of "awakenings" in the course of American religious history. Awakenings, it is argued, were spontaneous outcroppings of revival meetings and other proselytizing activities that generated a discernible increase in the nation's religious enthusiasm.[21] Each successive awakening is said to have brought large numbers of new converts to Bible-based religion and intensified the piety of those who already believed. What historians seem to have overlooked is that there have been periodic awakenings in America's unchurched religious life, too. Indeed, the periods between 1835 and 1860, 1885 and 1910, and 1970 and 1995 witnessed dramatic surges in public awareness of philosophies and practices outside the spiritual teachings of the nation's churches.

The first of these periods came directly on the heels of an outburst of Protestant revivalism that scholars have termed the Second Great Awakening. The revival meetings of the early nineteenth century set off a wave of religious enthusiasm that fostered what one historian termed "ultraism." Ultraism consisted of a "combination of activities, personalities, and attitudes, creating a condition of society which could foster experimental doctrines."[22] Mormonism, Shakerism, Adventism, and communitarianism were all among the experimental doctrines that sought out innovative ways to bring down the Holy Spirit and inaugurate a new spiritual life.

As broadly as revivalist preachers appealed to the American middle class, their message of personal sin and the need for redemption could never appeal to everyone. Many, particularly those infected by Enlightenment rationality and its humanistic faith, were immune to the hell-fire and brimstone rhetoric of the Protestant clergy. The revivalists' scare tactics presupposed prior belief in the inerrancy of the Bible. They had little effect on those who had already rejected scriptural accounts of humanity's supposedly sinful condition. These people were by no means indifferent to the great spiritual questions of life. Many yearned for an exciting new spirituality. This spirituality, however, would have to connect with scientific rationality. They had confidence in humanity's own powers to discern the lawful patterns according to which the physical universe operates. Spirituality, for them, should extend this process by providing insight into the lawful patterns of the more-than-physical universe, too.

Those whose intellectual and cultural outlook took them beyond existing religious institutions were in a state of spiritual disorientation. Significant economic, political, and intellectual changes in American life called for a new religious outlook. Two new intellectual systems appeared on the scene, promising to assuage the distress created by the shortcomings of organized religion. The first of these, Swedenborgianism, was a mystical philosophy based on the teachings of the Swedish scientist-turned-seer Emanuel Swedenborg (1688–1771). The second, Transcendentalism, was an American-born philosophy that spoke to the era's spiritual malaise by articulating a progressive and highly optimistic metaphysical philosophy.

With the possible exception of Theosophy, there has been no greater influence on unchurched American religious life than the writings of Emanuel Swedenborg. Swedenborg's influence can be seen in almost every innovative philosophy or movement of the nineteenth century. His inspirational vision surfaced "in Transcendentalism and at Brook Farm, in spiritualism and the free love movement, in the craze for communitarian experiments, in faith healing, mesmerism, and a half-dozen medical cults; among great intellectuals, crude charlatans, and innumerable frontier quacks."[23] The reason for Swedenborg's influence upon such a divergent group of individuals and causes was simple: his writings articulated a vision that reconciled our scientific and spiritual yearnings.

Emanuel Swedenborg was the son of a Swedish Lutheran bishop. After receiving a university education, he undertook a series of scientific explorations that produced significant contributions to such diverse fields as geology, anatomy, physics, and astronomy. In 1745, Swedenborg had the first of a long series of mystical experiences in which he was visited by angelic beings. These celestial beings provided him with long discourses concerning both the metaphysical structure of reality and what he described as "the spiritual sense of the Scripture."

What Swedenborg learned about the spiritual nature of reality is summarized in his two principal doctrines concerning "correspondence" and "influx."[24] His angelic guides taught him that the universe consists of seven interpenetrating dimensions (the physical, mental, spiritual, angelic, etc.). Spirit and matter are thus not opposed to one another, but rather complementary and inseparable dimensions of a single universal system. His doctrine of "correspondence" affirmed that each of the seven principal dimensions of the universe is constructed in such a way as to be intimately connected with every other dimension. God's divine spirit, as the source of all, works through every dimension. Although the divine nature is progressively obscured by the growing unresponsiveness of each successively "lower" realm, it is never obliterated. The doctrine of correspondence also implied that the laws that govern our physical order are but reflections of the spiritual laws that govern every other level of existence. All physical events are, when seen in their full metaphysical context, the images or results of the lawful workings of "higher" levels of existence.

This vision of metaphysical correspondence led directly to his doctrine of influx. Swedenborg taught that all causal power emanates from God. Causal power is constantly emanating from God and there is thus a continuous influx of divine spirit into each successively "lower" dimension of existence. All true progress proceeds according to influences received from above. The physical body achieves inner harmony by becoming attuned to the influx of energies coming from the soul, the soul through contact with superior angelic beings, and so on up the spiritual ladder. Through diligent study and by cultivating mystical states of awareness, anyone might obtain the requisite gnosis to make contact with higher spiritual planes. The benefits were numerous: spontaneous insight into cosmological secrets, conversations with angelic beings, intuitive understanding of scriptural verses, and the instantaneous healing of both physical and emotional disorders.

Swedenborg was convinced that he had been granted insight into the Bible's spiritual meaning. Believing that he had received "perfect inspiration," Swedenborg proclaimed that "the inner sense of the Word has been dictated to me out of heaven." He taught that the Bible, read symbolically, describes the metaphysical correspondences linking the many spheres of existence. Swedenborg believed that he was revealing the true spiritual meanings of the Bible that had been obscured by centuries of Christian dogma. He could thus affirm that the Bible contained ultimate spiritual truth and yet freely reinterpreted its message.

Swedenborg eventually wrote more than thirty volumes purporting to uncover the hidden spiritual meanings buried beneath the literal sense of Christian doctrines. In the 1830s, translations of these works finally became known in American intellectual circles. They found a receptive audience. Those whose spiritual outlook had been tempered by Enlightenment rationality were particularly drawn to Swedenborg's program to free religion from a literal reading of Scripture. His description of humanity's inner connection with higher, spiritual realities appealed to the more mystically inclined who yearned for intense, personal religious experience. John Humphrey Noyes, Christian minister and founder of the perfectionist commune at Oneida, explained how rationalists and mystics alike were affirmed by Swedenborg's daring spirituality:

> The Bible and revivals had made men hungry for something more than social reconstruction. Swedenborg's offer of a new heaven as well as a new earth, met the demand magnificently. ... [T]he scientific were charmed, because he was primarily a man of science, and seemed to reduce the world to scientific order. The mystics were charmed because he led them boldly into all the mysteries of intuition and invisible worlds.[25]

Swedenborg's exciting description of the "mysteries of intuition and invisible worlds" held a particular fascination for his American readers. For one thing, it undermined the Calvinist doctrine of human depravity and instead strengthened Americans' democratic faith in every individual's unlimited potential for development. It also enticed the general reading public to become more open to the mystical notions that had persisted in the background of Western culture for centuries. Various esoteric traditions such as Neoplatonism and Renaissance occultism had held out the possibility of inward connection with "higher" orders of existence. This was, after all, a time when Western culture was swinging in the direction of philosophical Romanticism. The conditions were thus ripe for the emergence of an indigenous metaphysical vision—Transcendentalism.

About a decade after the creation of the American Unitarian Association, a group of rebellious young Unitarian preachers founded the Transcendental Club. The early members of this club sympathized with most Unitarian principles including freedom in religious thinking, the humanity of Jesus, and the culturally conditioned nature of the Bible. But these free spirits possessed a pronounced mystical sensibility. They were influenced by Romanticism's reverence for the mysterious powers that engulf humanity and its celebration of profound emotions. Those drawn to the Transcendentalist movement wished to link liberal religious thinking to a decidedly Romantic emphasis on the importance of inner experience. George Ripley, Theodore Parker, William Henry Channing, Orestes Brownson, Henry David Thoreau, and Margaret Fuller were among the movement's leading voices. But it was Ralph Waldo Emerson who emerged as the principal architect of the Transcendentalist vision.

The similarities between Swedenborgianism and Transcendentalism are no coincidence. Emerson was introduced to Swedenborg's writings while he was a student at Harvard. Years later, in his treatise *Representative Men*, Emerson acknowledged his debt to the Swedish seer and made it clear that many of his own views were inspired by the doctrines of correspondence and influx. Swedenborg's insistence on the close connection between the material and spiritual worlds informed the Transcendentalists' belief that every human being has the capacity to become receptive to the inflow of spiritual energy. But Emerson never embraced Swedenborg's belief in celestial spirits.[26] Whereas Swedenborg credited angelic spirits with mediating his metaphysical revelations, Emerson proclaimed that each individual could receive God's inflowing spirit without any mediation whatsoever. He criticized Swedenborg for being too literal in his understanding of the spiritual energies that engulf us. In Emerson's view, belief in angelic spirits externalizes and objectifies the sources of religious knowledge, reducing an ineffable encounter with a higher spiritual order to trivial images. Emerson therefore wished to dispense with Swedenborg's belief in angelic communication and to emphasize instead Swedenborg's message "that God must be found within."

True to his Unitarian heritage, Emerson refused to accept the special divinity of Jesus. In a famous sermon delivered at Harvard Divin-

ity School, Emerson argued that "historical Christianity has fallen
into the error that corrupts all attempts to communicate religion. It
has dwelt, it dwells, with noxious exaggeration about the person of
Jesus."[27] This "noxious exaggeration" of Jesus's divinity diverts attention from our own capacity for expressing divine creativity. In Emerson's view the Church's preaching had gone dead. It spoke of
revelation as something delivered once and for all in the distant past
rather than as an imminent possibility. The Church encouraged slav-
ish worship of ancient dogmas rather than nourish our own spiritual
awakenings.

Emerson's Unitarian background also influenced his belief that the
Bible doesn't have a monopoly on religious truth. He even went so far
as to draw on Hindu mystical writings known as the Upanishads to
describe the relationship between God and the human soul. Emerson
found in the Upanishads a moving statement of how God can be
thought of as "the divinity that flows through all things." The
Upanishads inspired Emerson to think of God as the Oversoul, the
cosmic spirit suffusing the whole of living nature. Hindu mystical
thought thus provided Emerson with a vocabulary for communicating his belief that each of us is ultimately connected with the vast
spirit of God.

Emerson's metaphysical yearnings set him apart from his fellow
Unitarians whose commitment to Enlightenment rationality directed them toward science and moral reflection, not mystical experience. For this reason he eventually resigned his position as a
Unitarian minister to become a spokesman for the philosophy of
Transcendentalism. At the core of his teachings was a vision of how
every human being is, at depth, connected with the transcendental
reality that infuses our universe with Law, Beauty, and Joy. His insistence on the radical immanence of God had important psychological
consequences. It implied that God, as universal spirit, is always and
everywhere available to the properly attuned mind. Emerson borrowed from Hindu mysticism the view that the only thing separating
us from complete harmony with God's spiritual presence is a self-
imposed, psychological barrier. For this reason Emerson emphasized
the need to cultivate spiritually receptive states of mind. He personally found the quiet of nature conducive to such states of mystical
reverie. When alone in nature, he wrote, "All mean egotism vanishes.
I become a transparent eyeball; I am nothing; I see all; the currents of

the Universal Being circulate through me; I am part or parcel of God."[28]

For Emerson spirituality had nothing to do with church attendance, belief in the divinity of Jesus, or blind faith in biblical dogmas. He equated true spirituality with the cultivation of a lifestyle that promoted inner connection with the "currents of Universal Being." Such connection with spiritual power led naturally to what Emerson called "self-reliance." The self-reliant individual was not at the mercy of others' opinions or, for that matter, external conditions of any kind. This ability to transcend environmental conditions and become an agent of creative change was not, however, an achievement of sheer willpower. The "self" that gives us spiritual composure is not the physical or social self. It is, rather, the self that has first "become nothing" so that it might then become receptive to the "exertions of a power which exists not in time, or space, but an instantaneous instreaming causing power."[29] The metaphysical categories of "correspondence" and "influx" are the crucial variables affecting our capacity for true self-reliance. Psychological conditions such as beliefs, attitudes, or willpower are necessary, but by no means sufficient, causes of true self-reliance. It is, finally, a spiritual achievement. The ultimate power behind self-reliance does not derive from the activities of the rational ego but rather from the instreaming presence of "the divinity that flows through all things."

Emerson and his fellow Transcendentalists articulated a new metaphysical outlook that corresponded to changes occurring in American culture. Yet, even though its terminology appeared new and radical, the values behind this metaphysical outlook were essentially those traditional to middle-class Americans. The metaphysical awakening that occurred between 1835 and 1860 helped preserve inherited values by reformulating them in ways that were sensitive to changing social realities. As historian William McLoughlin has shown, one of the most important functions of religious awakenings is to give new expression to what might be considered the "core beliefs" of American religious life: the chosen nation; the covenant with God; the existence of a higher law against which private and social behavior is to be judged; the laws of science, presumed to be from the Creator, and evolutionary or progressive in nature; the free and morally responsible individual; the work ethic that holds that equal opportunity and hard work will bring economic success and public respect to all who assert and discipline themselves; and the benevolence of nature under the controlling human hands.[30]

The Swedenborgians and Transcendentalists used their notions of correspondence and influx to provide just such a reformulated "culture core" to those who no longer bought into churched religion. Emerson in particular possessed a genius for adapting metaphysical concepts to meet Americans' practical religious needs. As historian Eugene Taylor has noted, the way in which Emerson and other Transcendentalists selectively appropriated Swedenborgian concepts reveals a great deal about what is distinctively "American" in the history of our religious thought.

> The Transcendentalists, in short, took up Swedenborg avidly and adapted him to their own individual purposes. ... They took him partly by way of protest against the prevailing secular materialism as well as the pretensions of ecclesiastical orthodoxy, and partly as an affirmation of the divinity within each person. They saw in him a vast suggestiveness and his ideas became part of the major reform movements of the time.[31]

The process of Americanization altered Swedenborgian metaphysics in such a way that they spoke to American cultural issues. And, as Taylor puts it, "through a process that might be called the naturalization of ideas—in which specific intellectual influences have now become part of the flow of common culture, both Swedenborgian and transcendentalist thought survive as integral, albeit hidden, strands of the fabric that defines present-day folk consciousness in America."[32]

From Metaphysical Speculation to Practical Technique: The Mesmerists' Contribution

In 1836, a Frenchman by the name of Charles Poyen began a lecture tour of New England. Poyen realized that his audiences would be wholly ignorant of what he described as the "well-authenticated facts concerning an order of phenomena so important to science and so glorious to human nature."[33] He was confident, however, that their initial indifference would turn to evangelical zeal when they were finally acquainted with Franz Anton Mesmer's science of animal magnetism.

Mesmer (1734–1815) had attracted a good deal of attention when he presented himself to European intellectual circles as the bearer of an epoch-making discovery. The Viennese physician claimed to have detected the existence of an invisible, superfine substance that had previously eluded scientific notice. Mesmer referred to this fluidlike substance as animal magnetism and postulated that it permeated the physical universe. He explained that animal magnetism was the etheric medium linking the universe and making possible the transmission of causal influences from one object to another.

Mesmer was certain that his discovery would lead to progress in virtually every scientific field. He was most convinced, however, that it contained the secret to a radically new understanding of medicine. Mesmer maintained that animal magnetism was evenly distributed throughout the healthy human body. If for any reason an individual's supply of animal magnetism was thrown out of equilibrium, one or more bodily organs would consequently be deprived of sufficient amounts of this vital force and begin to falter. "There is, " Mesmer reasoned, "only one illness and one healing."[34] Every illness can ultimately be traced back to a disturbance in the body's supply of animal magnetism. It followed that medical science can be reduced to a simple set of procedures aimed at supercharging a patient's nervous system with this mysterious life-giving energy. Mesmer gradually developed a technique for inducing relaxed mental states in patients. Then, by passing either his bare hands or magnets over their heads and down along their bodies, he stimulated the flow of animal magnetism into, and through, their physical systems. "Mesmerizing" people was thus a means of creating the proper psychological conditions for restoring harmony with this invisible spiritual energy.

Even before Poyen brought mesmerism to American shores, the science of animal magnetism had already undergone changes that were destined to enhance its popularity in the United States. One of Mesmer's pupils, the Marquis de Puysegur, faithfully imitated Mesmer's techniques only to have his patients fall into unusual, sleeplike states of consciousness. Puysegur's entranced subjects exhibited the most extraordinary behaviors. When he asked them questions, they responded with more intelligent and nuanced replies than could possibly be expected given their educational and socioeconomic background. Many subjects suddenly remembered long-forgotten experiences with astonishing accuracy. A select few appeared to drift into a much deeper state of consciousness, which Puysegur described as one of "extraordinary lucidity." These subjects

spontaneously performed feats of telepathy, clairvoyance, and precognition. Puysegur had stumbled on the existence of a stratum of
mental life just below the threshold of ordinary consciousness. In
discovering the technique for leading patients into this unconscious
mental realm, he had initiated a revolution in the study of the mind.

Charles Poyen had studied directly under Puysegur and thus believed
that mesmerism's single most important discovery was that of the
somnambulic, or mesmeric, state of consciousness. His public lectures
provided audiences with an actual demonstration of mesmerism's powers. Many in Poyen's audience came in hope of a medical cure. He
obliged by making repeated "passes" with his hands in an effort to direct
the flow of animal magnetism to the appropriate part of the body. Many
of those receiving this treatment awoke from their mesmeric sleep and,
remembering nothing of what had transpired, claimed cure. Poyen's
own account, in many cases supported by newspaper reports and letters
to the editor, lists successful treatment of such disorders as rheumatism,
nervousness, back troubles, and liver ailments.

Poyen was convinced that mesmerism had value over and beyond
its contributions to medicine. He claimed that roughly 10 percent of
his subjects attained the "highest degree" of the mesmeric trance.
Many of these subjects claimed to feel animal magnetism enter into
and flow throughout their bodies. Others appeared to establish some
nonverbal means of communication with the "mesmerist," telepathically receiving unspoken thoughts and suggestions. Nor was it un-
common for subjects to perform feats of clairvoyance and
extrasensory perception. They would locate lost objects, describe
events transpiring in distant locales, or read the minds of persons in
the audience. On returning to the waking state, they remembered little of their trance-bound experiences. It was as if they had temporarily existed in an altogether different realm. They knew only that
they were now refreshed, energetic, and healed of their former ailments. In Poyen's view, mesmerism had discovered a set of "well-
authenticated facts" that were not only important to science, but
"glorious to human nature."

Word of Poyen's fantastic healing methods spread throughout
New England. His 1837 treatise on the progress of mesmerism in
New England declares that "nineteen months have elapsed since that
period and already Animal Magnetism has sprung from a complete
state of obscurity and neglect into general notice, and become the

object of a lively interest throughout the country."[35] Newspapers began to take notice. According to one account, mesmerism was fast becoming a "steady theme of interest in New England papers" and
making "a deep impression upon some of the soundest and best balanced minds."[36] Poyen cited articles published in Rhode Island, Maine,
and Connecticut supporting his contention that mesmerism had become a topic of conversation in all classes of society, especially—as he
was quick to point out—among the learned and well-to-do.

Poyen returned to his native France in 1839. His efforts had attracted a host of American followers eager to become spokesmen for
the science of animal magnetism. According to one estimate, by 1843
more than 200 "magnetic healers" were selling their services in the
city of Boston alone.[37] Growing public interest in this new medical
science stimulated demand for books and pamphlets, and the American mesmerists willingly complied. Most of the dozens of works to
appear over the next twenty years followed a common format: an introductory exhortation to open-mindedness; a short history of
Mesmer's discovery; a catalogue of typical cures; anecdotal reports of
clairvoyance and telepathy; and last, but not least, a set of do-it-your-
self instructions. Most of these works suggested that mesmerism held
the secret to personal rejuvenation and enhanced personal power.
One widely circulated pamphlet, for example, included in its title the
promise to explain "the system of manipulating adopted to produce
ecstasy and somnambulism."[38]

American advocates of mesmerism gradually arrived at a consen-
sus concerning the fledgling science's most important theoretical
contributions. They argued that mesmerism was essentially a technique for shifting mental activity along a continuum. Each stage or
point along the continuum was said to correspond to a successively
deeper level of consciousness. It was claimed the deepest levels of the
mesmeric state were characterized by the temporary suspension of
the external senses and the simultaneous awakening of some "inner
source of feeling."[39] The mesmerists hailed their experiments as having made possible a giant breakthrough in the scientific understanding of the human constitution. They thought that they had
empirically proven that there exists "a sense in man which perceives
the presences and qualities of things without the use of ... the external organs of sense."[40] The "inner source of feeling" that exists at the
deepest level of consciousness was said to be uniquely receptive to the

unmediated inflow of animal magnetism. This exalted state of consciousness was said to permit healings to occur spontaneously. It was also said to permit clairvoyance, prevoyance, telepathy, and intuitive knowledge of universal laws and structures.

The deeper levels of the mind disclosed by mesmerism had a decidedly mystical element. Subjects claimed that they temporarily transcended the mundane affairs of ordinary existence and entered into an intimate rapport with the cosmos. One investigator reported that mesmerized subjects "speak as if, to their consciousness, they had undergone an inward translation by which they had passed out of a material into a spiritual body.... The state into which a subject is brought by the mesmerizing process is a state in which the spirit predominates for the time being over the body."[41]

The mesmerists were launching their psychological and medical theory into uncharted cultural waters. Their commitment to the causal agency of animal magnetism (often referred to as vital fluid, vital force, divine electricity, etc.) placed them outside the theoretical spheres of both the science and the theology of their day. Mesmerism promised to unite matter, mind, and spirit into a single cosmological system. But this proved to be almost as much a liability as an attraction. Eclectic thinking took precedence over clarity, and mesmerism soon became allied with almost every metaphysical notion then circulating among progressive-minded Americans. For example, Midwestern physician Joseph Buchanan embraced mesmerism as the key to what he called "neurological anthropology." Mesmerism, he argued, disclosed humanity's psychosomatic unity. Buchanan argued that mesmerism revealed how "positive material existence and positive Spiritual existence—however far apart they stand, and however striking the contrast between their properties—are connected by these fine gradations ... both are subject to the same great system of laws which each obeys in its own sphere."[42]

Buchanan had become dissatisfied with existing science and existing religion even before coming across mesmerism. He believed that strictly materialistic theories of human nature lead inevitably to pessimism and atheism. He thus rejected contemporary medical science as an inadequate framework for describing the human constitution, "since it lacks the essential perspective of the modus operandi of life power."[43] Theological dogma, while recognizing that humanity has a higher nature, was likewise unacceptable because it undermined the inductive spirit of the scientific quest for truth. Mesmerism signaled an intellectual breakthrough of the highest magnitude. It forged the relative contributions of science and theology into a higher synthesis. At last Buchanan could confidently affirm that "the power of disembodied mind and intellectual manifestations ... fall within the scope of the fundamental principles of the constitution of man, and spiritual mysteries, too, are beautifully elucidated by the complete correspondence, and mathematical harmony, between the spiritual and material laws of our being."[44]

Buchanan's interest in mesmerism's religious and metaphysical implications was widely shared. As early as 1837, a letter addressed to the editor of the *Boston Recorder* had testified:

> George was converted from materialism to Christianity by the facts in Animal Magnetism developed under his [Poyen's] practice ... it proves the power of mind over matter ... informs our faith in the spirituality and immortality of our nature, and encourages us to renewed efforts to live up to its transcendent powers.[45]

A high school teacher wrote to the *Providence Journal* that "God and eternity are the only answer to these mysterious phenomena—these apparitions of the Infinity and the Unknown."[46] An early tract on the science of animal magnetism drew attention to the ways in which it casts "light on how we are constituted, how nearly we are related to, and how far we resemble our original ... God who is a pure spiritual essence."[47] The same author went on to boast that mesmerism "shows that man has within him a spiritual nature, which can live without the body ... in the eternal *NOW* of a future existence."[48]

Those who experienced the mesmerizing process described it as a decidedly numinous experience. Direct contact with the instreaming animal magnetic forces was thought to momentarily transform and elevate a person's being. A typical account relates that

> The whole moral and intellectual character becomes changed from the degraded condition of earth to the exalted intelligence of a spiritual state. The external senses are all suspended and the internal sense of spirit acts with its natural power as it will when entirely freed from the body after death. No person, we think, can listen to the revelations of a subject in a magnetic state, respecting the mysteries of our nature, and continue to doubt the existence of a never dying soul and the existence of a future or heavenly life.[49]

It is evident that even though mesmerism had no overt connections with institutional religion it was nonetheless interpreted as a progressive variation of the religious revivals that had shaped American religious life. The mesmerists, no less than Protestant revivalists, taught that human brokenness comes from having fallen out of rapport with the invisible spiritual workings of the universe. Mesmerism, like revivalism, provided inwardly troubled individuals with an intense experience believed to restore them to harmony with unseen spiritual forces. And the mesmeric state, no less than the emotion-laden conversion experience, gave powerful and convincing experiential grounds for the belief that humanity's lower nature can be utterly transformed and elevated when brought under the guiding influence of spirit.

Yet the mesmerists differed from the revivalists in one very important respect. Far from reproaching individuals for challenging orthodox religious thinking, they encouraged them to do so. Mesmerism's doctrines tended to appeal to those whose religious sensibilities could not be constrained by scriptural piety and who yearned instead for a progressive, co-scientific outlook. As one advocate put it, mesmerism "not only disposes the mind to adopt religious principles, but also tends to free us from the errors of superstition by reducing to natural causes many phenomena."[50] Mesmerism attracted those who, while committed to the intellectual standards of Enlightenment rationality, nonetheless hungered for a spiritual outlook on life.

Among the first to recognize mesmerist psychology's contributions to the era's religious turmoil was a Universalist minister by the name of John Dods. Dods, like many other Universalist ministers who came to embrace mesmerism, had struggled to make a convincing case for God's redemptive presence in nature. He was therefore quick to appreciate how the science of animal magnetism taught "that God is electrically and magnetically connected to His universe, that this is how He stamps upon the world its BEAUTY, ORDER, and HARMONY."[51] And, what is more, mesmerism also articulated the principle that each and every human being is inwardly connected with "the grand agent employed by the Creator to move and govern the universe."[52] The mesmerizing process was in this sense a sacrament. When properly employed, it had the power to "enlarge and elevate the mind ... to impress upon it more exalted ideas of the infinite wisdom and goodness of the Deity."[53]

Another zealous convert to the mesmerist cause was the Swedenborgian spokesman, Professor George Bush. The Swedenborgian notions of correspondence and influx held forth a vision of the universe in which there is lawful interaction between the physical and metaphysical orders of reality. There was, as yet, no scientific account of precisely how such interaction or influx takes place. In his 1847 volume, *Mesmer and Swedenborg*, Bush suggested that mesmerism was providing empirical support for Swedenborg's teachings. Mesmerism was proving "the grand principle that man is a spirit as to his interiors and that his spiritual nature in the body often manifests itself according to the laws which govern it out of the body."[54] Mesmerism struck Bush as providing the foundation of a new vision of human nature that could satisfy both our scientific and spiritual interests. He concluded that "On the whole it must, we think be admitted that the phenomena of mesmerism taken in conjunction with the developments of Swedenborg, open a new chapter in the philosophy of mind and in man's relations to a higher sphere."[55]

It is important to note here that cultural factors were far more important than strictly scientific considerations in generating popular support for intellectual systems such as mesmerism. Mesmerism, no less than Transcendentalism and Swedenborgianism, was pressed into the service of meeting a host of otherwise unmet spiritual needs. Historian Whitney Cross succinctly captures the "Americanization" of these ideas that offered Americans new, unchurched sources of spiritual understanding:

> Before they [nineteenth-century Americans] ever heard of Mesmer or Swedenborg, they expected new scientific discoveries to confirm the broad patterns of revelation as they understood them: to give mankind ever-more-revealing glimpses of the preordained divine plan for humanity and the universe. They expected all such knowledge would demonstrate the superiority of ideal over physical or material force, and that it would prove the relationship of man's soul to the infinite spiritual power.[56]

Swedenborgianism, Transcendentalism, and mesmerism melded together to create a free-flowing repertoire of ideas that could be used to fashion a bold, new spiritual outlook. All three found their way into yet one more manifestation of this first metaphysical awakening—spiritualism.

| The Discovery of Spirit Guides

Spiritualism is usually thought to have originated in 1847 in Hydesville, New York. Soon after John D. Fox, his wife, and six children moved into their new home they began to hear mysterious rapping noises. Two daughters, Maggie and Kate, gradually became brave enough to clap their hands and snap their fingers in an effort to elicit these knocking sounds. A series of raps responded to their initiative. Soon a simple code of communication was set up between the Fox sisters and the invisible spirit who apparently resided in their home. With time Maggie and Kate learned that the spirit who made these rapping noises was that of a murdered peddler whose remains were buried in the cellar of their home. News of the Fox sisters' sensational communication with the spirit world traveled rapidly. They had, it seemed, stumbled upon dramatic proof of life after death. Within months they were national celebrities.

The Fox sisters understood the commercial value of their newfound ability to make contact with the spirit world. An older sister joined them and organized a series of public demonstrations. The Fox sisters charged admission to these demonstrations and in no time at all spiritualism proved to be a lucrative enterprise. Following their lead, other spirit "mediums" learned to attract audiences eager to pay for the right to witness this fascinating spectacle. The spiritualists' seances were part sideshow entertainment, part shamanlike encounter with awesome supernatural powers. Some mediums were able to produce slates on which spirits had written special messages for members of the paying audience. Others used their spirit contacts to perform feats of telepathy and clairvoyance. All offered solace to those who came hoping to hear that departed loved ones were all right in their new heavenly existence.

Spiritualism's origins were actually far more complex than the story of the Fox sisters suggests. Before the Fox family ever moved into their famed Hydesville home, a person by the name of Andrew Jackson Davis was initiated into a very different, more religious form of spiritualism. Davis's autobiography paints his life as one long, religious obstacle course. As a youth he attended a Presbyterian church where he was taught of a "God clothed in Calvinist attributes, also in His eternal decrees of election and reprobation and also in many other points of faith ascribing unamiable qualities to the Deity."[57]

Whether out of persistence or petulance—or both, Davis took it on himself to quiz his religious teachers about the evidence supporting these theological doctrines. His queries were stifled. He was admonished that it must be a very depraved and hellbent boy who would dare to question the ways of God as described in the Bible. Davis's dissatisfaction led him to investigate other Protestant denominations. Unfortunately, he fared no better with the Methodists. Their "program for prayer and conversion" failed to satisfy his craving for experiential insight into divine truth. It soon became apparent that no ready-made religious doctrine, no matter how liberal its cast, could contain Davis's spiritual restlessness. He relates that "by another year I was introduced to Universalism. Its teachings were more congenial with my better nature ... [but] I couldn't believe the Universalist system of theology as a whole."[58]

A quirk of fate rescued Davis from a life of spiritual impoverishment. In 1843—four years before the Fox sisters' rappings—a mesmerist passed through Davis's hometown of Poughkeepsie giving lecture-demonstrations on the subject of animal magnetism. Davis was invited to come up on stage to serve as a volunteer subject. Davis, who was at the time an apprentice cobbler, appeared to have extraordinary aptitude for attaining the deepest levels of the mesmeric trance. When mesmerized, Davis performed such feats as reading from books while blindfolded, telepathically receiving thoughts from those in the audience, or traveling clairvoyantly to distant locales. Davis proved so adept at entering the mesmeric trance that he hired himself out as a professional subject and for a time toured New England, exhibiting his miraculous mental powers.

After several months of repeated journeys into the inner recesses of his mind, Davis abruptly declared that mesmerism had activated "some of the many powers which we know to rest in the soul's deep bosom."[59] The greatest of these was the ability to channel messages from spirits who resided in the "ethers" that invisibly surround earth. Davis had become a trance medium. He soon learned to dispense with the assistance of a mesmerist and learned to enter a self-induced state of mystical reverie. Davis claimed that in this receptive mental state he received messages from spirits. These messages were channeled automatically through his mind into spoken words. Friends feverishly recorded every word that Davis uttered so that they might later be published in thick, scholarly-looking tomes. The American public fairly gobbled up these dispensations from the spirit world. One of Davis's major works, *The Harmonial Philosophy*, went through twenty-four editions.

The theological statements written "by and through" Andrew Jackson Davis became the nucleus of a loosely knit system of spiritualist philosophy. Following Davis's lead, spiritualist writers developed a new language for describing God. They typically referred to God as an impersonal energy or intelligence. This pantheistic way of thinking about God allowed spiritualists to attribute both masculine and feminine qualities to divine spirit. Our universe, they taught, is structured and lawful (as opposed to being run by a fickle deity). It consists of several concentric spheres arranged in such a way that causal energies can flow from "higher" spheres to "lower" ones. By enhancing our inner connection with these higher spiritual realms, each and every one of us might become a medium through which spiritual power flows into our physical world.

If all of this begins to sound a bit like Swedenborgianism, in a manner of speaking it was. One of the first spirits to instruct Davis was none other than Emanuel Swedenborg. Or, at least, so Davis's contact in the spirit world frequently identified himself. From Davis on, spiritualism absorbed and popularized the metaphysical teachings of Swedenborgianism, Transcendentalism, and mesmerism. Anyone attending a spiritualist séance would witness a concrete demonstration of the metaphysical doctrines of "correspondence" and "influx." Spiritualists fully accepted Swedenborg's belief in the inner divinity of person as well as his conception of the basic continuity between the material and spiritual worlds.[60] They also drew heavily on his idea that there are spirits inhabiting "higher" spheres of existence and that we can communicate with these spirits.

Spiritualism did, however, veer away from Swedenborg on some issues. Spiritualism encouraged interest in the personalities and insights of the entities who authored spirit messages. Swedenborg had actually warned that spirits lack reliability as a source of truth. He discouraged his followers from making contact with spirits on their own, instructing them instead to rely on his special guidance in these matters. American spiritualists ignored these warnings and sought their own personal communication with celestial beings. Many taught that each of us has a special "spirit guide" who watches over our worldly and spiritual destinies. Not only was this a more democratic spirituality than Swedenborgianism had originally envisioned, but it also introduced a "personal" element. The Protestant traditions that dominated American religious thought had long repudiated belief in the efficacy of prayer to saints or the Virgin Mary. American Protestants consequently stood alone before a remote, wrathful God. They had to face life's rigors without the consolation that Catholics found when they sought intercession from the quasi-human personages of Mary and the saints. Even those nineteenth-century Protestants whose liberal religious beliefs rejected the traditional image of a sin-hating God often felt in need of greater spiritual comfort or assistance. The idea of an "impersonal deity" that was emerging in liberal theology furthered a rationalist tendency toward cold abstractions rather than the intimacy of warm personal communication. Spiritualism's belief in the existence of spirit guides who take a personal interest in our lives (and who are in a position to mediate on our behalf) was an appealing alternative to either conventional Protestant theism or rational metaphysics.

Andrew Jackson Davis had, in the words of historian Brett Carroll, "established a new religious ideology postulating the presence and activity of spirits ... and the ability of human beings to receive religious comfort and guidance through communication with them."[61] This ideology reflected the spiritual aspirations of a wide spectrum of Americans dissatisfied with the existing religious establishment. Foremost among these were women who were tired of religious institutions dominated by male clergy. Spiritualism emerged at a time when no churches ordained women and many forbade them to speak aloud in church. In contrast, the growing spiritualist movement offered women equal authority, equal opportunities, and equal access to positions of religious leadership.[62] Spiritualism was, furthermore, sensitive to women's interest in religious language that emphasized their relationship with God. Spiritualist leaders paved the way for innovations in the way we describe God so as to balance male and female imagery. In fact, the spiritualists' entire religious outlook encompassed what appear in retrospect to have been the most liberal, progressive, and liberating intellectual currents of their generation.[63]

An even stronger reason why many were attracted to spiritualism was its apparent potential to reconcile science and religion. Most middle-class Americans admired science and accepted its growing cultural prestige. They were, however, unsettled by its materialistic tendencies. Because science recognizes only those realities that can be measured and quantified, it implicitly undermines belief in all lofty ideals and meanings—including those of religion. Spiritualism, on the other hand, proclaimed that the phenomena experienced at se-ances were susceptible to empirical demonstration. It was thought that spiritualism could provide scientific proof of life after death. If spiritualism could deliver on this promise, it would force science to expand its scope to include the higher, nonmaterial orders of reality. Not only would spiritualism lead the way to an expanded science, but it would furnish new empirical foundations for religious belief. Those who embraced spiritualism argued that it moved religion past reliance on either blind faith or the supposed revelations of the Bible. We were now free to explore the spiritual spheres of life in the same way that science investigates the world of nature. Curiosity and free-thinking inquiry could now be affirmed as the keys to a genuine spiri-tuality.

The spiritualists' vision of a lawful, structured universe had one unintended theological consequence. They had painted themselves into a corner that seemingly left no room for free will. Spiritualists of-ten claimed to believe in free will, but it didn't have a logical role in their metaphysical system. Humans were said to be influenced by a network of cosmic forces that included the spirits who watched over them and occasionally intervened on their behalf. Given this belief in metaphysical causation, their arguments on behalf of free will were strained. On the one hand, spiritualists recognized that belief in the lawful nature of the spiritual world was consoling, especially to those who had come to feel personally powerless and now sought help from "higher" supernatural sources. One of the most appealing ele-ments of religion is the belief that there are higher powers who care for us and are able to intervene on our behalf. On the other hand, our culture's emphasis on moral responsibility presupposes free will. It seems that spiritualism—like most unchurched religion to this day—wanted to have it both ways. The need to affirm the importance of personal effort while simultaneously promising the availability of help from "higher" sources ultimately triumphed over theological consistency.

When all is said and done, however, the main reason for spiritual-ism's popularity was that it contained a thrilling experiential element. Attending a seance was an eerie, awe-inspiring experience. It brought one face-to-face with supernatural entities who possessed mysterious powers. Such encounters were exhilarating. They suggested that there was far more to our universe than was being taught by either science or religion. All this was in stark contrast to the "extraordinary dullness" most converts to spiritualism associated with established churches. Adherents of spiritualism criticized the churches as rigid and superficial. According to Andrew Jackson Davis's second wife, Mary Fenn Davis, religious organizations are inherently tyrannical; they stifle the sources of inner spiritual illumination. "Ecclesiastical regulations merge into customs; individualism ceases; and men become automatons, and exist for centuries on a dead level of mental slavery and conservatism."[64] Her husband continued the crusade against what he saw as the churches' historic efforts to conspire against individual freedom. He wrote that "American Republicanism will be transformed into tyranny unless individual man declareth himself independent of all political and ecclesiastical Institutions."[65] Other spiritualist writers agreed and urged their readers to throw off the cloak of "churchianity." Genuine spirituality, they proclaimed, requires us to reclaim our own potential to become bearers of divine inspiration. Spiritualists believed that in order to become a true follower of Christ one must, like him, leave existing religious institutions behind and insist on a personal connection with God. As one spiritualist wrote, the life of Christ "was a beautiful spontaneity, with its governing principle within, wholly independent of external authority or organization, with which he lived in daily conflict."[66] Spiritualism thus appealed to those who had long since decided that existing churches were both emotionally and intellectually stifling.

Swedenborgianism, Transcendentalism, mesmerism, and spiritualism came together to create the first "metaphysical awakening" in American religious life. Although their origins and theological outlooks were different, they melded neatly in the minds of Americans seeking new sources of religious edification. One historian has suggested that "mesmerism led to Swedenborgianism, and Swedenborgianism to spiritualism, not because of the degree of intrinsic relationship between their propositions but because of the assumptions according to which their American adherents understood them."[67] Middle-class audiences were attracted to these metaphysical systems as a means of preserving—not repudiating—the core values of American culture. The adherents of these movements felt stifled by the rigidity of existing churches. They were energetically searching for ways to accommodate their religious impulses to the modern world. Historical hindsight reveals that these "highly active seekers" were the avant-garde of what was to become a long tradition in unchurched American piety.

2

The Flowering
of Metaphysical
Religion

The Civil War brought a temporary halt to the growth of unchurched spirituality. Political discord and the carnage of war siphoned away much of the enthusiasm for religious innovation. But, by the mid-1880s, when some measure of normalcy had returned to American life, it was inevitable that the nation would regain its spiritual vitality. Transcendentalism, Swedenborgianism, mesmerism, Unitarianism, Universalism, and spiritualism had sewn the seeds of religious experimentation and these seeds had fallen on fertile cultural soil. Many Americans styled themselves as progressive thinkers. Their commitment to modern ways of thinking made a retreat to old-fashioned church religion impossible. Yet most were equally unwilling to settle for a purely scientific account of the universe. They needed a new religious outlook that would demonstrate the existence of something beyond physical reality. The period between 1885 and 1910 witnessed the flowering of religious philosophies that met this cultural need. These new religious movements were metaphysical in nature, focusing attention on a more-than-physical reality not yet recognized by science. Their descriptions of our connection with this reality generated a wave of religious enthusiasm and, in the process, provided a new terminology that permeates unchurched religious thought even to this day.

| New Thought and the Triumph of Harmonial Piety

Mesmerism was destined to exert a long-lasting influence on American religious life. One unlikely source of this influence was a clockmaker from Belfast, Maine, by the name of Phineas P. Quimby. In 1838, Quimby attended a lecture-demonstration on mesmerism and was inspired to conduct some experiments on his own. He discovered that he had a remarkable gift for putting people into a mesmeric trance. His subjects fell into a sleeplike condition and when they awoke they claimed to have been cured of various physical and emotional disorders. Over time, however, Quimby began to suspect that he had very little to do with his patients' rapid recoveries. He speculated that what really cured them was their own belief. They expected to be healed, and the healing followed. Quimby didn't stop there. He jumped to the more radical conclusion that their beliefs had caused their illnesses in the first place. He reasoned that our minds are the sum total of our beliefs. If a person is "deceived into a belief that he has, or is liable to have a disease, the belief is catching and the effects follow from it."[1] Quimby was thus struggling to formulate what we today would call a theory of psychosomatic illness.

Quimby did not mean that beliefs influence our well-being all by themselves. He held that the real source of human health is the magnetic fluid or vital force that enters the human nervous system through the deepest levels of the mind. Beliefs function like control valves or floodgates: they either connect or disconnect the conscious mind and its unconscious depths. Some beliefs focus our attention solely outward. Such beliefs render the mind wholly reactive, blocking its receptivity to the inflow of spiritual forces available through the unconscious. Severed from its internal source of vital energies, the body eventually lapses into disease. When, on the other hand, we hold beliefs that focus our attention inward, we remain continuously open to the inflow of spiritual energy. As a consequence, we radiate health and creativity. Quimby believed that if he could just show his patients "that a man's happiness is in his belief, and his misery is the effect of his belief, then I have done what never has been done before. Establish this and man rises to a higher state of wisdom, not of this world, but of that World of Science ... the Wisdom of Science is Life eternal."[2]

Quimby's gospel of mental cure had a beautiful simplicity about it. Right beliefs channel health, happiness, and wisdom out of the cosmic ethers and into the individual's unconscious mind. If we can control our beliefs, we will control the shunting valve that regulates psychological abundance. With this idea Quimby managed to translate the rather vague metaphysical language of an Emerson or Swedenborg into a practical philosophy of life. Earlier doctrines concerning the influx of spirit from the Oversoul could now be expressed in simpler, psychological terms. By making the appropriate mental adjustments we can connect with the very powers that activate the universe. Right thinking, combined with occasional moments of silence for the purpose of cultivating inner receptivity, is a surefire formula for generating personal power.

Many of Quimby's patients became students and eventually disciples of his mindcure philosophy. One of these students was Mary Baker Eddy who converted Quimby's teachings into the cardinal doctrines of her Church of Christ, Scientist. Mrs. Eddy and Christian Science belong more properly to the study of institutional religion. It is clear, however, that they played an important role in disseminating a new kind of psychologically phrased spirituality. In fact, Eddy's principal text, *Science and Health with Key to the Scriptures*, would sell more than 400,000 copies by 1900. Three of Quimby's other patients also succeeded in bringing his psychological gospel to the attention of the American middle class. Warren Felt Evans, Anetta Dresser, and her husband Julius Dresser blended psychological and religious language without creating churches or defining fixed doctrines. These three former patients of Quimby pioneered the self-help spiritualities that to this day speak to those who hunger for greater personal power than they have yet achieved through conventional religious means.

After he was healed by Quimby, Warren Felt Evans opened a healing office of his own in Boston. There for the next twenty years he gave direction to what was variously referred to as the mind cure or New Thought movement. In addition to his healing activities, Evans went on lecture tours and authored a series of books that brought

Quimby's insights to the attention of the nation's middle-class readership. His *The Mental Cure* (1869) and *Mental Medicine* (1871) had, by 1875, gone through seven and fifteen editions, respectively. In these and other works with titles such as *The Divine Law of Cure, Esoteric Christianity and Mental Therapeutics*, and *The Primitive Mind Cure*, Evans equated the healing powers of the unconscious with the kerygma of the early Christian church. He argued that the church had lost contact with its experiential origins. Evans believed that the principles of mind cure psychology recaptured the metaphysical teachings of Jesus and his earliest followers and thus promised to return Christian faith to its true beginnings.

Like Evans, Anetta and Julius Dresser opened an office in the Boston area. They, too, attracted a steady stream of clients who believed that neither existing medical nor religious establishments understood their psychological unrest. The Dressers organized their clients into discussion groups and, later, into structured courses. They began charging tuition and awarding credits toward eventual certification in the theory and practice of mind cure science. On graduation, mind cure students found a new profession awaiting them. Practitioners were able to charge clients up to five dollars per visit, and the more successful rapidly attracted a coterie of followers who would sign up for course instruction. Boston soon reached the saturation point, prompting many practitioners to move westward in search of new clients. Metaphysical healing clubs sprang up in scattered locales around the country, including New York, Chicago, Kansas City, and finally Los Angeles.

The Metaphysical Club of Boston, founded in 1895, issued a statement of purpose that was "to promote interest in and the practice of a true philosophy of life and happiness; to show that through right thinking, one's loftiest ideals may be brought into present realization; and to advance intelligent and systematic treatment of disease by spiritual and mental methods."[3] This statement reveals the idealism that late nineteenth-century Americans brought to metaphysical teachings. The New Thought philosophy, as the movement came to be known, offered inspiring new ideas about humanity's place in the greater scheme of things. Whereas traditional churches emphasize moral obedience in the present so that we might one day exist as souls in a heavenly afterlife, New Thoughters proclaimed that we "are living souls now, Children of God ... spiritual citizens of a divine universe." In this divine universe, mind is primary and causal, while matter is secondary and resultant. The way to accomplish anything—from healing to financial abundance—is "metaphysical, beyond the physical, in the realm of causes which are mental and spiritual."

New Thought reformulated traditional ideas about the nature of God and our relationship to God. Its whole outlook on life was predicated on "the idea of God as immanent, indwelling Spirit, All-wisdom, All-goodness, ever-present in the universe." These pantheistic images contrasted sharply with biblical ideas of God as a male authority figure. The churches taught that the basic problem of human nature is sin, understood as willful disobedience to the commands laid down by this supreme male ruler. For New Thought, on the other hand, the only thing that separates humans from God is limited self-understanding, understood as simple ignorance of our potential to become inwardly attuned to God's instreaming spiritual energies. These metaphysical understandings also implied a wholesale rejection of the need for vicarious atonement through Christ. The New Thoughters were not denying the divinity of Christ so much as they were celebrating the inner divinity of every man and woman. They looked to Jesus as a great example of a life governed by metaphysical awareness. But they denied that Jesus or any other great religious teacher had a monopoly on spiritual truth. Indeed, New Thought taught both the "universality of religion" and the "progressive revelation of truth." They felt free to look beyond the Christian Bible for new insights into the nature and meaning of life.

The New Thought philosophy rendered church membership irrelevant. Biblical religion had argued that humans were in the condition of disobedience or sin. It followed that repentance, contrition, and public displays of worship or adoration were preconditions for restoring a convenantal relationship with God. But the discoveries of the mesmerists and mind curists now pointed Americans in a different direction. New Thought proclaimed that obedience to the laws of the mind, not to scriptural commandments, is what enables God's presence to manifest itself in our lives. Men and women should stop straining to please a judgmental God or to worship God in a weekly church service. It is sufficient to spend a few moments alone in silence for the purpose of activating the powers of the unconscious mind. As Walter Felt Evans wrote, there is "a battery and reservoir of magnetic life and vital force" deep within us, awaiting spiritual activation.[4]

One of New Thought's best-known authors, Ralph Waldo Trine, succinctly captured the movement's metaphysical vision:

> In just the degree that we come into a conscious realization of our oneness with the Infinite Life, and open ourselves to the Divine inflow, do we actualize in ourselves the qualities and powers of the Infinite Life, do we make ourselves channels through which the Infinite Intelligence and Power can work. In just the degree in which you realize your oneness with the Infinite Spirit, you will exchange dis-ease for ease, inharmony for harmony, suffering and pain for abounding health and strength.[5]

For Trine and other New Thoughters, mental healing was empirical proof that "thoughts are forces." It seemed to them that thoughts generate a vibratory field of energy, which can be strengthened and amplified to exert causal influence on natural conditions. Trine asserted that "in the degree that thought is spiritualized, does it become more subtle and powerful ... this spiritualizing is in accordance with law and is within the power of all." Even more to the point: "Within yourself lies the cause of whatever enters your life. To come into the full realization of your awakened interior powers, is to be able to condition your life in exact accord with what you would have it. ... This is the secret of all success."[6]

"As a man thinketh, so is he" was no mere aphorism for the New Thoughters. It was metaphysical law. Evans taught that "if we form the true idea of man and apply it to ourselves, and hold it steadfastly in the mind and believe in its realization, by one of the deepest and most certain laws of our nature, it will tend to recreate the body of the mental type."[7] Many New Thoughters believed that their thoughts could transform virtually any condition in the outer world. Trine had taught that in just the degree that thought is spiritualized, it becomes more subtle and powerful. Following this logic, New Thoughters encouraged their readers to believe that they could telepathically transmit their desires and ideas into the psychic ethers with full confidence that they would be transformed into physical reality. By the late 1890s, the New Thought movement had generated dozens of self-help books that linked metaphysical spirituality with get-rich-quick schemes. One of these success authors, Frank Haddock, produced a steady stream of books with such titles as *Power of Will*, *Practical Psychology*, *The Personal Atmosphere*, and *Power for Success*. As another think-your-way-to-success pundit wrote, our "own thought power is a force, the intentionality and utility of which has been almost undreamed of." The significance of this discovery was unmistakable: "We may grasp and wield its divine forces, and through them assert our supremacy over the kingdom of our rightful domain."[8]

New Thought took metaphysical religion out of the realm of idle speculation and made it the basis of practical self-help exercises. Its popular success enabled "harmonial religion" to become a major force in modern spiritual life. In harmonial religion, spiritual composure, physical health, and even economic well-being are understood to flow from a person's rapport with the cosmos.[9] As such, harmonial religion is a vast and highly diffuse impulse in American religious life. It underlies interest in meditation. It informs many forms of alternative medicine. And, to be sure, it can be found in the crassest self-help schemes. Harmonial piety is in many ways like sympathetic magic; it encourages us to adjust our inner lives in hopes of better aligning ourselves with powerful energies operative in the universe at large. In the 1880s and 1890s, this message appealed to many middle- and upper-middle-class urban Americans (including roughly twice as many women as men).[10] Since then, the major themes of harmonial religion have gradually filtered into such a wide array of inspirational literature that they not only shape the spiritual lives of unchurched persons, but inform the inner meaning of the faith affirmed by many church members as well.

‖ The Lure of the Esoteric: Theosophy's Legacy

Occult philosophies have attracted a small but loyal following throughout Western history.[11] The first three centuries of the common era witnessed a resurgence of Neoplatonic and Gnostic speculation about the nature of the soul and its relationship to higher spheres. A collection of writings from this time known as the *Book of Hermes Trimegistus* became highly influential during the Enlightenment. Comprising a loose assortment of magical, astrological, and Neoplatonic ideas, it gave its name to Hermetic science. Hermetic science covered the entire gamut of occult topics including the existence of divine reality, the nature of the elements, and the symbolic interrelationships connecting the various orders of the universe. Over time, Hermetic science blended with other mystical philosophies, resurfacing in occult interests such as Jewish cabala, Rosicrucianism, Masonry, and the spiritual writings of Jacob Boehme. The Western occult traditions were largely esoteric, meaning that their teachings were thought to be secret and could only be transmitted through privileged instruction or the cultivation of special states of mystical awareness. Shrouded in mystery, occult philosophies cast an aura of intrigue and excitement. And, for this reason, they have for more than 2,000 years appealed to the intellectually adventurous as a viable philosophical and religious alternative to biblical religion.

We know that in the colonial era many personal libraries contained treatises on occult philosophy. There is little evidence to suggest, however, that esoteric spirituality was anything more than a passing curiosity among Americans prior to the 1880s. A major step toward the solidification of occult interests took place when Madame Helena Petrovna Blavatsky (1831–1891) immigrated to New York in 1872. Blavatsky's personal history is shrouded in mystery. It appears that she left her native Russia when she was twenty years old. Becoming something of a gypsy, Blavatsky traveled extensively and seemed to gravitate toward people who dabbled in mesmerism, spiritualism, and other occult philosophies. In New York she earned a reputation as a trance medium, channeling messages from advanced spiritual teachers whom she referred to as the mahatmas (the Hindu term for "great souls"). In 1874, Madame Blavatsky met up with Colonel Henry S. Olcott (1832–1907), a lawyer who was deeply interested in the scientific and religious implications of spiritualism. As it turned out, the mahatmas took special interest in Olcott. Through Blavatsky's trances the mahatmas sent Olcott a message instructing him to found an organization for the purpose of disseminating spiritual wisdom. By 1875, Olcott and Blavatsky had launched the Theosophical Society, dedicated to bridging the current gulf between science and religion through the study of mesmerism, spiritualism, and the universal ether.

In 1877, Blavatsky published *Isis Unveiled*, now widely recognized as a modern occult classic.[12] Blavatsky claimed that her writing was guided by the mahatmas, members of the Universal Mystic Brotherhood who lived in the Himalayan mountains of Tibet. The mahatmas were spiritually evolved humans who had achieved the ability to travel and communicate psychically. Blavatsky had first met the mahatmas in her travels abroad and they had revealed to her how the mystical core of both Hinduism and Buddhism constituted the true source of all living world religions. With the help of the mahatmas, Blavatsky articulated what might be called an emanationist view of the world. This view explains that life originated with the emanation of a "divine spark" into the world of matter—a spark that is now gradually evolving back to its divine source. This cosmology enabled Theosophy to embrace Darwinian theories of evolution in a larger metaphysical synthesis. While physical science was said to describe the "how" of evolution, metaphysics provided seekers with insight into evolution's ultimate meaning and purpose.

Throughout *Isis Unveiled* and her later work, *The Secret Doctrine* (1888), Blavatsky sprinkled the concepts of reincarnation and karma, which she had acquired from Hinduism. This enabled adherents to view their personal lives against the backdrop of cosmic evolution. They could now interpret their daily struggles as opportunities to grow spiritually and thereby contribute to the larger push of cosmic evolution. Blavatsky went even further, teaching that we exist in a multidimensional universe. Borrowing from Asian vocabularies that describe the "subtle" layers of selfhood, Blavatsky taught that we exist simultaneously on seven levels—including what she termed the astral and etheric planes. Other Theosophical writers expanded upon this theme and taught that we consist of seven subtle bodies. These other bodies connect with our physical body at the seven chakras (or spiritual centers) located at various points along our spinal columns. Theosophy explained how meditation can open up our chakras and enhance our connection with these other planes of existence. Such connection brings us into direct contact with "higher powers" that promote both physical health and emotional serenity.

Isis Unveiled sold a thousand copies in the first ten days after its release and has sold more than 500,000 copies to date. Those who investigate Theosophical teachings are likely to be "educated persons to whom religion is important but who have become estranged from established religious traditions. Their learning makes them both sensitive to the challenges of science to religion and aware of the insights of different religious traditions."[13] Theosophy claimed, after all, to represent wisdom descending from ancient civilizations. It was returning us to the pristine source of all religious and scientific wisdom, a source free from the distortions that have gradually crept into modern institutions.[14] Many who delve into occult philosophies don't believe that they are abandoning Christianity or Judaism so much as going to deeper teachings than can be found in present-day institutions. This, however, could not be said for Madame Blavatsky herself. In theory, Blavatsky proclaimed that all religions share a common esoteric source. Yet in practice she seemed especially anxious to argue that Jesus's teachings were not original, that the Bible merely copies other ancient works, and that Christian theology has largely distorted the mystical insights on which it was originally founded. Theosophy's anti-Christian polemic undoubtedly kept Theosophy from directly influencing as many churched Americans as either New Thought or spiritualism. At the same time, its bold confidence in non-Christian philosophies strengthened Theosophy's appeal to those eager to explore decidedly exotic forms of mystical spirituality.

Even at the height of its popularity, Theosophy never had more than 10,000 members in the United States. Its worldwide membership may have reached over 50,000. Despite these relatively small numbers, Theosophy has exerted considerable influence on the historical development of unchurched religion. Its most important contribution was the integration of Eastern religions into the metaphysical vocabularies of unchurched Americans. Theosophy was not simply advocating toleration of Hinduism and Buddhism; it went further, suggesting that these traditions possessed superior understandings of our potential to achieve mystical connection with God. Theosophy was thus largely responsible for the fact that subsequent generations of unchurched Americans have freely referenced Yoga meditation, Zen satori, the Atman-Brahman unity, or the existence of "subtle energies" such as *kundalini, chi*, or *prana.*

Theosophy also advanced the cause of metaphysical religion by taking Christian orthodoxy head on. Theosophical writers emboldened those who were already dissatisfied with Christian doctrines of special revelation, original sin, vicarious atonement, and the need for self-abnegation. In their place Theosophy preached that all religions have a common source, that God is an impersonal presence in nature, that everyone's real self is divine, and that we can continue to grow spiritually in this and future existences. Finally, Theosophy introduced a language of expectation of a "new age."[15] Both in substance and in style the "New Age" movement that gained widespread recognition in the 1980s and 1990s reflects Theosophical influences. From talk about *chakras* to trance-channeling messages from ascended masters, the New Age movement has drawn freely on the vocabularies and spiritual practices first introduced to American audiences by Helena Petrovna Blavatsky and her followers.

William James and the Quest for Higher States of Consciousness

The ministers and theologians who represent institutional religion usually possess greater intellectual and cultural sophistication than those who speak for unchurched religious movements. Denominational seminaries produce graduates trained in a disciplined theological method. Their religious writings consequently appear cogent and grounded in a time-honored theosophical vocabulary. The spokespersons for unchurched religion, meanwhile, are more likely to come from the ranks of low- or middlebrow American culture. Phineas Quimby, Ralph Waldo Trine, and Helena Petrovna Blavatsky are representative of those who have sought to communicate a spiritual vision without the benefit of formal theological training. This is probably one reason why Ralph Waldo Emerson and William James have come to occupy such a commanding place in the history of America's unchurched religious thinking.[16] We have already looked at Emerson's role in generating the nineteenth century's metaphysical movements. It was William James, however, who most clearly put the imprimatur of highbrow respectability on Americans' fascination with unconventional spirituality.

William James (1842–1910) was born to an affluent and socially connected family. His father, Henry James Sr., was a self styled intellectual and progressive thinker. He was a close friend of many of the era's religious innovators, including Emerson, who frequently visited the James home to engage in lively discussion. Henry became enamored of Swedenborgianism and even expanded on the Swedish seer's teachings in his own, largely ignored publications. He was determined that his children would make a distinctive mark in the world, and provided them with expensive educations, private tutors, and numerous trips to European cultural centers. One son, Henry Jr., became a gifted novelist. But it was the oldest son, William, whose contributions to psychology, philosophy, and religion put the boldest stamp on modern American thought.

After a brief stint as an artist, William James earned a medical degree from Harvard and joined its faculty to teach first physiology, then psychology.[17] His interests, however, were never fully scientific. James was intensely curious. His desire was to develop a philosophical system that would synthesize his scientific and religious interests. Even though William was not himself particularly mystical, he nonetheless envied mystics. He yearned to share their direct experience of higher orders of reality. Once while working in his laboratory he inhaled nitrous oxide gas and later recorded that it had temporarily afforded him "the tremendously exciting sense of an intense metaphysical illumination."[18] James later went on to the systematic study mystical states, culminating in the 1902 publication of his classic *The Varieties of Religious Experience*. The *Varieties* argues that there is an experiential core to religion that underlies all of the various creeds and rituals associated with religious organizations. James's understanding of religion reveals how fully he had absorbed his father's Emersonian and Swedenborgian ideas concerning correspondence and influx. In the *Varieties*, James suggests that religion arises out of mystical experiences in which we realize that (1) the visible world is part of a more spiritual universe from which it draws its chief significance and (2) union or harmonious relation with this "more" is our true end. Importantly, James confessed that his understanding of the authentic core of religion first came to him during his own nitrous oxide-induced altered state of consciousness:

> Some years ago I myself made some observations on this aspect of nitrous oxide intoxication, and reported them in print. One conclusion was forced upon my mind at that time, and my impression of its truth has ever since remained unshaken. It is that our normal waking consciousness, rational consciousness as we call it, is but one special type of consciousness, whilst all about it, parted from it by the filmiest of screens, there lie potential forms of consciousness entirely different.[19]

Our normal waking state of consciousness has the special task of adapting us to our physical surroundings. James suggested that other states of consciousness open our awareness to entirely different metaphysical "worlds." Although our usual world of experience and these "higher" worlds are usually separated from one another, "yet the two become continuous at certain points, and higher energies filter in."[20] James called this his "piecemeal supernaturalism." That is, he thought that under certain circumstances our consciousness shifts along a continuum to a point at which it becomes receptive to the "inflow" of supernatural energies. He noted the physical healing produced by the mind cure practitioners of his era as evidence of this piecemeal supernaturalism. The mind curists effectively demonstrated that mystical states of consciousness enable us to become continuous with higher metaphysical worlds. James believed that the study of mystical states of consciousness could potentially widen the scope of science to the point where it would empirically verify the major claim of religion: that a higher reality exists and that establishing harmony with this higher reality is the key to enhancing our personal lives.

James's interest in the scientific study of expanded states of consciousness was not restricted to religious mysticism. He was also fascinated by spiritualism and other psychic phenomena such as telepathy or clairvoyance. James was one of the leading members of the American Society for Psychical Research, even serving as its president.[21] He patiently studied mediums and psychics, attempting to expose instances of fraud and deception. It was his hope, however, that he would be able to substantiate the existence of genuine psychic phenomena. To prove even a single case of paranormal activity would be sufficient to show the limitations of modern science and force even the toughest-minded intellectuals to acknowledge the existence of metaphysical realities. As James put it, "If you wish to upset the law that all crows are black, you mustn't seek to show that no crows are; it is enough if you prove one single crow to be white."[22] James believed that he found such a white crow in the person of Mrs. Leonora Piper, a trance medium. He became convinced that her messages must originate in a source not currently understood by science. The periodic appearance of paranormal mental experiences was sufficient to inspire in James a spiritual vision that our personal "consciousness is a center surrounded by a fringe that shades insensibly into a subconscious more ... we inhabit an invisible spiritual universe from which help comes, our soul being mysteriously one with a larger soul whose instruments we are."[23] References to "a subconscious more" or "a larger soul" might strike many churchgoers as a pale version of their faith in an almighty Father. But for James and other Americans who feel themselves disenfranchised from biblical religion, such attestations of "higher" metaphysical realities are a starting point from which they might arrive at an intellectually tenable religious philosophy.

James's stature as a highbrow intellectual has cast an aura of respectability over the continuing public fascination with the study of parapsychology and altered states of consciousness. Following James's lead, writers such as Timothy Leary, Carlos Castenada, Charles Tart, Stanislav Grof, and Huston Smith argued that drug-induced mysticism can afford valuable insight into the existence of metaphysical realities.[24] Others such as Ken Wilber, Abraham Maslow, Robert Monroe, and the American followers of Carl Jung have all argued that the "farther reaches" of the unconscious connect humanity with a wider spiritual environment.[25] This quest for higher states of consciousness has been an enduring theme in Americans' pursuit of spiritual awakening.

Thirst for the Paranormal: Trance Channeling, Angelology, and Near-Death Experiences

The spiritualist movement was eventually hurt by a series of scandals. Scientific investigations of several well-known mediums uncovered evidence of fraud and deceit. People who had been attracted to spiritualism principally for its scientific promise were embarrassed and their enthusiasm waned. Some of them turned their attention to the field of parapsychology, which also sought to expand science's understanding of reality. Those who were more interested in the mystical aspects of spiritualism typically gravitated toward one of the occult philosophies spawned by Theosophy. One such source of Theosophy-inspired spirituality was the "I AM" movement founded by Guy and Edna Ballard.[26] Ballard claimed to have made contact with the ascended masters. The ascended masters were spirits who had evolved to the level of perfect oneness with the divine power that sustains the universe, the "I AM" presence. The spirits, particularly one known as Saint Germain, used Ballard as the medium for a series of metaphysical teachings. Transcribed into pamphlets and books, these teachings were eventually read by more than a million American seekers. Both Guy and Edna had studied New Thought philosophy, Rosicrucianism, Theosophy, and snippets of Hindu mystical thought. The ascended masters' teachings wove these philosophical perspectives together into a grand metaphysical synthesis that was surprisingly accessible to the average reader. The "I AM" movement splintered after Guy Ballard's death in 1939, but belief in the existence of the ascended masters and

Saint Germain continues to this day among many intrigued by spirit communication. A notable example is Elizabeth Clare Prophet. With her first husband Mark, Prophet left the "I AM" movement to found the Church Universal and Triumphant, which was based on teachings that Elizabeth herself had received from Saint Germain, the Buddha, and other spirits belonging to the Great White Brotherhood. Prophet's efforts to sustain a clientele for her occult teachings were hampered by controversy over the authoritarian and even militaristic nature of her headquarters in Montana. Yet her publications and charismatic public channeling sessions have provided a powerful forum for the continued dissemination of metaphysical religiosity.

Spiritualist and Theosophical ideas were also injected into popular culture through the phenomenal career of Edgar Cayce (1877–1945).[27] Seeking release from an intractable case of laryngitis, Cayce availed himself of the services of an amateur hypnotist. Hypnotized, Cayce spontaneously diagnosed his own condition and prescribed a cure. News of his remarkable recovery began to spread, bringing flocks of patients to him for similar trance-bound diagnoses and remedies. Cayce became adept at entering into self-induced trances during which he would make diagnoses and suggest treatments. He even claimed to "travel" clairvoyantly to persons who had written to him for medical assistance. Fairly early in his career he met Arthur Lammers, a wealthy printer and student of Theosophy and related occult topics. From this time on, Cayce began to use his clairvoyant abilities to gather religious and metaphysical knowledge. While he was in his trance, those who were in the room with him took turns asking questions about such things as reincarnation, karma, the lost civilization of Atlantis, and astrology. Cayce's clairvoyant commentary on these topics was transcribed and collected in the extensive library of the organization created to promote his teachings, the Association of Research and Enlightenment (A. R. E.) headquartered in Virginia Beach, Virginia. The Association of Research and Enlightenment was an important conduit for the transmission of metaphysical knowledge throughout the last half of the twentieth century.

Somewhere between the late 1960s and the mid-1970s, the term "trance channeling" came into use to describe spiritualism and trance mediumship. The major features of contemporary trance channeling began to take shape with the career of Jane Roberts. Late in 1963, she and her husband were experimenting with a Ouija board when a spirit calling himself Seth began to use Jane as his channel. Jane transcribed Seth's messages into a series of books that together sold well over a million copies before her death in 1984.[28] Seth was a particularly knowledgeable guide to the metaphysical issues that have dominated unchurched American spirituality over the last few decades: reincarnation, the role of karma in shaping our present experience, the role of free will in growing beyond our past karma, the knowledge accumulated by those who lived in the lost civilization of Atlantis, and the ancient metaphysical wisdom that Jesus drew on to awaken the potential for Christ consciousness that exists within us all.

In 1977, J. Z. Knight became bored with her role as a suburban housewife. Her life took a sudden turn when an enormous figure dressed in robes of light appeared to her in the middle of a Sunday afternoon. This was Ramtha.[29] Ramtha professed to be an Enlightened One, a former Atlantean warrior. He now wanted to use Knight to teach humans to tap into their full, unlimited spiritual potential. Ramtha's prophetic message was a New Age variation on Christian apocalypticism. He warned that our planet will soon undergo cataclysmic changes, including floods, volcanic eruptions, and adverse climatic shifts. Just as conservative Christianity has used such prophecies of doom and gloom to motivate audiences to make radical changes in their lives, Ramtha taught that these earthly disasters are meant to propel us to realize our own divine potential. According to Ramtha, the coming "kingdom of God" on earth will not be initiated by the arrival of the historic Jesus but by each individual awakening the Christ potential within. Some embarrassing financial troubles in the 1990s hastened the inevitable decline in public interest in J. Z. Knight's trance-channeling ministry. But, even as other channelers have taken over the limelight, the basic messages received from Ramtha have joined those of Seth as important sources of "seeker spirituality."

Other trance channelers have contributed to the kind of unchurched ministries inaugurated by the likes of Edgar Cayce, Jane Roberts, and J. Z. Knight. For example, Helen Schucman's trance-channeled *A Course in Miracles* has spawned study groups across the nation. The principal message of *A Course in Miracles* is that we make our own reality through the power generated by our thoughts. One of the text's leading disciples, the New Age author Marianne Williamson, says that the metaphysical insights she gained from Schucman's channeled teachings transformed her life. The most important thing she learned was that "because thought is the creative level of things, changing our mind is the ultimate personal empowerment."[30] Like many other New Agers, Williamson believes that this metaphysical principle is at last being discovered by modern physics.

> Old Newtonian physics claimed that things have an objective reality separate from our perception of them. Quantum physics, and particularly Heisenberg's Uncertainly Principle, reveal that as our perception of an object changes, the object itself literally changes. ... all creation is expressed through the mind.[31]

From all of this she concludes that miracles are not really exceptions to the lawful operations of the universe. Instead, what we commonly call miracles are nothing more than instances in which love and thought combine to produce an "invisible force" capable of setting a "higher set of laws" into motion.

Even more recently, Jach Pursel has launched a successful career as a public speaker, author, and website manager for the channeled messages of a spirit named Lazaris. Lazaris, whose teachings mesh well with Pursel's own background in Theosophy and Silva Mind Control, emphasizes everyone's potential to seize abundance. Through publications, tapes, weekend seminars, and even online conferences, Lazaris offers seekers spiritual insight into an array of topics including the power of crystals, strategies for optimizing success, empowerment, the use of amulets and talismans for creating material abundance, and the truth about the metaphysical wisdom once known in Atlantis.

In his excellent study of recent trance channeling, Michael Brown shows that trance channeling can be far more effective than institutional churches in bringing persons into a felt-connection with a higher spiritual level of existence.[32] Brown offers the example of the spiritual journey of a woman he interviewed, Anna Swenson. Swenson had been brought up in a conservative Lutheran family. Later she belonged to an evangelical church before finally becoming disillusioned with what she labeled its hypocrisy. After graduating from college, she found herself attracted to new forms of spirituality. First she studied at a center for psychics, then she affiliated with a Hindu meditation center. Eventually she joined a New Thought organization, the Church of Religious Science. About this time she came across Jane Roberts's *The Seth Materials*. As Swenson explained,

"The Seth books talk about your own power to create reality. At that point, my life was out of control. I didn't have a clue as to where I was in the midst of it. So those two things, Religious Science and the Seth material, were an important awakening." Swenson continued to explore. She took classes in Transcendental Meditation and finally affiliated with another New Thought group, Unity church. Then, in the midst of one of her daily meditations, she began to feel the presence of spirits she calls the Wise Ones. Her description conveys the allure of communing with metaphysical realities: "The energy would come over me and the muscles of my face would be moved. It was like a pulling in my throat and a pushing on my solar plexus. The energy was always beautiful and peaceful, though." The Wise Ones identified themselves as spiritual teachers who were at the next level of evolvement beyond the human level. They chose Anna Swenson as the medium through whom they would deliver a series of religious teachings to human beings. Their message revolved around a simple spiritual theme: "Our purpose is to bring the peace of God. The peace of God is God-experience. The peace of God is the experience of total acceptance, the experience of total oneness, the experience of no conflict within the consciousness of the individual."

Swenson's involvement with trance channeling led to a series of spiritual transformations that were in some ways unique to her. Yet her experience also reveals how all of us thirst for paranormal encounters to one degree or another. Humans have always been fascinated by the mysterious, the holy, the more-than-human. Yet religious institutions understandably find it difficult to facilitate such experiences within the context of routinized worship services. Swenson's encounter with the Wise Ones brought her face-to-face with an awesome, numinous reality that went well beyond anything she had experienced in her religious upbringing. This experience was fraught with awe-inspiring ecstasy and resulted in a sense of inner peace. Ecstasy transforms religion from a dull habit to a vital world outlook. Not only can an ecstatic experience such as Swenson's become the cornerstone of a new spiritual orientation, it even seems philosophically reasonable that it should.

Many people who come into contact with trance channeling are already moving in intellectual directions that make it difficult for them to believe in biblical religion. Their enthusiasm for trance channeling is often due to their first exposure to spiritual viewpoints that strike them as relevant to life in the twenty-first century.[33] One of the most appealing of these is the recurring message that human beings have unlimited spiritual potential. In sharp contrast to traditional theologies of original sin, trance channeling proclaims humanity's inner-divinity. This message is expressed in different ways by different channels, but all affirm that humans are living expressions of God's creative energies. Belief that humans are "fragments of the God-Head" or "Christed beings" leads directly to another basic theme of channeled messages: that the purpose of human life is to actualize our divine potentials. Channelers teach that every challenge we face in life is in fact an opportunity for ongoing spiritual growth. Life is viewed as an evolutionary process that takes us through multiple reincarnations so that we eventually develop our full divine potential. Yet another theological principle responsible for channeling's popular appeal is the contention that thoughts shape reality. Channelers not only teach that we have the opportunity to shape reality in accordance with our innermost desires, but that this opportunity carries with it a grave spiritual responsibility. It is imperative that we guard our thoughts and ideas so that they will contribute to the planet's ongoing spiritual evolution. And, finally, many are inspired by channeling's idealistic and even utopian goal of transforming our world. The spirits who speak through contemporary trance channelers envision a new, holistic culture that brings together the elements of life ripped apart by Western civilization: science and religion, body and soul, culture and nature, male and female, reason and intuition. They invite us to see the universe as a single interconnected field. Each of us has an important role to play in healing the social and ecological damage created by "old age" consciousness.

Metaphysical religion is no less prone to confusion and inconsistency than biblically based theologies. Channeled teachings, for example, are never quite clear whether evil is real or only a human perception. We are told that the difficulties we face in life are determined by our past karma. Sickness, financial troubles, and tragic accidents are brought about by our own poor judgments. Their purpose, furthermore, is to provide us with new opportunities for finally mastering these spiritual lessons. These ideas, however, presuppose a highly individualistic way of viewing the world. Nothing really exists in its own right; instead, everyone and everything in the world exists for the sole purpose of contributing to our personal spiritual edification. This leads to the further problem that although trance channelers give lip service to the interconnected nature of the universe, they rarely direct our attention to the specific forces or structures that influence such interconnection. By putting so much emphasis on "thought" as a causal force in our world they end up ignoring the causal role of social, economic, and political realities. And, finally, trance channelers inevitably run into a dilemma concerning the relative roles of faith and free will. Most channelers teach that spirit guides can assist us in our struggles and that they even arrange events in such a way as to facilitate our spiritual growth (once again implying that other persons are there to be manipulated for the greater purpose of fostering our growth). At the same time, most also speak of free will and exhort us to take responsibility for our thought and actions. It is thus never clear how much energy should be expended trying to induce spirits to act on our behalf as opposed to solving our problems on our own. Which is the more spiritual of the two approaches? In this regard adherents of trance channeling receive no clearer guidelines than members of Christian churches. On the one hand, they are told to have faith and rely on higher powers. Yet, on the other hand, they are encouraged to act as moral agents by strengthening their personal resolve.

Recent fascination with angels reveals many of the same themes and dilemmas found in trance channeling. Communicating with angels is apparently more plausible than with spirit guides or ascended masters. Surveys show that only 11 percent of Americans believe in trance channeling, yet 67 percent believe in angels and 32 percent believe that they have personally "felt an angelic presence" in their lives.[34] Given these figures, it is not surprising that there has been a steady increase in the number of books encouraging us to establish personal relationships with angels. In the entire decade of the 1970s, fifty-one books about angels were published. In the 1980s, there were ninety-one. And in just the first half of the 1990s, 110 were published, combining for sales of more than five million copies.[35]

Trance channeling appeals almost exclusively to the unchurched. Interest in angels, however, straddles the gray area separating churched and unchurched religion. After all, belief in guardian angels is fully in keeping with conservative, Bible-based religion. The best-selling angel book of all time is the evangelist Billy Graham's *Angels: God's Secret Agents*. Graham flatly states: "I believe in angels because the Bible says there are angels."[36] Graham found more than 300 references to angels in the Bible. The Bible teaches that God uses angels to intervene in human affairs, to send special communications, and to lift our spirits. To Graham, the most important characteristic of angels is that they work on our behalf, striving to assist us in times of danger and hardship. It should be pointed out that Graham never suggests that his readers cultivate relationships with angels. His principal message is that angels witness how we walk through life. If we truly desire salvation, we must be careful that angels will observe only righteousness in our words and actions. Graham and other Christian writers instruct their readers to develop closer connections with Christ, not angels. And thus those churched Americans who do develop a fascination for guardian angels must look to unchurched sources of angel enlightenment.

The vast majority of books on angels promise that they are eager to comfort us and intervene on our behalf. Typical in this regard is Linda Georgian's *Your Guardian Angels*.[37] Already known to the viewers of television's *Psychic Friends Network*, Linda Georgian wrote this book to teach her readers how the power of angels can enrich and empower their lives. She reveals that she had developed a personal relationship with her guardian angels by the age of five. She made contact with the angels watching over her by listening to what she describes as the little voice we each have inside us, our intuition. She explains that intuition is the voice of angels, passing divine assistance from God. From the moment she discovered the true source of inspiration, angels have guided her through life. She has learned that angels actively orchestrate the situations we find ourselves in, the people we meet, and the degree of good fortune or prosperity we experience. In Georgian's angel-directed universe, there are no such things as coincidences. Guardian angels are able to do such things as arrange for us to meet someone "coincidentally" at just the right time, improve our health suddenly, or make sure we miss a connection for an airplane that later crashes. She even suggests that angels have the power to make some people poor, homeless, or addicted to alcohol so that we might see them and develop a greater sense of sympathy for others. In all these ways our guardian angels arrange our lives so as to contribute to our spiritual development. Unlike Billy Graham, however, Georgian offers practical advice for making contact with our own guardian angels. First and foremost, she suggests that we seek God first, for angels are only the messengers of God's will. She then explains that we need to create an angel altar in our home and set aside a few minutes each day for quiet meditation near this altar. In silence we should go over our list of the things we need assistance with, assigning each task to a specific angel. Reminding us that we don't always get everything we want, Georgian nonetheless provides numerous anecdotes sent to her from individuals who believe that angels were responsible for their unexpected good fortune.

Just as the topic of trance channeling shades imperceptibly into that of angels, the topic of angels connects with near-death experiences. Angels, after all, are among the entities one might expect to encounter at the moment of death. And so it was with Betty Eadie, author of the *New York Times* bestseller *Embraced by the Light*. Back in 1973, Eadie underwent a hysterectomy. After surgery she began to feel a terrible sinking sensation, as if the very last drops of blood were draining out of her. Almost twenty years later, she decided to write down and share with others what happened to her. The scenario she described is similar to hundreds of other accounts of "near-death experiences": She felt her consciousness separate from her body, she then felt that she was traveling through a long tunnel, at the end of this tunnel was a bright light (which she associated with the spiritual presence of Jesus Christ), a voice told her that each of us is a spirit being who came to earth for spiritual "schooling," she was told that she had not yet finished her earthly experiences and thus it was not yet time for her death, and then she finally felt her consciousness re-attach itself to her physical body. At the end of the tunnel, Eadie met up with three males who were her guardian angels during her life on earth. They told her that guardian angels orchestrate experiences for our growth and stand by us through our trials. They cheer when we do good, and are saddened by our mistakes. These angels not only protect us from the evil forces of Satan, they work in organizations to answer our prayers. Eadie even learned that some angels are "spirit prodigies" who come up with important inventions and technological developments and pass them on to individuals on earth through spiritual inspiration.

Eadie's near-death experience was very comforting. She had learned that we are surrounded by a dimension of light in which God, Jesus, and the angels are all working on our behalf. She had returned from her journey to the light with a simple and beautiful message: "Love is supreme. ... Love must govern. ... We create our own surroundings by the thoughts we think. ... We are sent here to live life fully, to live it abundantly, to find joy in our own creations, to experience both failure and success, to use free will to expand and magnify our lives."[38] And while our spiritual responsibilities are great, we are constantly aided by guardian angels who are always there for us, lightening our load, and cheering us on.

Eadie's warmhearted account of her near-death experience struck a responsive chord in the American reading public. She had succeeded in personalizing the age-old quest for empirical evidence of life after death. Virtually every culture, ancient and modern, has produced individuals who claim to communicate with spiritual beings on the "other side" of death. Testimony concerning ghosts, poltergeists, and spirit communication abounds in the folklore of every civilization. Americans, no less than people in other cultures, yearn for proof of an afterlife. In the early 1970s, about the time Betty Eadie had her startling encounter with the light, Raymond Moody began collecting similar accounts from people who had come close to death.[39] After interviewing 150 individuals who had undergone "clinical death," he began to discover recurring patterns in the near-death experience. The experiential features were similar to those Eadie recounts: feelings of peace and quiet, a sensation of separating from the physical body (what is called an out-of-the-body experience), traveling down a dark tunnel toward a "Being of Light," and a panoramic review of one's life. Moody also found that those who had a near-death experience had been affected in several ways. They lost all fear of death and instead described it as a condition of extraordinary beauty and peace. They came to view life as a precious gift and became much more loving and considerate of others. And, finally, they became dedicated to seeking ever more knowledge about life and investigating the ultimate philosophical questions about the nature and meaning of life.

Moody's book spawned other explorations of the near-death experience. The surgeon Michael Sabom set out to scrutinize Moody's methods and results. Sabom's investigations confirmed the basic themes of Moody's work, but Sabom went further, suggesting that research on near-death experiences had established the empirical reality of a spiritual dimension that exists independently of the space/time physical world.[40] Psychologist Kenneth Ring, meanwhile, argued that near-death research corroborated the occult belief that the human self consists of three bodies: the physical, the astral (which he likens to the concept of the soul), and the causal (which he likens to the Christian concept of spirit).[41] In Ring's view, out-of-the body experiences occur when consciousness shifts from the physical body to the astral body. Ring's metaphysical explanation shows how readily near-death experiences, spirit communication, or fascination with angels leads "seekers" to the vocabularies rooted in America's unchurched traditions.

What is the significance of Americans' continuing thirst for the paranormal? Most people probably don't attach too much significance to purported instances of the more-than-normal. Their interest rarely goes beyond mild curiosity. Evidence suggesting the existence of spirits, angels, or out-of-the-body experiences do hint that reality may be far more complex than our sciences presently understand. But although such phenomena are intriguing, they don't affect the way most people go about their everyday lives. Sociologist Robert Wuthnow notes that the paranormal doesn't impose any religious demands. In his view, the secular character of modern life

> is precisely why current understandings of the supernatural fit so well with it. One experience of the supernatural will do. Just one ... These experiences not only reinforce belief that the supernatural exists but also persuade people that the supernatural cannot in any way be understood and, therefore, it need not take much of their time. ... The spiritual reality is thus a reality that people can muse about in everyday life, but its location remains on the periphery of their daily routines. It diverts little of their attention. It does not require them to set aside portions of their day to pray, worship, read sacred texts, reflect on ways to deepen their relationship with God, or be of service to others.[42]

Wuthnow's observation is fundamentally correct. Fascination with the paranormal may serve some spiritual needs, but it hardly replicates all the functions we associate with institutional religion. Yet to expect this is to misunderstand unchurched spirituality on two counts. First, this criticism of interest in the supernatural makes the mistake so common in academic interpretations of unchurched spirituality—it implicitly accepts the defining features of America's churched religion as criteria for evaluating any and all forms of spirituality. Wuthnow's criticism implies that spiritual interests that don't result in Bible reading or formal worship services are somehow suspect. And, second, this criticism does not recognize how many unchurched individuals do struggle to piece together a comprehensive vision of the universe. This is a difficult task, and few do it very well. But it seems a project worthy of our respect and admiration. An argument could even be made that unchurched spirituality—even in its lowbrow expressions—comes far closer to being an example of mature personal faith than the conventional piety of churchgoers.[43] Wuthnow himself recognizes that many Americans "struggle with how to think about the sacred, vacillating between long stretches in their lives when they pretty much live as if the sacred did not matter at all and extraordinary moments when some unexplained experience with 'the other side' takes on special significance."[44] Wuthnow, however, doesn't seem to accredit unchurched religion sufficiently for leading people to a felt-experience of "the other side." Like William James, many of those who strive to be "spiritual, but not religious" yearn for just one white crow. Finding even one instance of the supernatural is the only way they can honestly affirm any reason whatsoever to entertain religious hypotheses about the nature or meaning of life. And, with this white crow, many are indeed able to piece together an outlook predicated on the specifically spiritual understanding (1) that the visible world is part of a more spiritual universe from which it draws its chief significance and (2) that union or harmonious relation with this "more" is our true end.

The Celestine Prophecy: Metaphysical Spirituality Penetrates the American Religious Vernacular

Metaphysical ideas have gradually filtered into the general stock of concepts with which Americans—educated and uneducated, churched and unchurched, lowbrow and highbrow—take their bearings on life. One national study shows that 24 percent of church members read their horoscopes every week, 20 percent believe in reincarnation, and 11 percent believe in trance channeling. What is more, this study showed that a majority of church members hold at least one such metaphysical belief.[45] Interest in metaphysical ideas would thus hardly seem to be something restricted to the cultural fringe. On the contrary. Metaphysical ideas are part of what one historian describes as a "a dominant popular outlook."[46] For almost 200 years ideas tinged with occult or metaphysical meanings have been a continuous factor in American spirituality despite the fact that they develop quite outside either our religious or scientific institutions.

There could be no clearer evidence of how fully such ideas have been assimilated into America's "dominant popular outlook" than the phenomenal popularity of *The Celestine Prophecy*.[47] The author, James Redfield, is in many ways a prototype of the "seeker" style of Baby Boomer spirituality. Born in 1950, Redfield was raised in a Methodist church that he describes as loving and community-centered. By his college years, however, Redfield became frustrated with his church's "lack of answers to his questions about the true nature of spiritual experience."[48] His quest for spiritual authenticity led him to study Eastern philosophies, particularly Daoism and Zen. Opting for a career in counseling, his graduate studies brought him into contact with various psychological theories about the laws governing our movement toward optimal happiness or fulfillment. Redfield found himself particularly drawn to the human potential movement with its interest in our untapped psychic powers. After more than fifteen years as a therapist, Redfield quit his job to devote all of his energies to writing. He hoped to produce a work that synthesized the insights of psychology, futurism, parapsychology, ecology, and Eastern mystical philosophies.

Redfield wanted his book to have epic qualities, an adventure story whose hero battles the evil forces of militarism, authoritarian religion, and environmental destruction. He says that at one point he hit writer's block and lost his creative drive. He traveled to Sedona, Arizona, the site of "high energy vortexes" according to many advocates of New Age philosophy. Redfield was sitting on a ridge near one of these vortexes when a crow flew over his head. He followed it into a nearby canyon. Redfield sat down in this canyon and the rest of his book just came pouring out of him. The finished book tells of an American child therapist who by sheer coincidence hears that an ancient manuscript has been discovered in Peru. Learning that this manuscript contains exciting prophecies and spiritual teachings from the lost Celestine civilization, he travels to Peru to investigate for himself. There he finds himself caught up in a dangerous struggle to find the manuscript and protect it from governmental and religious authorities who fear its liberating message.

Commercial publishers initially showed no interest in Redfield's book and he decided to publish it himself. This self-published edition developed a sizable following and was finally picked up by Warner Books. *The Celestine Prophecy* quickly climbed to the top of the *New York Times* bestseller list and remained there for more than three years. Six years after its publication, *The Celestine Prophecy* was still on the *New York Times* "expanded" bestseller list, which includes the top thirty books in the country.

The Celestine Prophecy clearly did not become a bestseller because of its literary merit. The book is poorly written in terms of character development, plot, dialogue, and action. Yet it excelled at inviting readers to view the universe in overtly metaphysical ways. Redfield drew on, and amplified, the diffuse set of metaphysical concepts in our popular cultural outlook. His genius lay in his ability to connect these ideas and show how they constitute a surprisingly coherent philosophy of life.

Redfield presents his metaphysical synthesis in the guise of nine insights ostensibly contained in the ancient Peruvian manuscript. The first insight concerns the importance of understanding the so-called coincidences (chance meetings, coming across the right idea, intuitions) in our lives. Redfield, like those involved with trance channeling and angels, believes that such events are in fact not accidental, but instead reveal the vast extent to which our lives are influenced by metaphysical energies and forces. The first step in our spiritual journeys is learning to "intuit higher meanings in these mysterious happenings." Soon we will learn that every situation in life is designed to further our spiritual development. Life is really about "a spiritual unfolding that is personal and enchanting—an unfolding that no science or philosophy or religion has yet fully clarified." By discerning the metaphysical patterns revealed in everyday life we will understand that all the answers we need are provided to us and merely await our recognition.

Redfield's second insight is that the human species is entering a new stage in its long process of spiritual evolution. Early in our history we relied on unquestioning religious faith. But, since the medieval era, we have taken a step forward in our ability to understand the world and have relied instead on skeptical reason and the scientific method. This stage in our evolutionary development is now also coming to an end. More and more people are realizing that neither scientific materialism nor religious dogmatism can fully grasp the meaning of existence. Redfield is hoping, of course, that these stages in humanity's spiritual growth mirror his readers' own quest for a holistic understanding of the universe.

The third insight is more boldly metaphysical. It teaches that the universe is made up of one dynamic energy, a pure energy that radiates from all things and responds in some way to our thoughts. Redfield's description of this "pure energy" is sufficiently vague as to make it compatible with mesmerism's notion of animal magnetism, Eastern concepts of subtle energies, or various pantheistic-leaning understandings of God. Spiritually attuned individuals, he explains, are able to see energy fields or auras around people. It is also possible to perceive this energy radiating from rain forests and mountain ranges where nature still exists in its original, pristine form. This cosmic energy responds to our thoughts. Some people are even able to grow vegetables teaming with protein, vitamins, and minerals by consciously projecting energy into the auric fields that surround these plants. This third insight connects directly with the fifth, which explains how mystical experiences open us up to this pure energy. In a manner that hearkens back to Emerson's doctrines of correspondence and influx, Redfield teaches that each of us can learn to use mystical states of awareness to draw on the pure energy of the universe and thereby bring ourselves to a higher state of spiritual vibration.

The Celestine Prophecy's most original contribution to unchurched spirituality is the connection it forges between religious metaphysics and contemporary popular psychology. As befits his background as a psychological counselor, Redfield devotes three of his nine insights to a spiritual perspective on interpersonal human relationships. The fourth insight is that humans are unconsciously engaged in a tragic competition for "personal energy." We unconsciously try to control others in ways that allow us to steal their energy. Feeling the need for more energy and power, we try to "fill up" at other people's expense. Spiritual growth, therefore, entails improving our interpersonal relationships. Redfield's sixth and eighth insights elaborate a new interpersonal ethic. We must learn to overcome our tendencies to manipulate other people. Rather than stealing energy from others, we must utilize spiritual techniques that enable us to acquire all the "personal energy" we could possibly desire. Once we have attained a mystical connection with the "pure energy" of the universe we will no longer need to take energy from other people. We will even be able to project this life-enhancing energy to everyone we encounter. Redfield presents these insights in jargon drawn from twelve-step programs and other psychological theories about co-dependency. Readers easily relate to these strategies for personal improvement and thus find their newfound spirituality to be profoundly practical. Spiritual insight, they learn, is relevant to their daily lives even while it brings them closer to mystical illumination.

The Celestine Prophecy ends by drawing out the utopian elements of metaphysical spirituality. Redfield suggests that we are at the dawn of a new era in which humans will protect the environment, decrease our population, and all behave ethically because we will all be guided by the universe's evolutionary energy. We will soon learn to interact with others so that every personal relationship contributes to the growth of both persons. All of us will experience the thrill of spiritual growth. One by one we will all learn to live at "a higher state of vibration." We will attain the very same level of spiritual development that Christ achieved. Metaphysical insight will enable us to realize the truth of Christ's prophecy that "greater things than these ye shall do also."

Redfield assures us that the basic message of *The Celestine Prophecy* "is not religious in nature, but it is spiritual." It does not ask for blind acceptance. Nor does it ask us to renounce our pursuit of personal fulfillment in favor of subservience or self-abnegation. Instead, it proclaims that "experience is the evidence"—that we must test spiritual concepts by how they work in our lives. It also invites us to embrace a self-enhancing spirituality, one that leads to the fulfillment, rather than suppression, of our personal desires. Many critics of this and other bestsellers in the booming "spirituality market" have had a field day lampooning the obvious ways in which it caters to popular interests. There is a sense in which *The Celestine Prophecy* offers a very watered-down version of spiritual discipline. Some have called it "spiritual lite," a convenience food for the soul. After all, it contains little to combat the modern tendency toward self-absorption. Its utopian vision that we will all learn to think our problems away suggests that spiritual growth is finally about avoiding life's challenges rather than facing them. And while its message has obvious appeal to middle-class, educated readers, it offers almost nothing to the underclass. Yet for all these easy criticisms, *The Celestine Prophecy* has succeeded in tapping into the reservoirs of metaphysical curiosity that continually well up into the Americans' religious vernacular. This text, like Jesus's parables, uses this vernacular to bypass our usual way of looking at the world and invites us to reexamine our basic beliefs about its nature and meaning. It would thus seem that the metaphysical movements that first emerged in the late nineteenth and early twentieth centuries have flowered into a popular religious attitude that inspires "spiritual seeking" among middle-class Americans even to this day.

3

Exotic Messages, Familiar Themes

Contemporary Involvement in the American Dilemma

By the mid-twentieth century it was already possible to discern common themes in unchurched American religious thought. To this extent, unchurched religion gradually established its own traditions. These traditions are often overlooked. Scholars tend to focus on each movement's distinct philosophical lineage, missing the way in which alternative spiritualities are actually "consumed" by middle-class seekers. Spiritual seekers don't encounter alternative religious ideas in a vacuum. They usually approach new spiritual philosophies with an agenda shaped by their exposure to other traditions of unchurched religious thought. This agenda causes them to filter out a great deal of what is unique to a particular system and selectively emphasize those ideas that speak to their concerns. These concerns tend to coalesce around five interrelated themes.

First, and most important, spiritual seekers are concerned with the individual's right, even duty, to establish his or her own criteria for belief. Religious beliefs, they maintain, must be tested by experience.

They do not want to be required to accept religious doctrines on faith. They insist on experimenting for themselves. They are willing to take responsibility for making their own judgments as to which ideas can make a practical difference in their lives. Furthermore, those attracted to unchurched religious philosophies don't expect complete uniformity in matters of religious thought. They argue that no two persons experience the world in precisely the same way and therefore total uniformity in religious belief is neither possible nor desirable.

Second, seekers think of spirituality as something more along the lines of a sensibility than a set of creeds. Being "spiritual, but not religious" is equated with a particular mode of perceiving and responding to the world. Personal spirituality has to do with cultivating a mystical feel for God's presence in the natural world. What makes a religious idea "true" is whether it helps individuals become inwardly receptive to what Emerson described as the "divinity that flows through all things." This is particularly important to those who find it difficult to affirm Bible-based religious beliefs. They seek alternative religious philosophies that will encourage them to follow reason and science wherever they lead. Intellectual integrity is the first step in making religion a prevailing sensibility, a total way of life, rather than a pledge of faith in historic creeds.

Third, seekers are typically impatient with institutional religion. They tend to fault churches for becoming stagnant, failing to keep pace with humanity's ongoing evolutionary growth. And, too, many feel they have been emotionally victimized or belittled by the church due to their gender, curiosity, or simple unwillingness to conform for conformity's sake.

Fourth, seekers have new understandings of the self and the self's inner connection with God. In sharp contrast to the belief that humans are born into the condition of sin, they affirm the self's infinite potentials. The traditional idea of sin centered on the belief that since Adam and Eve all humans have disobeyed the commands given to us by an Almighty Ruler. Seekers lean to an alternative view that the principal impediment to spiritual growth is limited awareness of our own inner potentials. Of paramount concern is learning new methods for living a full and abundant life.

And, finally, unchurched Americans are surprisingly interested in exploring what lies beyond our physical universe. Many are almost

incurably metaphysical. They believe that—at least in certain conditions—our world is susceptible to an "influx" of spiritual energies. It
is this metaphysical conviction that underlies their harmonial faith
that spiritual composure, physical health, and even economic well-
being flow automatically from a person's rapport with the cosmos.

These concerns continue to shape the way in which Americans appropriate novel spiritual philosophies. Although seekers typically
sample many alternative philosophies, they filter these messages
through a fairly similar set of interpretive categories. Similarities between unconventional spiritual outlooks tend to be accentuated, differences overlooked. The spiritual needs of those who are "spiritual,
but not religious" have in this way given rise to traditions within unchurched American religious thought. And for this reason Americans are able to embrace exotic-sounding religious systems while
continuing to affirm a fairly familiar set of spiritual principles.

Fascination with the Mystic East

Christianity affirms that Jesus is God's only son and that his death
and bodily resurrection have made our salvation possible. The evangelical tradition that flourished among American Protestants has
been particularly narrow in its interpretation of how humans come
to share in Jesus' atoning sacrifice. By the mid-nineteenth century
evangelicals had reduced the requirements for salvation to a simple
formula: Accept Jesus as your personal Lord and Savior. It follows
that those who don't consciously embrace Jesus as their savior have
no chance for salvation. Unbelievers and heretics are categorized as
unrepentant sinners. Adherents of other religions are likewise cut off
from the benefit of Jesus's atoning sacrifice. This is true even of Jews
and Muslims who embrace the God of the Bible, but deny Jesus's special divinity. It is even more blatantly the case for those who embrace
nonbiblical religions. These persons, often labeled heathens or pagans, are to be pitied. By fate of birth they have grown up in a family
or even a whole nation whose ignorance about Jesus will cost them a
chance for eternal life.

The vast majority of early American colonists came from Western
Europe and were heirs of evangelical Protestantism. They knew almost nothing about such Asian religions as Hinduism, Buddhism,
and Daoism. The atlases and reference volumes available to most co-

lonial Americans identified just two kinds of religion: true and false. In 1784, Hannah Adams published her *Alphabetical Compendium of the Various Sects* in hope of counteracting this ignorance and prejudice. It was her goal to be fair in her treatment of the many religious groups found in the Western world while trying to "avoid giving the least preference to one denomination above another."[1] In the third edition of this volume, issued in 1801, she added a thirty-page sketch on Asian religions. Although her sources were limited, Adams's book prompted at least some segments of the American reading public to take a fresh look at non-Christian faiths. Hannah Adams was a Unitarian. Like many who were attracted to Enlightenment thought, she believed in the importance of both reason and tolerance. The American intellectuals who shared this outlook were confident that every area of life, including religion, was governed by a few underlying, rational principles. Joseph Priestly, Benjamin Franklin, John Adams, and Thomas Jefferson were among those who believed that we would eventually be able to reduce religion to its rational essentials. All particular creeds and rituals could be considered superfluous and discarded as a hindrance to rational religion. Hoping to gain further insight into the underlying principles of natural religion, many intellectuals took the time to acquaint themselves with the basic outlines of Asian religious philosophies. Their Enlightenment sensibilities led them, as religious studies scholars Thomas Tweed and Stephen Prothero have noted, to be particularly drawn "to the naturalistic philosophy and ethical emphasis of Confucianism. In that Chinese tradition they found a historical instance of the 'natural religion' they had sought, a tradition free from the intolerance and superstition they saw in the supernaturalist traditions of the West."[2]

Enlightenment scholars thus promoted a new attitude of tolerance toward non-Christian faiths. It was, however, the Transcendentalists who first proclaimed that Eastern religious philosophies contain ideas that are actually superior to their Western counterparts. Ralph Waldo Emerson was drawn to Hindu mysticism. At the same time that he abandoned his Unitarian pulpit to become a spokesperson for Transcendentalism, Emerson added a number of Hindu terms and phrases to his own experimental religious vocabulary. From this point onward, Eastern ideas and terminology would factor significantly into the development of the major themes of unchurched spirituality in America. Emerson's popularization of Hindu metaphors for describing the self and its inner connection with God was particularly influential. The Hindu notion of the Atman, or true self, captured his growing confidence that the self is essentially divine. Emerson found further confirmation of his developing views in the Hindu mystical essays known as the Upanishads. The Upanishads explain that the chief problem of the human condition is not sin, but spiritual ignorance. They describe our spiritual condition in what are essentially psychological terms. The Upanishads teach that so long as we remain exclusively attached to the outer world, we live in ignorance of our true spiritual nature. The physical senses so dominate our awareness that they distract us from the deeper recesses of the mind where the ability to become inwardly receptive to God's instreaming presence resides. The self who lives in spiritual ignorance is at the mercy of outer appearances and is therefore controlled by the external environment. The Upanishads teach, however, that it is within the power of all of us to turn our attention inward and discover that the inner self (Atman) is finally identical with God (Brahman). The Hindu phrase "That Art Thou" reinforced Emerson's conviction concerning the inner divinity of every person. Hinduism gave him a vocabulary to express his philosophy of self-reliance, a philosophy that urged Americans to move beyond the shallow identities society provides us with and instead to see ourselves as agents of a higher, instreaming spiritual power.

There is some scholarly debate as to whether Emerson's "discovery of the East" came before or after he had developed the basic principles of Transcendentalism.[3] There can, however, be no doubt that Emerson's writings did a great deal to generate public interest in Eastern thought. He wove Hindu terminology into his pantheistic-leaning discussions of God and his description of how divine energy is available to all of us through the deepest levels of the self. The implication was that Eastern mystical writings are better sources of spiritual wisdom than the biblical literature associated with America's established churches. Yet, importantly, Emerson was never really calling for Americans to abandon Western thought. He saw in Eastern teachings a sublime statement of the very best of the Romantic tradition of Western thought. He championed Eastern religious ideas as a means of supplementing or complementing what our Western traditions offer, not as their antithesis.

Emerson was not the only Transcendentalist to encourage American seekers to turn toward Eastern sources of spiritual edification. While Emerson read Eastern texts as essays about spiritual philosophy, Henry David Thoreau (1817–1862) turned to them for models of spiritual practice and moral action. Thus, for example, Thoreau sought solitude so that he might himself become "a yogin." Thoreau was also quick to seize on the lofty ethical teachings of the *The Bhagavad Gita*, the great Hindu text whose moral principles were consistent with his own tenet of nonviolent civil disobedience. And, too, Thoreau was one of the editors of *The Dial*, a Transcendentalist journal that published translations of several Eastern classics.

In 1871, another Transcendentalist writer, James Freeman Clarke, published the *Ten Great Religions* in which he encouraged readers to find spiritual edification in the teachings of Hinduism, Buddhism, and Confucianism. Although never formally associated with the Transcendentalist movement, Walt Whitman (1819–1892) sprinkled references to mysticism and Asian religions throughout such works as *Leaves of Grass* and *Passage to India*. His writing furthered the growing alignment of Eastern religions with the Romantic mood in American cultural thought. Americans' "turn to the East" expressed a number of Romantic themes: interest in exotic locales and ideas, advocacy of modes of thought or feeling that break through the confines of narrow reason or cultural convention, and a deep yearning for mystical connection with higher spiritual powers.

Strangely enough, Theosophy probably had the greatest influence on the way Americans have appropriated Eastern religious philosophies. Transcendentalism was largely a movement of the upper-class literary elite. Theosophy, however, was a middle-class movement that transformed esoteric traditions into a philosophy geared to everyday spiritual concerns. Madame Blavatsky attributed *Isis Unveiled* to the Mahatmas or Masters residing in the Himalayas. The Mahatmas were spiritually perfected individuals who possess "mysterious powers" and "profound knowledge." The implication was that their spiritual understanding went well beyond anything that Western religious teachers had to offer. Blavatsky annointed Hinduism and Buddhism as the "purest form" of the world's Wisdom Traditions. She delighted in contrasting the vital insights preserved in Hindu and Buddhist writings with what she saw as the culturally encrusted doctrines of Western Christianity. It should be noted, however, that her portrayal of Hinduism and Buddhism was slanted to accommodate her occultist and spiritualist interests. Blavatsky focused almost exclusively on the esoteric features of these Asian traditions, giving the mistaken impression that their spiritual practices were primarily concerned with arousing the body's subtle energies or eliciting paranormal abilities such as clairvoyance, telepathy, and astral projection (the ability to separate one's consciousness from, and "travel" beyond, the physical body). Blavatsky conjured up powerful images of a "mystic East" in which individuals might awaken spiritual abilities long neglected by Western religious institutions. Such expectations would color Americans' fascination with Eastern philosophies for decades to come.

When the Parliament of Religions opened in 1893 as part of the Columbian Exposition hosted by the city of Chicago, no one was prepared for the enthusiasm with which representatives of Asian religions were received. The most popular of all was Swami Vivekananda, who spoke for the highly refined and idealistic Hindu philosophy known as Vedanta.[4] Swami Vivekananda preached tolerance, proclaiming that the world's various religions are but different paths leading to the same goal. Vivekananda believed that the similarities between these paths far outweighed their differences. His implicit message was that enlightened persons should feel free to fashion their own, personal religious paths by picking eclectically from the best ideas of all world religions. A host of popular magazines ran stories about this charismatic guru, and he followed his speech in Chicago with a lecture tour across the United States. One woman who heard Vivekananda speak in Detroit in early 1894 recorded that

> The audience listened spellbound while he ... [delivered a lecture full of] lofty idealism, of wisdom. Through it all ran India's most sacred teaching: the divinity of man, his innate and eternal perfection; that this perfection is not a growth nor a gradual attainment, but a present reality. *That thou art.* You are that now. ... We are not the helpless limited beings which we think ourselves to be, but birthless, deathless, glorious children of immortal bliss.[5]

A few decades later another Vedanta teacher, Swami Paramahansa Yogananda, sought to bring enlightenment to American audiences. His lectures and *Autobiography of a Yogi* introduced thousands of Americans to Hindu beliefs and meditation practices. Yogananda described meditation as a "secret to cosmic consciousness." Making repeated references to the existence of subtle "life energies" that can be aroused through meditation and used to stimulate the "omniscient spiritual eye," Yogananda promised that Eastern mystical philosophies could help Americans "express the infinite potentials of cosmic energy."[6] Yogananda, much like Theosophy before him, thus predisposed Americans to associate Eastern religions with meditation, mysticism, and the discovery of the self's latent psychic powers. Yogananda founded an organization known as the Self-Realization Fellowship whose purpose is "to reveal the complete harmony and basic oneness of original Christianity as taught by Jesus Christ and original Yoga as taught by Lord Krishna; and to show that these principles of truth are the common scientific foundation of all true religions."[7] The society also endeavored "to demonstrate the superiority of mind over body, of soul over mind; to promote spiritual understanding between East and West, and to advocate the exchange of their finest distinctive features; to harmonize science and religion through realizing that nature and its laws originated in the Divine Mind; and to overcome evil by good, sorrow by joy, cruelty by kindness, ignorance by wisdom." Each of these principles resonated clearly with the teachings of American metaphysical movements. In turn, these preexisting sources of unchurched religious provided a set of categories that helped the American reading public selectively appropriate precisely those Eastern teachings that would mesh easily with their own spiritual quests.

Among the dozens of Asian gurus who introduced twentieth-century Americans to the mysteries of the East, two others deserve special mention. The first, Jiddu Krishnamurti (1895–1986), was trained by Annie Besant and other leading Theosophists to become the long-awaited world teacher who would usher in a New Age of religious awareness. Although he later broke with Theosophy, Krishnamurti's writings provided American readers with yet another eclectic blend of occultism, Vedanta teachings of the divinity of the self, and Western psychologies of self-reliance. The second great Asian teacher, D. T. Suzuki (1870–1966), became almost the sole source of Americans' knowledge about the sect of Buddhism known as Zen. Suzuki was well versed in Theosophical teachings. He shared Theosophy's belief that the essence of true spirituality consisted of an immediate, mystical experience of a reality that in some fundamental way transcends the world of everyday existence. He was thus predisposed to understand Zen as a pristine form of spirituality wholly removed from, and unaffected by, human culture. In his view, the goal of Zen was not to help us experience a different reality, but rather to make us suddenly awaken to the sacred character of this reality. Suzuki taught that satori, or Zen enlightenment, is the realization that the sacred is present in the here and now of everyday life. This realization cannot be arrived at through logical thought, but can only be achieved through direct spiritual experience. Suzuki's writings about Zen were to have a powerful effect on the most important popularizers of Eastern thought: composer John Cage, novelist Jack Kerouac, poet Allen Ginsberg, Catholic monk Thomas Merton, psychologists Erich Fromm and Abraham Maslow, and eclectic philosopher Alan Watts.[8]

Cage, Kerouac, and Ginsberg all helped inject Eastern concepts into the vocabulary of the Beat Generation during the late 1950s and early 1960s. The Beats, who were self-consciously countercultural, were particularly attracted to Zen. Beat intellectuals seized on Zen as a form of "pure" spirituality, free from what they saw as the stultifying doctrines and rituals that defined bourgeois American Christianity. The writings of Alan Watts were even more influential in making Eastern religions "hip" among those attracted to the counterculture movement of the 1960s and 1970s. Watts was a disillusioned Episcopal priest who had come to see the church's rituals as hollow. At a critical point in his personal spiritual journey he came under the tutelage of Christmas and Aileen Humphreys. The Humphreys were English Theosophists who had organized a Buddhist lodge in London. The lodge became a magnet for those embracing metaphysical philosophies. There Watts gained invaluable insight into the most exciting concepts of Vajrayana Buddhism, Daoism, Zen, Vedanta, Sufism, Christian mysticism, astrology, psychic research, magic, New Thought, Jungianism, and the writings of Krishnamurti.[9] Watts succeeded in extracting from these philosophies precisely those elements that could ignite spiritual idealism in those who were disenchanted with religion. Many Americans, including a disproportionately high percentage of those who attended college during the 1960s and 1970s, had come to blame Western religions for their complicity in producing our excessively materialistic culture. They yearned for a spirituality that would release them from their cultural conditioning and prepare them for an ecstatic experience of "cosmic consciousness." It was Watts's genius to take unconventional philosophies and repackage them in such a way that they spoke directly to these concerns. In his famous essay "Beat Zen, Square Zen, and Zen," Watts depicted Zen as an elegant deconditioning agent. Zen, he proclaimed, "is the liberation of the mind from conventional thought."[10] Mingling Eastern metaphysics with Western psychological themes, Watts tried to awaken his readers to "an enlarged frame of mind" in which the concrete, physical world could be seen to be teeming with divinity. Yet for all his advocacy of spiritual understanding, he remained wary of Christianity's militant approach to "truth" and cautioned his readers against the narrowness of all organized "religion."

> I do not even style myself a Zen Buddhist. … I am temperamentally not a joiner. For the aspect of Zen in which I am profoundly interested is nothing that can be organized, taught, transmitted, certified, or wrapped up in any kind of system.[11]

Many Americans eventually moved beyond flirtation with Eastern concepts and took up the actual practice of meditation. Thick Nhat Hanh's books on mindfulness, for example, are found on coffee tables and nightstands across the country.[12] Vajrayana, Zen, and Vipassana meditation centers have sprouted up across the country.[13] The Hare Krishnas also drew sizable numbers into the practice of Eastern meditation. However, the movement popularly known as Transcendental Meditation (TM) was undoubtedly the most successful at teaching Americans to use Eastern meditation practices. Its founder, Maharishi Mahesh Yogi, orchestrated TM's efforts to teach a simplified form of yoga at college campuses, corporate offices, and suburban conference centers. The practice of TM consisted of two 15- to 20-minute periods each day during which the practitioner was taught to sit comfortably, relax, and recite a one-syllable mantra. The purpose of the mantra was to help individuals let go of their preoccupation with the outer world and turn their attention inward. Newcomers were told that it would help them cultivate inner receptivity and establish harmony with the "pure creative intelligence" that pervades our universe. TM spokespersons were always quick to point out that they were not promulgating a religion. Rather, they were teaching a spiritual technique that could enhance people's appreciation of their own personal religious faith. The truth of the matter, however, was that TM presupposed a very Eastern view of the nature of God and of God's presence within every person. Although many initially came to TM as a new route to psychological health, they inevitably absorbed at least fragments of a very new vocabulary for depicting our relationship with an indwelling spiritual power.

All in all, Americans received a fairly consistent and familiar set of spiritual messages from these exotic-sounding Eastern religions. They were rarely introduced to the sectarian differences that exist between various schools of Hindu or Buddhist thought. Nor did they learn about the folk beliefs and devotionalism that permeate these religions as they are actually practiced in Asia. Instead, Eastern teachings were typically severed from their historical and cultural context. Hinduism and Buddhism were transformed into a psychological tonic designed to assuage the spiritual malaise common among middle-class Americans. Take, for example, the concepts of reincarnation and the law of karma. In Asia, these concepts often express fatalistic resignation to powers beyond one's personal control. In their adaptation for American audiences, however, they come across as the secret to an upbeat spirituality. Karma and reincarnation become ideas that can be used to reframe our lives. To Americans, they suggest that every moment of life affords us yet another opportunity for mastering spiritual lessons and making additional progress toward total enlightenment. As appropriated by American audiences these Eastern ideas resemble the affirmations popularized by New Thought as techniques for sustaining optimistic attitudes as we go about our daily lives. In general, the messages that American audiences take from Eastern teachings vary little from those of indigenous metaphysical movements: a pantheistic understanding of God; continuity of the self with this ever-present divine reality; our innate susceptibility to subtle spiritual energies that reinvigorate our physical and emotional systems; experience and personal reflection as the crucial criteria for arriving at religious beliefs; and the need to develop a personal spiritual outlook that builds on, rather than repudiates, scientific understandings of our universe.

Eastern religious systems have often been invoked as offering a much-needed corrective to the destructive features of Western culture. As awareness of our ecological crisis deepened, more and more Americans began to blame Western monotheism for engendering exploitative attitudes toward the natural environment. The pantheistic beliefs of Eastern religions seemed to cultivate a deeper reverence for nature. What is more, Eastern religions affirmed the interconnection of all forms of life. Many were convinced that Eastern thought was compatible not only with environmentalism but also with the new conceptions of reality emerging from modern quantum physics. In the 1970s, a spate of books argued that Eastern mystical thought is perfectly congruent with the most recent advances in Western scientific thought. According to the best-known of these, *The Tao of Physics*, "Eastern thought and, more generally, mystical thought provide a consistent and relevant philosophical background to the theories of contemporary science; a conception of the world in which man's scientific discoveries can be in perfect harmony with his spiritual aims and religious beliefs. The two basic themes of this conception are the unity and interrelation of all phenomena and the intrinsically dynamic nature of the universe."[14] Eastern religions seemed to offer a scientifically validated vision of humans and their place in the cosmic scheme of things. Their understanding of the world as "a system of inseparable, interacting, and ever-moving components" teaches us that we are not separate from nature, but rather "an integral part of this system."[15] In sharp contrast to the biblical message that humans are to exercise mastery over the whole of nature, Eastern thought suggests that we should learn to conform to its rhythmic patterns.

It is impossible to know how many Americans have seriously engaged Eastern religious philosophies or consciously appropriated any of their teachings. One possible indication is the steadily increasing amount of space that major booksellers devote to books dealing with Eastern religious ideas. A recent search of books in print revealed over sixty with the word Daoism in the title and almost 200 with the word Zen.[16] Books with titles such as *The Tao of Management* and *The Zen of Running* have tried to apply Eastern perspectives to almost every dimension of human life. Some of these are surely whimsical. But the fact remains that the past two generations of Americans have been exposed to nonbiblical religious ideas to an extent unprecedented in Western cultural history. Respected cultural authorities and Hollywood celebrities alike have endorsed Eastern philosophies and have portrayed them as exciting alternatives to biblical religion. As a consequence, increasing numbers of Americans feel encouraged to adopt an eclectic approach to religious belief. This appears to be true not only for those without church affiliation, but also for an increasing number of churchgoers who no longer believe that their tradition has a monopoly on religious truth.

It is another measure of the impact of Eastern religions that approximately 800,000 Euro-Americans might be considered "convert" Buddhists (this in addition to the approximately three million Asian-American Buddhists in the United States).[17] Convert Buddhists overwhelmingly tend to be well educated, white, and middle class.[18] Their involvement with Buddhism differs from that of Asian Americans. For one thing, serious interest in Buddhism or any other Eastern religion entails a person's break from his or her family's traditional religious affiliation. Even becoming a "sympathizer" signals a distinctive shift in identity. And, whereas Asian-American expressions of Buddhism tend to be integrated into both family and community life, convert Buddhists more typically practice Buddhism as individuals, and their involvement is more apt to express a personal search for fulfillment.[19]

It is apparent that Euro-Americans reinterpret Buddhism to meet their own preexisting spiritual needs—many of which are shaped by America's unchurched spiritual traditions. Convert Buddhism has departed from its Asian heritage in several ways. It places more emphasis upon meditation and personal experience, is more democratic and antiauthoritarian, gives more parity to women, encourages social action, and welcomes Western psychology as useful in explaining Buddhism's goals of self-transformation.[20] Interest in Buddhism is often a way of realizing values that persons had already assimilated from American culture. Religious studies scholar Peter Gregory has noted that, at least in the case of Buddhism, Americans justify their interest in Eastern religious ideas "in terms of values that are thought of as 'American'—such as self-realization, freedom, transforming relationships, getting in touch with one's experience, living more fully in the moment or the world, healing, and so forth."[21] As exotic as they at first appear, the Eastern religious ideas that find their way into popular American culture travel paths already hewn by the nation's unchurched spiritual traditions.

Holistic Visions: Feminist and Ecological Spiritualities

Historically, women have played an important role in generating new and creative forms of unchurched spirituality. Since the time Anne Hutchinson was banished from the Massachusetts Bay Colony for daring to express opinions that differed from those of the male clergy, many women have found that traditional religious institutions tend to thwart their own religious experience. Judaism and Christianity are, after all, patriarchal religions. The symbols, myths, and metaphors of these religions largely reflect the experiences of men. The God of Judaism and Christianity is a male God. All the major prophets and apostles are said to have been men. And traditionally in these religions only males have been empowered to perform rituals, speak from the pulpit, and write authoritative theological treatises. It should come as no surprise that many women feel that they have been relegated to a second-class status within their churches. Many of these women have decided to take responsibility for their own religious development. They have learned to question their traditions and to engage in their own, self-directed religious journeys. Women were among the best-known Transcendentalist writers. And, as the nineteenth century progressed, both the Spiritualist and New Thought movements opened up new opportunities for women to blaze new spiritual paths for themselves and others. Women such as Mary Baker Eddy and Madame Helena Blavatsky used the categories of metaphysical religion to explain how they possessed the same potential as men to experience an "influx" of spiritual inspiration.

By the middle of the twentieth century women became more open about turning to unchurched religious philosophies for the terminology to reclaim their spiritual identities. Mary Daly, arguably the most influential feminist writer in the field of religion, is an excellent example. Daly's first major work, *The Church and the Second Sex* (1968), was reformist in nature. She argued that the historical exclusion of women from full participation in the Catholic Church represented a distortion of the Christian gospel. Her early hope was that the Catholic Church would realize how its sexist practices betrayed Christianity's affirmation of the fundamental dignity of every human being. She was confident that the Church would be eager to modernize and incorporate women's experience into its proclamation of faith. Daly's book, along with the writings of Rosemary Reuther, articulated many women's frustration at being second-class citizens with their religious traditions. Daly finally decided that adequate reform was never going to happen within existing church structures. She took a more radical turn, proclaiming that there was no more point in a woman wanting a better role in the Church than an African American wanting a higher position in the Ku Klux Klan.

In her next major book, *Beyond God the Father,* Daly condemned the Christian message as implicitly oppressive to women. Here Daly offered a penetrating critique of the core symbols of Christian theology: God the Father and the male Christ. Daly was among the first to argue that masculine religious symbols legitimize the sexist structures of Western culture. The maleness of God and Christ suggests that male rule is part of the structure of the universe. Daly went further and argued that many of the other traits attributed to God also foster exploitation. The whole notion of a "Supreme Being" who is infinitely superior to His creation envisions the entire universe in terms of power struggles: higher versus lower; good versus evil, spiritual versus worldly; male versus female. Daly insisted that if women are to overcome oppression, they must reject not only the idea of a male God, but also the Bible's entire notion of the hierarchical and dualistic nature of our universe.

Daly was joined by a host of other women who sought to define a new religious vocabulary to support women's personal spiritual journeys.[22] The first step toward such a spiritual renovation is to reject traditional biblical descriptions of God as a transcendent male being. Feminist writers argue that women must learn to think of God in pantheistic ways. A doctrine of divine immanence affirms that divine spirit is equally present in all of creation—male and female. This new understanding of God's relationship to the universe also helps to correct outmoded ideas of "sin." The biblical view of sin is the act of breaking the commands of a male authority figure. A theology that stresses divine immanence recasts sin as a failure to recognize the presence of God within us and our fellow creatures. Feminist thought thus understands spirituality as entailing reverence for the sacredness of all life. Being spiritual requires sensitivity to the way that various kinds of exploitation (racial, environmental, sexist) do violence to the presence of God in our world. Feminist writers tend to believe that we will only be able to usher in a new era in human spirituality if we first embrace a new, holistic vision of life that recognizes the presence of God within ourselves, other persons, and the whole of natural creation.

Many feminists have called for the repudiation of male-oriented metaphors for God such as Lord, King, Master, and Almighty Father. Some have suggested that we think of God in ways reminiscent of Paul Tillich's "ground and power of being" or process theologians' ideas of a feeling, responding, relational God. Others have preferred the image of the goddess. The image of the goddess draws our attention to the role of such "feminine" activities as nurturing, weaving together, and loving. Images of the goddess are said to evoke awareness of the sacredness of our bodies, our fellow human beings, and our natural environment. It is claimed that genuine worship of the goddess contrasts sharply with traditional religious institutions that require self-abnegation or teach us to regard the natural world as an inferior realm of being. Feminist images of deity direct us to understand true worship as the enjoyment of, and commitment to care for, the immediate world that surrounds us.

Many of the themes that characterize feminist religious thought are echoed in recent ecological spiritualities. Since the time of Emerson and the Transcendentalists, the concept of nature has factored strongly in unchurched American religion. As historian Catherine Albanese has noted, there is a long-standing tradition of "nature religion" in the United States.[23] Some versions of nature religion are wholly pantheistic, postulating a near identity between matter and spirit. Others are more properly metaphysical, proposing a lawful "correspondence" between nature and higher spiritual dimensions. In this view, nature is susceptible to periodic "influxes" of higher spiritual energies. Both versions contrast sharply with biblical notions about the relationship between God and His creation. The Bible states that God created humans in His own image, intending them to have dominion over the earth. The world of nature thus becomes the arena for human action and conquest. Ecologists argue that because the God of the Bible is wholly beyond our finite world, human conduct toward nature is often viewed as without real religious significance.

Nature religion embraces the natural world as itself a medium of divine revelation. Consider the famed conservationist John Muir. Muir's walks through the wilderness convinced him that nature possessed an intrinsic worth over and beyond any utility it might have for humans. Immersion in nature brought Muir to the insight that, despite the teachings of orthodox Christians, the world does not revolve around humans. Creation is not the work of a humanlike God, but of the impartial force of Nature.[24] In Muir's own words,

> Nature's object in making animals and plants might possibly be first of all the happiness of each one of them, not the creation of all for the happiness of one. Why ought man to value himself as more than an

infinitely small composing unit of the one great unit of creation? And what creature of all the Lord has taken the pains to make is not essential to the completeness of that unit—the cosmos? The universe would be incomplete without man; but it would also be incomplete without the smallest tranmicroscopic creature that dwells beyond our conceitful eyes and knowledge.[25]

A major tenet of modern environmentalism is that humans are not the center of the universe. Environmentalism also prompts us to emphasize God's presence within, rather than beyond, the created universe. Most of those who "convert" to these more holistic visions are thus aware that they are simultaneously rejecting the biblical scheme of creation. As the ecological essayist Wendell Berry put it, "The great disaster of human history is one that happened to or within religion: that is, the conceptual division between the holy and the world, the excerpting of the Creator from the creation."[26] He argues that it is healthier to view God within the natural order than to elevate God far beyond earth. The problem of Western monotheism in his view is that it makes it possible to fear and worship God without fearing or worshipping nature; indeed, it becomes possible to love God while exploiting the whole of creation. Berry writes,

> If God was not in the world, then obviously the world was a thing of inferior importance, or of no importance at all. Those who were disposed to exploit it were thus free to do so. And this split in public attitudes was inevitably mirrored in the lives of individuals: a man could aspire to heaven with his mind and his heart while destroying the earth and his fellow men, with his hands.[27]

Preserving the environment has become for many Americans what Paul Tillich termed an "ultimate concern." Some environmental activists coined the term "deep ecology" to signify the radical new worldview now required of us.[28] Deep ecology insists on the radical interdependence of life on this planet. It also invites us to see how each living organism both contains and expresses the creative force of evolution itself. Violating even a single organism is thus not only an offense against the organic whole to which we all belong, but a sacrilegious act as well.

Closely aligned with deep ecology is Green politics. Green politics refers to a set of loosely connected local, state, national, and international groups that aggressively promote environmental legislation.

At one level, Green politics is associated with such causes as protection of wildlife, preservation of rain forests, elimination of nuclear power plants, and the search for renewable resources. But, at another level, Green politics is also about effecting a total change in humanity's spiritual outlook. In her *Spiritual Dimensions of Green Politics*, Charlene Spretnak maintains that it is not enough to develop "sustainable" systems of agriculture, economics, and technology. We also need a "sustainable religion." Spretnak indicts traditional Western religion for sanctioning the violence that has been committed against the environment. She argues that biblical monotheism is ultimately responsible for our alienation from nature, suppression of empathy, and injustice toward women. In contrast, a sustainable religion is one that focuses on the profound interconnectedness of life. Sustainable religion must be able to weave scientific and mystical perspectives together to produce a holistic vision of our universe. Such a vision, she argues, will "reveal the true nature of being: all in One, all forms of existence are comprised of one continuous dance of matter/energy arising and falling away, arising and falling away."[29] What is more, Spretnak writes, sensitivity to nature can trigger flashes of "God consciousness," which she equates with "awe at the intricate wonders of creation and celebration of the cosmic unfolding."[30]

There is a considerable overlap between ecological and feminist spiritualities. Spretnak, for example, writes that a truly sustainable religion must promote "spiritual development through inner growth, ecological wisdom, gender equality, and social responsibility."[31] Writing in *Yoga Journal*, Stephan Bodian and Florence Windfall note that "many Greens practice some form of paganism, neopaganism, shamanism, or goddess religion, and many worship the Earth as a spiritual being."[32] Many of those attracted to an ecological spirituality cite James Lovelock's "Gaia hypothesis" that the earth behaves as a single entity, a living goddess.[33] Still others link their holistic beliefs with Buddhism or the "new physics." And, finally, Bodian and Windfall point out yet another connection of exotic spiritualities, remarking that most "Greens owe their spirituality to Native Americans and other indigenous peoples."[34]

Over the past several decades, Euro-Americans have propagated a highly romanticized version of Native-American spirituality. Religious seekers have been attracted to tales such as those spun by Carlos Castenada that depict the Native-American quest for mystical ecstasy. Most were quick to assume that Native-American cultures were rife with wisdom about how humans can live in harmony with nature. In fact, traditional Native-American societies often displayed little ecological sensitivity and exploited the natural resources in their own vicinity. Despite this historical legacy, it is widely believed that "Indian spiritual values, especially the attitude toward the Earth, may hold out a key to the survival of the planet and all its peoples."[35] One of the most popular sources of this belief is Native-American author Vine Deloria's *God Is Red*.[36] In Deloria's view, biblical monotheism is dysfunctional. Western religion separated God from creation, leaving the natural world beyond redemption. In contrast, Deloria claims, Indians see the natural world as suffused with "an undefinable power." Deloria asserts that this sacralization of nature causes tribal religions to revere all persons and all species. He further tells us that Native-American culture celebrates individual differences, considering them to be the desire of the creator. Native-American religion, in short, is said to have a holistic vision capable of healing virtually every conflict besetting contemporary American culture.

Ecological spirituality has reached wider audiences through such periodicals as *Mother Earth News* and the *Whole Earth Catalog*.[37] Many turned to these periodicals because they were interested in organic foods or "natural" crafts such as woodcarving, weaving, or pottery. Still others were interested in activities ranging from camping to organizing recycling campaigns. Interspersed with how-to instructions for making composts or using medicinal herbs, however, are alluring descriptions of unconventional spirituality. Among the fare offered to whet readers' appetites are articles on Western occult philosophies, Yoga, Transcendental Meditation, Carlos Castaneda's accounts of the pharmacological pursuit of mystical ecstasy, and Zen. These publications are also loaded with references to such frankly supernatural practices as the Chinese divination method based on the *I Ching*, astrology, tarot cards, and psychic healing.

Catherine Albanese points out that, in general, "the two publications have provided a focus for like-minded and like-hearted people who shared in the religion of nature. They have supported believers in a creed, urged them to live the creed in a daily behavioral code, and shown them how they could find ritual expression for their beliefs and behavior in various cultures."[38] And, perhaps even more important, these two publications "show us that the occult side of American life has spread to touch the lives of many not closely identified with one specific movement."[39] Individuals whose primary interest in reading these magazines might be to pick up tips on organic foods cannot avoid being introduced to a host of unchurched spiritual traditions. Books, periodicals, conventions, and websites link these persons—and these diverse interests—into a modern version of spiritual community. They might not actually meet, but they are affirmed by the fact that other like-minded and like-hearted seekers exist across the nation. Together they share the utopian vision of reaching the entire globe with their new, holistic vision of humanity's interconnection with the sacred depths of nature.

Paths to Personal Empowerment: Neo-Paganism and Witchcraft

The term Neo-Paganism is applied to the renewal of interest in pre-Christian, nature-oriented religious beliefs that began in both England and the United States during the 1950s.[40] This revival of paganism was due in part to the writings of Margaret Murray and Gerald Gardner.[41] Murray and Gardner described pagan and witchcraft traditions that they claimed had been faithfully transmitted from ancient, pre-Christian times. This was largely a fabrication. The pagan systems they described were really their own invented traditions. Combining information from historical pagan texts with various strands of Western occultism, Murray and Gardner offered modern seekers beliefs suited to contemporary religious unrest. Gerald Gardner's publication of *Witchcraft Today* stimulated a great deal of interest in nature-based religions; the most popular of which came to be known as Wicca. About half of those who claim to adhere to pagan beliefs identify themselves as witches (i.e., Wiccan).[42] Others, however, style themselves shamanic, Druidic, Gaian, or practitioners of ceremonial magic. About 40 percent of all pagans are eclectic, drawing freely from more than one category of pagan tradition.[43]

Neo-Paganism is so diverse that it is difficult to summarize the beliefs and rituals that characterize the movement. It is probably fair to say, however, that four themes are common to contemporary American paganism: (1) belief that the divine, while both immanent in nature and unified, can be understood through polytheistic images, most of them female; (2) belief in the efficacy of mind or consciousness to influence events in non-ordinary ways, a process commonly referred to as "magic"; (3) affirmation of the interconnectedness of all life and hence the need for both ecological sensitivity and commitment to social justice issues; and (4) opposition to traditional Western religious institutions whose beliefs and structures are seen to be implicated in the social, ecological, gender, and economic oppression that violates the inherent sacredness of our universe.

Recent studies suggest there may be as many as 200,000 Neo-Pagans in the United States.[44] One study found them to be mainly young to middle-aged adults, urbanites, mostly white, middle-class, and by slight majority (57%) female.[45] Pagans are, in other words, ordinary Americans. They have, however, rejected institutional religion, preferring an alternative spirituality that espouses greater reverence for the sacredness of nature. Most are introduced to Neo-Pagan ideas by books on various forms of alternative spirituality. Those who embrace Neo-Pagan beliefs typically say they were motivated by a quest for intellectual satisfaction, pursuit of spiritual growth, concern for the environment, or a growing commitment to feminism.[46]

Exposure to feminist thought has played an important role in the recent growth of paganism. This is especially true of witchcraft. Feminism has convinced many Americans, male and female, of certain weaknesses in biblical monotheism. And feminism has actively encouraged people to explore alternative religious philosophies, especially worship of the goddess. Gardner and others held witchcraft up as nature-based religion derived from pre-Christian traditions that worshipped a central great goddess. The decision to turn one's back on Christianity and instead honor goddess traditions is thus in part a reaction against the patriarchal symbols of institutional religion. Identifying oneself as a witch is, after all, as much a cultural as a theological statement. The very term witch elicits a negative reaction from most of us. This is deliberate.[47] Modern witches are self-conscious in their opposition to traditional imagery of God as a male Supreme Being. The God of biblical monotheism, witches say, has become a symbol of "power over." The biblical God is intimately connected with sexism, racism, ecological exploitation, and other cultural traditions that legitimate the exercise of "power over" others. Modern witchcraft seeks to help people turn to a wisdom found within.

Witchcraft encourages individuals to tap into mysterious reservoirs of inner power and use the magic of their own minds to focus this energy into healing activity within the world. The word witch might very well be an upsetting metaphor to many. But it is a powerful and exciting metaphor for those who seek harmony with inner spiritual power.

Witchcraft, like paganism generally, is a religion of nature. When trying to give a name to the divine energy immanent within nature, most Neo-Pagans use the term goddess. As the best-known modern witch, Starhawk, writes,

> There are many names for power-from-within, none of them entirely satisfying. It can be called *spirit*—but that name implies that it is separate from matter … It could be called *God*—but the God of patriarchal religions has been the ultimate source and repository of power-over. I have called it *immanence*, a term that is truthful but somewhat cold and intellectual. And I have called it *Goddess*, because the ancient images, symbols and myths of the Goddess as birth-giver, weaver, earth and growing plant, wind and ocean, flame, web, moon and milk, all speak to me of the powers of connectedness, sustenance, and healing.[48]

Neo-Pagans often speak of multiple goddesses. For many, however, this is to be taken metaphorically rather than literally. They believe that we are not meant to live up to just one moral or religious standard, but rather to express life in all of its infinite diversity. Neo-Pagan references to multiple deities are a way of drawing attention to our many, alternating psychological tendencies. Each of these is associated with a different goddess and honored as a different facet of the divine "jewel." Polytheistic imagery is thus a way of asserting that reality is itself multiple and diverse. In this way Neo-Pagan encourages personal and religious differences. It stands against totalistic religious and political views, encouraging diverse understandings of divine reality. As Margo Adler writes, the very premise of Neo-Pagan philosophy is that "the spiritual world needs diversity to thrive. … your own spiritual path is not necessarily mine."[49]

Neo-Pagan philosophies affirm the existence of a divine energy that infuses all of life. They believe that the whole of nature—including our very bodies—is an expression of this divine energy. For this reason Neo-Pagans view the human body as a sacred vessel. They do not endorse the kinds of humility, self-effacement, or guilt about enjoying basic human pleasures that we typically find in Western religious traditions. Instead, Neo-Pagans celebrate both the sacredness and creative potentials of every individual. Their theological vision proclaims that "Thou art God/dess." The ultimate goal of pagan beliefs and rituals is to help us discover the "one within."

Neo-Pagans are strongly attracted to magic, which they define as "calling forth the power-from-within." The purpose of magic is to make connection with the power within. What Neo-Pagans call magic is actually quite similar to techniques that the New Thought movement used some seventy years earlier in seeking to become in tune with the infinite. Neo-Pagans recite self-help formulas and visualize specific images with the goal of first drawing on divine energy and then directing it toward productive activity. They believe that our inner spiritual powers can be called upon to heal the self and to activate our full potentials. The movement's literature consistently stresses, however, that transforming the self is only the first step of authentic spirituality. We must also learn to direct the "power from within" outward to promote political and ecological healing. As Starhawk explains, "Unless we change the structures of the culture, we will mirror them again and again. ... Reclaiming personal power gives us the courage to demand a change in the basis of society's power ... to create a vision of a new culture based on another source of power."[50]

Contrary to popular belief, Neo-Paganism has nothing to do with Satanism. Satan, after all, is a figure that emerges out of Jewish and Christian thought—not paganism. There isn't anything even like the concept Satan in pagan thought. It is also important to note that paganism isn't finally about individualism. Its best known moral maxim, "An ye harm none, do as ye will," may be a bit misleading. It affirms Neo-Paganism's belief in the sacredness of every person. It also conveys the conviction that personal growth is important to the overall plan of cosmic evolution. Yet Neo-Pagan philosophies stress the interconnectedness of life. They teach the spiritual importance of compassion, empathy, and community. And while some Neo-Pagan systems emphasize techniques aimed at personal enlightenment and personal growth, all recognize that such growth occurs through intimate interaction with a wider community. And, for Neo-Pagans, the concept of community includes the plants, animals, and soil that constitute our global environment.[51]

Neo-Pagans give a variety of reasons for their interest in nature-oriented philosophies. Most frequently cited is the desire to heal the earth, transform society, promote world peace, and find an alternative to fundamentalist religion.[52] Many also list feminist motivations. Few, however, pursue paganism in isolation from other "alternative spiritualities." Margo Adler notes that over the past few decades Neo-Pagan teachings are increasingly combined with a variety of other interests. Among these she includes shamanism, the writings of Carlos Castenada, the use of psychedelic drugs for the purpose of expanding consciousness, and Eastern meditation techniques.[53] Thus although Wicca and other Neo-Pagan traditions surely have distinct historical and intellectual lineages, the American consumers of these alternative spiritualities have a tendency to overlook these differences and to discover similar and familiar messages.

| Portents of New Age Spirituality

These exotic religious philosophies are often referred to collectively as the "New Age" movement. The origins of this term are not entirely clear. Nor is there any clear definition of what marks an alternative spirituality as New Age. But the term does serve a useful function. It draws attention to the fact that a sizable segment of the population is looking for new sources of spiritual understanding. Recent surveys suggest that 14 percent of the Baby Boomer generation identify themselves as "metaphysical seekers."[54] These individuals are disenchanted with existing churches. Organized religion and its biblical heritage are, to them, decidedly "old age." Most have attended college and have been influenced by evolutionary biology, the scientific method of reasoning, cultural pluralism, and liberal skepticism concerning claims about absolute truth. They find themselves unable to believe in the literal teachings of any one organized religion. Yet they are still interested in religious issues.

Few seekers believe that there is any one, single truth that will address all of their intellectual and emotional needs. But most are sure about at least three things. First, they believe that it has come time for religions to abandon "old age" dogmatism and incorporate contemporary knowledge. For a religion to be viable in our era it must draw eclectically from science, modern psychology, and the best insights of all world religions. Second, religion must have practical applications in our everyday lives. It must be more psychological than theological.

That is, it should be primarily concerned with helping us to find fulfillment in the here and now of this life (rather than devoting most of its attention to some speculative afterlife). And, third, metaphysical seekers yearn for an experiential spirituality; they are bored with what they perceive to be the lifeless rituals of established churches and feel the need for some kind of mystical connection with God.

The quest for a spirituality suited to our contemporary age embraces the entire gamut of exotic philosophies examined in this chapter. Included, too, are the alternative healing systems and psychological theories that will be treated next. New Age religion also extends to a wide spectrum of interest in the supernatural. Astrology, Ouija boards, tarot cards, the *I Ching*, and even the fantasy worlds of science fiction have all sustained interest in the supernatural among those who are turned off by religion. So too have the writings of the psychologist Carl Jung and the mythologist Joseph Campbell. When considered together, these various spiritual interests have had a significant impact on American religious life.

It is difficult to know just how many Americans are sympathetic to New Age spirituality. Very few people ever use the term when describing their own religious beliefs. Even the 14 percent of Baby Boomers who describe themselves as metaphysical seekers rarely identify themselves as New Agers. There is, after all, no such thing as an organized New Age movement. Those interested in one alternative spiritual topic may have absolutely no interest at all in other topics that usually get lumped together as New Age. Yet it is probably fair to say that those who describe themselves as "spiritual, but not religious" are in general agreement with the broad principles of these alternative philosophies. This would mean that a full 20 percent of the population can be said to be sympathetic with the New Age movement. But it doesn't end there. Church members, too, often have spiritual interests or curiosities that go beyond the teachings of mainstream religious denominations. As previously noted, 22 percent of all church members believe in astrology, 24 percent read their horoscope at least once each week, 20 percent believe in reincarnation, 12 percent have consulted a fortune-teller, and 11 percent believe in channeling.[55] It seems that America's unchurched traditions also influence the way that some church members privately go about constructing their religious identities.

Unchurched sources of spiritual thought have competed quite

successfully in America's "spiritual marketplace." Like all market-places, the spiritual marketplace is ultimately driven by consumer demand. Churched and unchurched alike look to this marketplace for ideas that meet their practical religious concerns; and, increasingly, these concerns seem to lead them to supplement the teachings of our established churches by drawing on one or more alternative spiritual philosophy. Recent surveys have convinced Wade Clark Roof that the nation's spiritual marketplace is changing. He believes that over the past two decades there has been "a qualitative shift from unquestioned belief to a more open, questioning mood."[56] The sheer variety of spiritual philosophies available in today's marketplace makes it difficult for thoughtful people to believe that any one religious system has a monopoly on truth. And, with a growing shift in emphasis from the producers of religious ideas (e.g., the churches or the Bible) to the consumer of religious ideas, there is a corresponding emphasis on spiritualities that are tailored to everyday concerns. The concerns that characterize the "spiritual, but not religious" sector of the population would thus appear to be causing the marketplace to operate differently. The traditions that emerged to address these concerns now affect how a large number of educated Americans understand personal spirituality. These changes in American religious life raise fascinating questions. Where are we headed? What will personal spirituality be like in the future? Has religion become captive to the marketplace, at the mercy of passing whims or fads? How might we evaluate the pros and cons of the trends set in motion by America's unchurched spiritual traditions?

We will return to these and other questions about the portents of unchurched religion in the concluding chapter.

4 | Alternative Medicines, Alternative Worldviews

In the early 1990s, *Time* magazine ran a cover story on the growing interest in alternative medicine. "New Age medicine is catching on," readers were told. "Fed up with surgery, drugs, and quick fixes from their doctors, Americans are turning to an array of alternative therapies ranging from the believable to the bizarre."[1] The article went on to say that this turn toward alternative medicine is usually motivated by sheer desperation. People with terminal illnesses who have exhausted conventional treatment options might understandably turn to therapies at the margins of scientific respectability. They are willing to try healing systems that run the gamut from those that have some scientific respectability (osteopathy, chiropractic, acupuncture) to the "frankly bizarre" (reflexology, crystal healing, color healing). The implication is that Americans who consider alternative medicine are consciously turning away from the cultural mainstream and turning, at least temporarily, toward the cultural fringe. The further implication is that such people are behaving in a way that is somehow inconsistent with "normal" middle-class behavior.

In fact, however, the "turn" to unconventional therapies is something that happens *within* mainstream, middle-class culture. Beginning with mesmerism, hydropathy, homeopathy, and mindcure in the nineteenth century, interest in alternative medical systems has largely been a middle-class phenomenon. Moreover, the vast majority of those who become enthusiasts of alternative medicines aren't medically desperate. On the contrary, they are typically healthy individuals who are exploring avenues to even higher levels of health and well-being. They are drawn to these novel medical theories not so much for their alternative treatments as their alternative theories about body-mind-spirit interaction. Alternative medicines almost invariably promulgate alternative worldviews. They provide clients with unconventional theories of human nature, often including frankly metaphysical views of the human potential to achieve harmony with higher healing powers. Alternative medicines have thus provided many middle-class Americans with their first introduction to exciting new philosophical and spiritual perspectives on life.

Religion and Medicine: Uneasy Connections

The last 300 years of Western history have witnessed the "official" separation of religion and medicine. Before the Scientific Revolution, religion dominated the popular understanding of disease and medical treatment. The church focused attention on the role of spiritual factors in causing illness. Disease was thus often thought to be due to personal sin or the phenomenon of spirit possession. Appropriate treatments were thought to require supernatural techniques such as petitionary prayer, confession, or exorcism. Medical science as we know it today emerged by repudiating this worldview. Medicine, much like religion, gradually developed its own orthodox system of beliefs and practices. Medical orthodoxy was defined by its commitment to the belief that disease is caused by physical or material factors. The impressive advances made by medical science gradually pushed religious explanations to the far fringes of intellectual and cultural respectability. Western religious institutions have had little choice but to concede the realm of medicine to science. Churches have for the most part been content with a clear-cut division of labor whereby they have become responsible for the cure of souls while medical professionals are entrusted with the cure of bodies. Conventional religion and conventional medicine seem comfortable maintaining this official wall of separation.

The popularity of alternative medicines suggests that a sizable number of Americans subscribe to beliefs that don't quite fit into conventional science or conventional religion. By questioning the materialistic theory of disease, they have challenged our culture's orthodox worldview. Both medical and religious authorities have predictably labeled advocates of alternative medicine irrational. Strictly speaking, however, any medical system is rational if its methods of treatment are logically entailed by its fundamental premises concerning the nature of disease. Alternative medicines are thus not necessarily less logical than scientific medicine, but many do adhere to a very different set of assumptions about the nature of reality. Many alternative medicines operate according to a worldview that recognizes the existence, and causal activity, of metaphysical forces. Their theories and practices consequently introduce patients into a religiously charged interpretation of reality (albeit one very different from the theology of most churches).

The point here is that the continued popularity of alternative healing practices in American culture cannot be explained exclusively in terms of simple ignorance or desperation on the part of the terminally ill. A study of alternative medical systems reported in the *New England Journal of Medicine* found that the demographic profile of the most frequent users of these unconventional therapies was "nonblack persons from 25 to 49 years of age who had relatively more education and higher incomes."[2] These individuals were far less likely to have life-threatening conditions than to be seeking relief from a chronic condition. They may well be desperate to get better, but they had time to make informed decisions about the cures they might experimentally use. Furthermore, most had consulted a medical doctor, indicating that they were supplementing rather than abandoning conventional medicine. It would seem, then, that the persistence and popularity of alternative healing systems must be due to more than simple ignorance or last-minute panic.

A closer look at the role of alternative medicines in American culture suggests that a major reason for their continued popularity is that they articulate spiritually significant ways of viewing the world.[3]

Healing systems have performed this role throughout the course of world history. In archaic societies, healing rituals involve the reenactment of cosmological dramas: the shaman is not only a healer but also a mystagogue who mediates between the divine and human realms. In early Christianity, healing was both a sign of Jesus's divine nature and a manifestation of the world-altering power of God. The Christian Church institutionalized Jesus' healing activity and made it an important part of Christian proclamation and ministry.[4] It was therefore fairly predictable that as the Church gradually abandoned its healing practices, alternative systems would "rediscover" the power of healing to bring individuals to an existential encounter with a sacred reality.

Not every system of alternative medicine has a spiritual dimension. For example, nutritional and exercise therapies usually seek to strengthen the body's own recuperative abilities and rarely make references to metaphysical energies. Many massage and breathing systems likewise make no claims concerning extrasomatic forces.[5] Yet alternative healing systems are considered "unorthodox" precisely to the degree that they propound alternative worldviews. Their healing techniques are frequently predicated on the belief that under certain conditions more-than-worldly energies enter into, and exert sanative influences on, the human body. Thus, while not all alternative medicines embody a spiritual orientation to life, most do.

| Chiropractic Medicine's Metaphysical Heritage

Daniel David Palmer (1845–1913) began his career as a grocer and fish peddler in What Cheer, Iowa. Palmer lacked formal education, but he read widely and was drawn to novel ideas. One of these novel ideas was spiritualism. Palmer's exposure to spiritualism taught him the vocabulary of nineteenth-century metaphysical movements. He subsequently met up with a mesmeric healer who tutored him in magnetic healing. Palmer procured several books on mesmeric healing that were to remain central texts in his personal library for the rest of his life. Having found his calling, Palmer opened his own magnetic healing practice in Burlington, Iowa, and later moved it to Davenport. Palmer innovated as he went along. Slowly but surely, he pieced together his own variation of mesmeric healing philosophy. As fate would have it, one day a janitor by the name of Harvey Lillard stopped by his office. Lillard told Palmer that he had been deaf ever since he had injured his back seventeen years earlier. Palmer asked Lillard to lie down on his couch. He then moved his hands up and down Lillard's spine. He felt an unusual lump at one vertebra and applied pressure with his hands. Palmer felt the vertebra move back into place and, lo and behold, Lillard could hear perfectly.

Similar healing successes followed. Palmer reasoned that misaligned spinal vertebrae must somehow block the flow of vital energy within the body. He concluded that this blockage was the direct cause of disease. It followed that for healing to take place these misplaced vertebrae must be forced back into position so that the energy can once again flow freely throughout the body. Palmer called his new medical philosophy *chiropractic* from the Greek words *cheiro* (hand) and *prakitos* (done or performed). Palmer was, however, not propounding a material or physiological theory of disease. Quite the contrary. Palmer's chiropractic philosophy was predicated on an overtly metaphysical wordview. According to Palmer, the key to understanding both health and disease is realizing that physical life is an expression of a divine force that he called Innate:

> What is it that is present in the living body and absent in the dead? ....
> An intelligent force which I saw fit to name Innate, usually known as
> spirit, creates and continues life when vital organs are in a condition
> to be acted upon by it. That intelligent life-force uses the material of
> the universe just in proportion as it is in a condition to be utilized.[6]

Palmer reasoned that Innate, as it exists as an energy within the individual human being, is in fact "a segment of that Intelligence which fills the universe." According to Palmer, "innate is a part of the Creator. Innate spirit is a part of Universal Intelligence, individualized and personified."[7] Palmer went on to explain that Universal Intelligence is the cosmic power that the various world religions call God. As such, Universal Intelligence is what has brought the universe into existence. All living things are rooted in the creative drive of Universal Intelligence. Their purpose is to contribute to this creative process by embodying the drive toward ongoing evolution and development.

The cosmology underlying chiropractic theory was hardly unique to Palmer; it also appeared in much of the mesmerist and spiritualist literature with which Palmer was familiar. Chiropractic theory built on these metaphysical views, trying to trace the physiological routes through which Innate spirit directs the life processes within the human body. Palmer concluded that Innate works through the brain to generate vital impulses, which in turn travel along nerve pathways to their various destinations. It is consequently imperative that the spinal column be perfectly aligned so that this vital energy can travel unobstructed throughout the physical system. Displacements of the vertebrae, called subluxations by Palmer, disrupt the flow of the Innate-generated nerve impulses. As a consequence, one or more area of the body will be severed from Innate and will begin to atrophy. As the cover of the Palmer School of Chiropractic Medicine's official publication, *The Chiropractor*, put it, "We are all well when Innate Intelligence has unhindered freedom to act thru the physical brain, nerves and tissues. Diseases are caused by a LACK OF CURRENT OF INNATE MENTAL IMPLUSES."[8] The manipulative therapy that Palmer designed to correct vertebral dislocations was thus one more variation on the mesmerists' magnets and hand gestures—a physical technique intended to align persons in such a way as to make them more receptive to the working of a higher spiritual power.

Palmer's son, B. J. Palmer (1881–1961), left his own mark on the theory and practice of chiropractic medicine. For over fifty years he directed the training of chiropractic physicians and tried to keep chiropractic medicine firmly rooted in its metaphysical foundations. B. J. Palmer believed that chiropractic had discovered that God, in the form of Innate, is present within each human being. There was now a scientific basis for understanding humanity's relationship with God. In one fell swoop chiropractic had made both conventional religion and conventional medicine obsolete. As he put it, "Everything that man could ask or pray for he has within. … The Chiropractor removes the obstruction, adjusts the cause, and there are going to be effects."[9]

Not all chiropractic's physicians were enthusiastic about the Palmers' metaphysical theories. They were well aware that opponents of chiropractic medicine repeatedly attacked the concept of Innate as untestable and hence unscientific. Most chiropractic physicians wanted to acquire scientific respectability. They were especially eager to earn the respect of medical doctors and become eligible for reimbursement from insurance companies. Most consequently ignored the metaphysical foundations of their medical movement. The majority of the 40,000 chiropractic physicians currently practicing in the United States have relegated the Palmers' writings to dusty archives and instead focus their efforts on treating the physical causes of muscoloskeletal disorders.

Nevertheless, the aura of metaphysical discovery continues to count among the reasons why nine million people visit chiropractic physicians each year. A significant minority of chiropractic doctors remain committed to introducing their patients to theories that are steeped in America's occult and metaphysical heritage. As Eugene Linden reported in a feature on alternative medicine for *Time* magazine, the chiropractic physician he visited for lower-back pain considered it just as important to give him "a line of Eastern philosophy" as a spinal adjustment. Linden recounts that "at first I found Christoph's messianic zeal as off-putting as the detached manner of the doctor in my H.M.O. Then Christoph checked my 'energy centers.'...Deficiencies in my sixth (or was it fifth?) 'chakra' notwithstanding, once Christoph had finished his Procrustean pullings, crackings and pushings, the pain was gone and I felt 20 lbs. lighter."[10]

It appears an increasing number of chiropractors share Christoph's spiritual interests and are proudly reclaiming their movement's metaphysical heritage. Many have now added acupuncture to their healing repertoire. Acupuncture is rooted in Chinese religious belief concerning a subtle spiritual energy known as *ch'i*. As the case of Christoph illustrates, many chiropractors draw eclectically from America's occult and metaphysical traditions. Christoph's reference to chakras reveals how fully he expects his clientele to be familiar with, or at least receptive to, terminology drawn from alternative spiritual philosophies. When G. F. Riekman, a chiropractic physician and former professor at Sherman College of Chiropractic, was asked to summarize chiropractic's distinctive philosophy for *The Holistic Health Handbook*, he described it as "New Age philosophy, science, and art":

> The chiropractic philosophy is based on the deductive principle that the Universe is perfectly organized, and that we are all extensions of this principle, designed to express life (health) and the universal laws. Since vertebral subluxations (spinal-nerve interference) are the grossest interference with the expression of life, the practice of chiropractic is designed to analyze these subluxations, so that the organism will be free to evolve and express life to its fullest natural potential.[11]

Most people who visit a chiropractic physician probably learn little or nothing about chiropractic's metaphysical heritage. Yet, for a sizable minority, this visit to an alternative healer becomes an introduction to an alternative spiritual philosophy.

Discovering the "Higher Self": Holistic Healing

During the late 1970s, there was a noticeable surge of interest in "holistic" medicine. The holistic healing movement was partly a reaction against the impersonal character of medical science. As the *Time* magazine article on New Age medicine noted, people are fed up with surgery, drugs, and quick fixes from their doctors. They want attention paid to psychological and emotional aspects of healing. They would like medical professionals to spend as much time promoting optimal health as they do curing disease. And many hope to reintroduce a boldly spiritual perspective to contemporary understandings of medicine and healing.

The basic premise of holistic medicine is that "every human being is a unique, wholistic, interdependent relationship of body, mind, emotions, and spirit."[12] This appears at first glance to be a fairly bland truism. It seems to be more exhortatory than intellectual, intended to remind health care practitioners that patients deserve to be treated with dignity and respect. Yet on closer inspection it proposes a fairly radical understanding of health and medicine. By introducing the term *spirit* alongside *body, mind*, and *emotions*, advocates of holistic medicine were going well beyond current models of psychosomatic medicine (which recognize the connection between our body, mind, and emotions). They were openly breaching the time-honored wall of separation between religious and scientific understandings of medicine. Spokespersons for holistic medicine were suggesting that there is a spiritual aspect to human nature that somehow transcends our physical and psychological nature. More important, they were claiming that this spiritual element plays a causal role in our sickness and health. Holistic healing theories invited people to adopt both an alternative medical theory and an alternative religious worldview.

Typical of overviews of holistic medicine was Herbert Otto and James Knight's edited volume, *Dimensions in Wholistic Healing: New Frontiers in the Treatment of the Whole Person*. Knight and Otto say that holistic approaches to medicine are unique in that they place "reliance on treatment modalities that foster the self-regenerative and self-reparative processes of natural healing."[13] The final source of these self-regenerative processes is neither physical nor psychological. It is metaphysical. Knight and Otto explain that "everyone is part of a larger system." Holistic healing requires individuals to make appropriate changes in their spiritual understanding so that they can "open the pathways or flows and harmonics necessary to unfold the channels of the self within the body and the self within the world, the Universe, and God."[14] Thus what began as a rather mild acknowledgment of the body's self-recuperative abilities slides imperceptibly into the same metaphysical doctrine of "influx" found in such other carriers of unchurched American religious thought as Swedenborgianism, Transcendentalism, mesmerism, and Theosophy.

Kenneth Pelletier's *Holistic Medicine* also exemplifies the way in which holistic medicine introduces alternative spiritualities. Like nearly all of the movement's defenders, Pelletier begins by appealing to recent research in the field of psychosomatic medicine. The discovery that an individual's mental and emotional states can directly affect physiological processes has established the fact that medicine must now acknowledge the role that nonmaterial factors have in both the cause and treatment of disease. He writes, "A fundamental philosophical revision is taking place in our paradigm of medicine. Central to this revision is the concept that all stages of disease are psychosomatic in etiology, direction, and the healing process."[15] It quickly becomes evident, however, that psychosomatic interaction alone hardly covers the fundamental revision he has in mind. Pelletier's "new paradigm" is far less concerned with our mental or emotional curative powers than with the supervenient power of spirit. Pelletier urges us to abandon Western notions of matter and energy and adopt the Chinese yin/yang philosophy, which traces all physiological processes back to their ultimate spiritual source (the Tao). He also endorses the general theories of Fritjof Capra's *The Tao of Physics*. Capra's book is cited by many advocates of holistic healing because it invokes both the "new physics" and Eastern mystical philosophies to argue that there is no final distinction between matter and energy (spirit). This suggests to Pelletier and others that spiritual energies are capable of exerting causal influences within the physical universe. Pelletier's anecdotal illustration of this new view of healing is revealing. He reports that a Zen practitioner healed herself of diabetes and cardiac irregularities by turning within and opening "a tiny hole of light" through which spirit entered and enveloped her whole being with healing energies.

Two of the best-known spokespersons for holistic healing have been Norman Cousins and Bernard Siegel. Cousins, former editor of the *Saturday Review*, contracted a serious illness for which his physicians gave a rather bleak prognosis. His *Anatomy of an Illness* (1979) became a classic indictment of the medical profession's needlessly materialistic vision of the human person.[16] In this book Cousins recounts how he willed himself back to health through a deliberate regimen of optimistic and cheerful thinking. The account of his lengthy remission drew a great deal of popular attention to the role of our attitudes in both creating and curing disease. But much like Phineas Quimby in the 1840s, Cousins implied that our attitudes have curative power largely by regulating our inner access to metaphysical energies. In a later work, *Human Options*, Cousins stated that the mind is connected with a "life-force" that drives us toward perfectibility: "The human brain is a mirror to infinity. ... No one knows what great leaps of achievement may be within the reach of the species once the full potentiality of the mind is developed. As we create an ever-higher sense of our cosmic consciousness, we become aware of our ever-higher possibilities and challenges."[17]

Physician Bernard Siegel has been even more influential in linking ideas of holistic healing with a decidedly metaphysical view of the human condition. Siegel's patients read books on meditation and psychic phenomena to learn practical techniques for tapping into higher healing energies. Outlining the scientific "theophysics" he believes will emerge in the near future, Siegel writes, "If you consider God, and you can use this label scientifically as an intelligent, loving light, then that energy is available to all of us. We are part of it, we have a collective unconscious. ... If you get people to open to this energy, anything can be healed."[18]

Holistic healing methods aspire to expand patients' understanding of themselves and the universe they live in. Actress Shirley MacLaine is a case in point. MacLaine writes that "natural, holistic approaches worked better for me than medicines or drugs. ... Orthodox Western medicine relied far too heavily on drugs."[19] Her introduction to alternative healing techniques convinced her that she possessed energies or powers that she had never known to exist. Meditation and other inner-healing practices made it possible for her to experience "the most beautiful white light above me. I can't describe how that light felt. It was warm and loving and real. It was real and it was God or something."[20] Having felt herself "vibrating with a strange magnetic energy," MacLaine realized that the real self is the spiritual self, the soul. She came to believe that we are, even now, spiritual beings who "interface with the energy which we refer to as God."[21] Not everyone is as quick to embrace the gospel of the "higher self" as Miss Mac-Laine. Indeed, most of those who visit a metaphysically oriented chiropractor or pick up books such as those of Siegel and Cousins probably aren't seeking a new worldview. Many, maybe even most, are secure in their churched religious beliefs and their faith in scientific medicine. They quickly filter out those concepts that don't mesh with their existing views, and only attend to new strategies for strengthening their self-recuperative powers. But they have at the very least become acquainted with terminology drawn from America's unchurched religious tradition. And many, churched and unchurched alike, discover new and untapped resources residing in their own "higher self."

Therapeutic Touch and Twelve-Step Programs

Therapeutic Touch and the many twelve-step recovery movements spawned by Alcoholics Anonymous are striking examples of how holistic healing movements introduce people to new spiritual philosophies. Dolores Krieger, a nursing instructor at New York University, developed a healing technique predicated on the existence of a universal life energy. Krieger, who has a background in Theosophy, believes that Eastern religions have long understood the concept of life energy in a way that still eludes Western science. She uses the Hindu term *prana* to identify the energy that she believes is responsible for the entire process of cosmic evolution. Krieger teaches that every living organism is an open system and is continuously connected with this cosmic energy. So long as we remain inwardly connected with *prana*, we will be healthy. Illness ensues when this connection is severed and some area of the body develops a deficit of *prana*. The art of healing thus entails the "channeling of this energy flow by the healer for the well-being of the sick individual."[22]

Krieger devised techniques for nurses to "channel" *prana* into patients. What Krieger calls "Therapeutic Touch" recapitulates Mesmer's science of animal magnetism in nearly every detail. She explains, for example, that healers cannot transmit *prana* to a patient unless they first cultivate their own receptivity to the inflow of this spiritual energy. Healers must learn to purify themselves and open up the various *chakras* (spiritual centers) through which *prana* enters our bodies. Healing is thus part of a spiritual way of life. It requires persons to develop a whole new set of mental and spiritual habits. It also requires becoming adept at entering into meditative states of consciousness. Once nurses learn to enhance their own connection with this life-enhancing power, they are then in a position to channel it to their patients through an elaborate ritual of touching. Much as mesmerists made their passes and D. D. Palmer made his adjustments, nurses trained in Therapeutic Touch use special massage techniques to restore the free flow of *prana*. According to Krieger, during the healing process both patient and healer experience tingling sensations, pulsation of energy, and a radiation of heat—all tangible evidence of the activation of *prana*.

Therapeutic Touch is therefore intended to do more than humanize modern medicine by restoring human contact between healer and patient. It is also seeking to introduce a new worldview in which spiritual energies are understood to have a causal power all their own. According to Krieger, instruction in Therapeutic Touch is an "experience in interiority ... [that] presents you with a rich lode of circumstances through which you can explore and grapple with the farther reaches of the psyche."[23] Opening oneself to the nonmaterial energy underlying physical existence is a "symbolic experience" that initiates an "archetypal journey" that leads newcomers to the spiritual resources residing in the depths of our own consciousness.

Nurses involved with Therapeutic Touch are not the only ones to find themselves suddenly pursuing archetypal journeys. The best known of all holistic therapies—Alcoholics Anonymous—is largely responsible for the widespread popularity of the phrase "spiritual, but not religious." The principal founder of the movement, Bill Wilson (or simply Bill W., as he is known within the movement), was himself an alcoholic who became acutely aware of his inability to overcome his addiction. Finally, in a moment of desperation, Bill W. found himself crying out, "If there is a God, let Him show Himself! I am ready to do anything, anything!"

Suddenly the room lit up with a great white light. I was caught up into an ecstasy which there are no words to describe. ... All about me and through me there was a wonderful feeling of Presence, and I thought to myself, "So this is the God of the preachers!" A great peace stole over me and I thought, "No matter how wrong things seem to be, they are all right. Things are all right with God and His world."[24]

This experience became the paradigm of self-renewal for Alcoholics Anonymous and the twelve-step program it created. To this day A.A. stresses the importance of acquiring "an overwhelming 'God-consciousness' followed at once by a vast change in feeling and outlook."[25] Yet despite the ways in which A.A. resembles the evangelical piety of America's Protestant churches, Bill W. was extremely wary of organized religion.[26] He was particularly suspicious of the moralism associated with biblical religion. Most alcoholics had had more than their fill of pious admonitions to cease sinning. He rejected traditional religious dogma and confessed that "in all probability, the churches will not supply the answers for a good many of us."[27]

A.A.'s disappointment with organized religion was rooted in personal experience. Ministers and lay counselors who tried to rescue alcoholics through forced conversions to Christianity struck Bill W. as more an obstacle to recovery than a help. Yet he observed that "the spiritual worked."[28] In Wilson's mind, the distinction between religion and spirituality is a real one. For him spirituality has to do with recognizing that there is a Higher Power, God. He believed that our highest good comes from letting go of our personal will and finding inner harmony with this fulfilling Other. Wilson devoted a great deal of time and energy describing what he meant by spirituality in nontheological terms. For this purpose he borrowed heavily from the writings of two spiritually oriented psychologists, Carl Jung and William James. Jung had treated Rowland H., another pioneer of A.A., for alcoholism. Jung believed that the alcoholic suffered from personality conflicts so profound as to be curable only through a spiritual experience. Jung himself, however, had also struggled with organized religion. Although his father was a Lutheran minister, Jung ultimately rejected his Christian heritage because he believed it no longer spoke to the modern individual. Jung instead came to speak of God as "the collective unconscious," a source of healing power available to us at the depths of our own personal consciousness. It was from Jung that A.A. borrowed its religious insight that the self must first give way before the regenerative process can begin. Jung's argument was psychological rather than theological. For him it was simply the case that the waking personality is too rationalistic and egocentric to permit higher influences to enter. A.A.'s insistence on the alcoholic's self-surrender was not motivated by belief in human depravity. A.A.'s spirituality was instead based on the experiences of alcoholics who had given up control of their lives to a Higher Power and, in the process, obtained "God-consciousness."

William James was an even greater influence on Bill W.'s innovative spirituality. Shortly after his recovery, Bill W. came upon James's monumental *The Varieties of Religious Experience*. James's psychological analysis of religious experience emboldened Bill W. to abandon belief in the Bible and church doctrines. He concurred with James's thesis that the "truth" of religion is to be found in personal experiences of a higher power. James argued that religious doctrines are nothing more than attempts to translate these experiences into words. Doctrines are human constructs and thus constrained by their authors' particular cultural background. For James it followed that all religious beliefs must be held tentatively and continuously revised as dictated by new experiences. James thus imparted to modern religious thought its characteristic open-mindedness and acceptance of the culturally conditioned character of all religious doctrines. Religion of this kind acknowledges diversity and makes allowances for personal differences. It also aspires to be co-scientific, willing to follow truth wherever it leads. Bill W's statement that William James was a "founder of Alcoholics Anonymous" is not merely a figure of speech. For it was James who gave A.A. a language and metaphysical rationale for a mode of spirituality that is at once deeply personal, optimistic, progressivist, and couched in the essentially therapeutic language of self-actualization.

Bill W. described A.A. as "a spiritual rather than a religious program"—a phrase that to this day resonates through the movement and all the twelve-step programs it has spawned.[29] Over the years A.A. has accommodated its mainstream clientele by toning down some of its metaphysical overtones and softening its critique of Christian churches. It has nonetheless retained its distinctively spiritual flavor. The group's self-help manual *Twelve Steps and Twelve Traditions* continues to warn against relying on willpower or one's own personal resources. The key to personal regeneration, it insists, is "the feeling of being at one with God and man."[30] A.A. has perpetuated the unique blend of mysticism and pragmatism propounded by such major contributors to unchurched American religious thought as Ralph Waldo Emerson and William James. It holds, for example, that true self-reliance is possible only once we have connected ourselves with the Other: "The more we become willing to depend upon a higher power, the more independent we actually are."[31] A.A.'s mystical, nonscriptural approach to spiritual regeneration makes it anathema to most of America's religious establishment. Its rejection of physiological factors in favor of such an overtly psychological and even spiritual approach to recovery makes it anathema to the American medical establishment. But its open-minded and eclectic approach to spiritual regeneration makes it one of the most powerful mediators of wholeness in America today.

New Age Crystal Healing

The basic themes of holistic healing are also found in a number of New Age religious interests. "New Age religion" is a convenient catch-all term for the resurfacing of the metaphysical currents set in motion a century ago by Transcendentalism, Swedenborgianism, mesmerism, spiritualism, and Theosophy. The New Age movement is characterized by (1) avid interest in Eastern philosophy and meditation practices, (2) continuing belief in the existence of subtle energies that connect the human body with higher cosmic planes, and (3) faith in the power of mind or thought to influence external reality. All have factored into the movement's distinctive understandings of health and healing.

New Age healing philosophies draw on traditions dating back to mesmerism. As we have seen, the mesmerists' use of mystical trance states to open patients to the inflow of healing energies continues to influence alternative medical systems such as Therapeutic Touch. Spiritualists added another dimension to New Age healing lore by using their connection with the spirit world to make diagnoses and prescribe remedies. And, too, Edgar Cayce used his clairvoyant powers to produce volumes of information on topics ranging from herbal remedies to the effect of past-life karma on health.

In recent years Deepak Chopra has been a prominent advocate for

New Age medicine. Formerly Chief of Staff at New England Memorial Hospital, Chopra has branched out from medical science to embrace a variety of Eastern and Western healing practices. His bestselling books have introduced American reading audiences to the healing powers associated with meditation, Yoga, massage, primordial sound therapy, aromatherapy, and Ayurvedic herbal wraps.[32] Chopra is typical of New Age healers in that he seems less interested in healing per se than with helping people attain optimal states of fulfillment and well-being. He writes that healing philosophies operate on the basis of metaphysical laws that, once understood, can be utilized to accomplish anything we desire. He has expanded on these cosmic laws in a series of books with titles such as *The Seven Spiritual Laws of Success: A Practical Guide to the Fulfillment of Your Dreams* and *The Way of the Wizard: Twenty Spiritual Lesson for Creating the Life You Want.*[33] As Chopra explains it, alternative healing techniques furnish the secret to a life of spiritual mastery: "To understand the magical nature of the mind is to acquire awesome power. It is to understand that at every moment of our lives, we have the power to accomplish everything we want."[34]

Common to all New Age medical systems is the conviction that we live in a multidimensional universe. Drawing on America's unchurched metaphysical traditions, New Age healers describe God in such impersonal terms as "divine spirit" or "pure white light." It is believed that this pure white light continuously emanates throughout the universe, infusing a vital force into each of the many dimensions or planes of existence—mineral, vegetable, animal, mental, etheric, and astral. New Age cosmology teaches that divine spirit enters our consciousness through the astral body (aura) and is diffused into the seven interior energy centers (or *chakras*) that supply the body with vitality. As one New Age healer explains, "When white light flows harmoniously [from the astral body] into the interior centers (the *chakras*), our condition becomes healthy and more harmonious. When there is some obstruction in the *chakra*, blocks are formed, and these blocks prevent energy from flowing freely, and the body is unable to heal itself."[35]

One example of the medical techniques predicated on this metaphysical vision is crystal healing. Rock crystal is almost entirely devoid of color. New Age healers claim that because of this unique property, crystals are almost perfect capacitors of divine white light.

The precise explanation of just how this works varies from healer to healer. Some practitioners maintain that crystals serve as receptors through which divine white light can be channeled from the etheric plane into a patient's body. Others suggest that crystals work by amplifying the patient's own personal energies. This apparent disagreement about whether crystals amplify personal energies or harness extrapersonal energies is possibly due to semantic confusion in the New Age lexicon. The vocabulary used by New Age healers—largely of theosophical and mesmerist parentage—describes humans as simultaneously inhabiting physical, etheric, and astral bodies. Crystals supposedly have the ability to harmonize the physical body with the etheric fields from which healing energy ultimately emanates. Crystal healer Korra Deaver explains:

> Crystals act as transformers and harmonizers of energy. Illness in the physical body is a reflection of disruption or disharmony of energies in the etheric bodies, and healing takes place when harmony is restored to the subtler bodies. The crystal acts as a focus of healing energy and healing intent, and thereby produces the appropriate energy.[36]

Learning to become a crystal healer is somewhat like a shaman's initiation. First, meticulous attention must be given to selecting a particular crystal that will enhance one's own personal vibrations. After an appropriate stone has been selected, healers must purify themselves by eliminating all nonspiritual desires and emotions and center themselves inwardly. Centering techniques include breathing exercises, relaxation exercises, meditation, and the repetition of spiritual affirmations. Many engage in these practices while focusing attention on their crystals in a manner reminiscent of the ancient art of divination using crystal balls. "Crystal gazing," as Deaver describes it, is "the science of inhibiting normal outward consciousness by intense concentration on a polished sphere. When the five senses are thus drastically subdued, the psychic receptors can function without interference."[37] To aid in this process of inner transformation, crystal healers often repeat such affirmations as "I am the Light of God," "I am filled with the Light of Christ," or "I am a radiant Being of Light temporarily using a physical body."

Healer Katrina Raphael writes: "Crystal healings are designed to allow the recipient to consciously access depths of being previously unavailable, and draw upon personal resources to answer all questions and heal any wound. ... The person who is receiving the crystal healing has the unique opportunity to contact the very essence of being."[38] Crystal healers counsel patients to put ego aside in order to become purer channels of divine energy. We must open ourselves fully and suspend our human will in order to follow the higher guidance that flows directly from the Supreme Soul. Crystal healing, then, is a spiritual path and spiritual discipline in its own right. Hence, Korra Deaver discourages a narrow focus on physical healing and suggests that "even if the breakthrough is only in your own understanding of yourself-as-a-soul, as a Cosmic Being, your efforts will not have been in vain."[39]

| Alternative Healing, Alternative Spirituality

Throughout world history, religion has featured special healing rituals. Individuals whose lives are broken, divided, or afflicted become "born again" after coming into contact with spiritual powers. Such healings serve as rites of initiation. They bring people into experiential contact with a higher power that is capable of transforming their lives, thereby initiating them into the deeper mysteries of faith. Jesus, Mohammed, and the prophet Elisha are all said to have performed healing "miracles." The purpose of these healings was to display the power of God in such a dramatic fashion as to bring both those who were healed and those who witnessed to a deeper faith. Judaism, Christianity, and Islam have all given rise to prophets and holy persons who continue to heal in the name of their God. These public healings, as well as the healings that accompany private prayer and reading of scripture, strengthen individuals' commitment to biblical religion.

The alternative medical systems currently popular in the United States might be viewed in a similar context. They, too, provide rites of initiation into religious belief systems. Mircea Eliade has written that classic rites of initiation introduce newcomers to a ritual setting that will "involve their entire lives." These rites lead initiates through a series of cognitive and emotional changes that enable them to see themselves as "a being open to the life of the spirit."[40] Alternative healing systems perform precisely these initiatory tasks. Their healing techniques guide patients through an experiential process aimed at eliciting a spiritual transformation. Alternative healing practices often induce sensations of heat and tingling, a classic feature of initiatory rites.[41] Patients are taught to attribute these sensations to the presence of "subtle energies," variously described as animal magnetism, *prana*, ectoplasm, or Innate. This experience provides a felt sense of encountering a numinous, life-altering spiritual reality. The healing ritual thus evokes a fundamental sense of wonder and mystery. Many are enabled for the first time in their lives to believe that they have, in Eliade's words, become "a being open to the life of the spirit" and have discovered a worldview that will "involve their entire lives."

The literature describing alternative healing philosophies is more widespread and more avidly consumed than the healing practices themselves. The ideas that alternative systems promulgate are generally thought to be as important as the physical techniques. *The Holistic Health Handbook* states this explicitly: "Perhaps more important than the techniques is the expansion of consciousness they foster."[42] The handbook provides overviews of such holistic health systems as acupressure, Shiatsu, reflexology, iridology, and meditation practices. It tells us, however, that the many differences between these practices shouldn't obscure the fact that they all advance ideas whose goal is to help us "open up a relationship to inner worlds" and thereby "awaken the spirit within." Even chiropractic medicine has often been more successful at adjusting patients' sense of personal identity than their spines. Consider, for example, the testimony of an early chiropractic patient whose exposure to the philosophy of Innate completely altered her fundamental sense of personal identity. Whereas she had formerly thought of herself as possessing a soul, she now understood that she is a soul. In her words, it is "not that I have an Innate Intelligence, but that I am Innate Intelligence in this physical shell."[43] Shirley MacLaine's use of crystals and related meditational practices embarked her on a similar spiritual journey. MacLaine's religious transformation led to the conviction that "a healthy state of spirit controlled my mind and body. I realized I was essentially a spiritual being, not a mind-body being."[44]

Perhaps the clearest example of how alternative medical systems propagate alternative spirituality is offered by the more than 5,000 professional nurses who have been instructed in Therapeutic Touch. Many who complete their training in Therapeutic Touch come to understand themselves in new ways. These nurses cease thinking of themselves as agents of a pharmaceutical technology and instead perceive themselves as "channels." Krieger's students describe their new identity this way: "A channel, definitely, for the universal power of wholeness. I am certain it is not 'I' who do it"; and "[I] see myself ... as a vehicle through which energy can go to the patient in whatever way he or she can use it."[45] The terms "channel" and "vehicle" are significant in that they echo the terminology associated with the spiritualist and Theosophical traditions that Krieger had previously studied. The fact that her students now understand themselves as channels indicates how easily Americans can assimilate alternative spiritual philosophies into their stock of "working ideas."

As one student expressed it, "Using Therapeutic Touch has changed and continues to change me ... [and] requires a certain philosophy, and this change in philosophy permeates one's total existence."[46] This "certain philosophy" is drawn completely from America's unchurched religious traditions. Nurses trained in a down-to-earth scientific tradition find themselves contemplating the existence of nonphysical forces that affect human well-being. They learn to see how techniques like meditation can be powerful tools for improving the quality of our lives. The benefits that these nurses attribute to their change in philosophy read like a page taken from psychologist Abraham Maslow's studies of peak experiences: increased independence and selfreliance; the ability to view things in their totality; a more caring (bodhisattva-like) attitude toward others; the sense of being an integral part of the universe; and the abandonment of the scientific method as the sole approach to understanding the nature of life. Many report that they now avidly read books on Yoga meditation, Tibetan mysticism, and the spiritual implications of the "new physics."

In a famous essay titled "The Will to Believe," William James noted that many modern individuals find it difficult to sustain belief in religion. James pointed out that educated people increasingly find that religious beliefs are avoidable, dead, or trivial. By this he meant that we can usually get along without them, that they no longer speak to our experience, and that they pale by comparison to the great advances being made by scientific thought. But, James argued, there are situations in which religion comes to us in such a way as to make it forced, living, and momentous. Then, and only then, religion becomes a genuine intellectual option.[47] We can see why alternative medicines so often help people awaken to a vital spirituality. Illness, of course, often causes people to turn to religious belief. Pain and fear of imminent death can make us desperate to find a supernatural source of help. Religious belief is both forced and momentous to the seriously ill. It is forced in the sense that we must believe right now, or forever suffer the consequences; it is momentous in that it entails whether we live or die. However, not everyone will be open to the ideas propounded by alternative medicines—even if they are desperate for supernatural assistance. Both rational humanists and the traditionally religious may never find our unchurched traditions to be a live intellectual option for them. But for those who are ill and willing to entertain metaphysical ideas, these beliefs will indeed be forced, momentous, and living; in other words, a genuine option.

It is even more fascinating to see how alternative healing systems have made religious belief both live and momentous for those without any serious physical ailments. Many modern people find that "being religious" isn't a genuine option for them. A decision to be religious isn't forced; they have no immediate crisis demanding an all-or-nothing commitment. It isn't momentous; they are getting along in life just fine—perhaps even better—without religion. And it isn't live, because they can't intellectually affirm many of the tenets they associate with biblical religion. Alternative healing systems have proven successful at helping such people discover that being "spiritual, but not religious" is a genuine option for them. First and foremost, these systems provide existential encounters with a numinous reality that suddenly opens their eyes to the momentous differences that "being spiritual" can make in our lives. They also redefine spirituality in ways that make it seem to be a living intellectual option; they base "being spiritual" on metaphysical beliefs that extend rather than break connection with the scientific method. Thus, through their doctrines (myths) and therapeutic techniques (rituals), these alternative healing systems have succeeded in helping persons affirm that "being spiritual, but not religious" is a genuine option. In historical perspective, it is clear that those who are attracted to these alternative medical systems are not turning away from middle-class normalcy, but rather are turning toward unchurched traditions that have persisted for nearly two centuries.

5

Powers of the Hidden Self
Psychological Spirituality

Historically, Americans have turned to religion when they were confused, lonely, or in need of an emotional pick-me-up. Ministers, priests, and rabbis have engaged in a variety of pastoral counseling activities aimed at bringing the resources of religion to bear on the problems we face in daily life. Many Americans have been brought up in churches that teach them how to use the Bible in times of personal turmoil. They learn, for example, that when you worry, you should read Matthew 6:19–34; when you want courage for your task, read Joshua 1; or when thinking of investments and returns, read Mark 10:17–31.

Today the situation has changed. Psychology has become the secular successor to religion, providing a new vocabulary and new set of theories by which to understand ourselves. Almost all educated people have some familiarity with academic psychology. Popular psychology, too, has found its way into the stock of ideas with which the general public takes its bearings on life. Television talk shows, radio call-in programs, and a burgeoning market of self-help books provide a steady diet of psychological strategies to aid us in our quest for happiness.

Some mistakenly assume that the rise of modern psychology has gone hand-in-hand with a loss of interest in spiritual issues. It is argued that psychology induces people to think primarily about themselves, thus contributing to the decline of the Western religious tradition and its focus on God. As one critic observes, "When educated man lost faith in formal religion, he required a substitute belief that would be as reputable in the last half of the twentieth century as Christianity was in the first. Psychology and psychiatry have assumed that special role. ... [transforming us into] a psychological society, a civilization in which, as never before, people are preoccupied with Self."[1] Others believe that psychology has weakened the moral and spiritual tenor of our society, arguing that "the contemporary climate is therapeutic, not religious. ... People today hunger not for personal salvation, but for the feeling, the momentary illusion, of personal well-being, health and psychic security."[2]

The turn to psychology may indeed represent a turn away from traditional religious concerns. Yet, on the whole, psychology has had a special affinity with America's unchurched spiritual traditions. For one thing, alternative spiritual philosophies have encouraged us to seek God within. They have also taught that if we wish to reach our full human potential we must first learn to become inwardly receptive to the deeper reaches of the universe. Unchurched spiritualities therefore tend to utilize a psychological vocabulary. This vocabulary (1) highlights the spiritual dimensions of the unconscious mind and (2) suggests self-help strategies for living in creative harmony with God. In this way our unchurched religious traditions prepared popular audiences to see a deeper, spiritual significance in theories concerning our untapped psychological potentials.

Spiritual Restlessness and the Birth of American Psychology

Prior to 1880, there were no academic departments of psychology in American universities. The popular movement known as mind cure was steadily building public interest in new theories about the mind's untapped powers. Universities, however, relegated the study of the brain to departments of physiology, while entrusting departments of philosophy and theology to look after the soul. The few psychology courses that did exist were typically taught by the university president, who was likely to be an ordained Protestant minister. These classes were really an extension of Protestant moral theology and sought to teach practical strategies for inspiring people to live up to the church's loftiest ethical ideals.

By 1890, however, virtually every American university had a separate department of psychology. In just one decade, American intellectuals had thoroughly embraced what they called the "new psychology" or "psychology without a soul." The most important task facing the first generation of psychologists was to separate the study of the mind from theology. This was difficult for reasons that were partly cultural, partly autobiographical.[3] Many early psychologists were sons of Protestant ministers or had themselves been seminary students before opting for a more secular career. They had been raised in a religious culture that held out the experience of conversion as the critical event in a person's life. The conversion experience was thought to signal an abrupt change wherein individuals let go of their former, self-centered identity and surrendered control of their life to Christ. Especially in rural communities, the conversion experience was a well-defined rite of passage. It marked the transition from adolescence to responsible adulthood. It was an all-or-nothing affair, and thought to be beyond the individual's personal control. Genuine conversions originate in a stunning act of God, leaving us at the mercy of a judgmental Heavenly Father.

G. Stanley Hall, George Coe, James Leuba, Edwin Starbuck, and James Mark Baldwin rank among the most influential members of the first generation of American psychologists. Each had some form of conversion experience during adolescence, but experienced a "crisis of faith" early in his academic career.[4] All these pioneering psychologists encountered new ideas or experiences that shook their belief in the Bible. Exposed to Darwinian thought and other forms of scientific naturalism, they soon found themselves thinking in ways that went counter to what they had been taught about the importance of unquestioning faith. Most anguishing of all was their realization that their conversion experiences hadn't been "once-and-for-all events"; instead, they had continued to grow intellectually in ways that led them beyond the narrow confines of their religious upbringing.

These pioneering psychologists were blazing intellectual trails that Americans still travel in their quest to be "spiritual, but not religious." Their interest in psychology grew out of their need to get a new perspective on their own religious backgrounds and justify their acceptance of modern scientific and philosophical thought. More specifically, they were motivated by the need to "explain away" the all-or-nothing model of conversion experiences and replace it with one that would legitimate their own personal quests.[5] The "new psychology" they helped create was focused on two important concepts: the existence of lawful processes of human development and the role of the unconscious in guiding individuals through these developmental stages. These concepts enabled first-generation psychologists to offer a new explanation of the personality changes that used to be understood in terms of religious conversion. At the same time, they provided a vocabulary that enabled them to affirm that they were still pursuing spiritual interests, even if they could no longer embrace the religion of their childhood.

Edwin Starbuck was one of the first to use the "new psychology" to interpret religion. A student of both G. Stanley Hall and William James, Starbuck turned his attention to the study of conversion experiences. He concluded that these experiences could be fully explained in psychological terms. He theorized that the most critical phase of normal personality development entails the process of "unselfing." This process consists of the gradual steps whereby we learn to transcend our adolescent self-absorption and develop the capacity to act as socially responsible adults. Starbuck believed that growth toward moral adulthood begins first in the unconscious mind and then slowly transforms the conscious personality.

Starbuck observed that evangelical religion had long made use of this psychological process. Ministers and revivalist preachers intuitively understood how to apply sufficient emotional pressure to bring this process to a dramatic resolution, culminating in conversion to Bible-based religious belief. Starbuck's argument was that this sudden transformation was in reality a psychological—not a theological—process. The new, or "born-again," self was not given by God from above; it had been gradually forming in the person's unconscious mind. "Spontaneous awakenings are, in short, the fructification of that which has been ripening within the subliminal consciousness."[6]

The picture seems to be that of a *flow of unconscious* life rising now and then into conscious will, which, in turn, sets going new forces that readjust the sum of old thoughts and feelings and actions.[7]

The unconscious, Starbuck explained, contains innate "tendencies of growth" that propel the mind to ever higher levels of development. By allowing the full range of these unconscious growth tendencies to flow into awareness, "the individual learns to transform himself from a centre of self-activity into an organ of revelation of universal being."[8] Starbuck knew that his ideas constituted an attack on conventional theistic belief, but he also recognized that his theory of the creative powers operative through the unconscious articulated a religious vision all its own. He described his outlook as "a sort of pantheism—or pan-psychism or pankalonism—a sense of Interfusing Presence."[9] By using psychological rather than theological categories to explicate our relationship to this Interfusing Presence, Starbuck believed that psychologists were making "thinkable and usable the elusive reals of religion."[10]

The life and career of G. Stanley Hall shows even more clearly how psychology emerged as a way of enabling persons to remain spiritual, even when they rejected traditional religion. Hall was originally slated for the Protestant ministry. His exposure to science and philosophy, however, made it increasingly difficult for him to affirm the literal truth of the Bible. Like many in his generation, Hall was deeply torn between head and heart, reason and faith. He could no longer in good intellectual conscience become a minister, but he nonetheless yearned to devote his life to the spiritual upliftment of the human race. Hall was drawn to Romantic philosophy, particularly the writings of Emerson, Tennyson, Schleiermacher, and Schelling. They taught him to see God within the depths of nature rather than as existing in some remote region "out there." According to his biographer, Dorothy Ross, the Romantic worldview was to him "as much a statement of faith in the ultimate rationality and moral beneficence of nature as of God, less a confession of theism than of pantheism."[11] This was an important philosophical step. It pointed out a way to reconcile head and heart, science and faith. Once he accepted that God provides nature with rationality and moral beneficence from *within*, he could embrace science as a genuinely spiritual activity.

Hall turned to the fledgling field of psychology in full confidence that it would yield important moral and spiritual truths. He had been impressed by the German philosopher Hegel's ideas about cosmic evolution. Hegel inspired Hall to see evolution as the means by which a pantheistic deity gradually pushes creation forward through an on-going process of growth and development. Hegel, along with Schelling, gave Hall the intellectual framework within which he could understand "all organic and even inorganic nature as steps in the unfoldment of a mighty process."[12] Hall thus approached psychology as the scientific analog of Hegel's developmental philosophy. Child and developmental psychology was not just science, it was a contribution to our understanding of God's activity in the universe. For this reason Hall saw himself as the prophet of a new era in humanity's religious development.

> The new psychology, which brings simply a new method and a new standpoint to philosophy, is I believe Christian to its roots and centre; and its final mission in the world is not merely to trace petty harmonies and small adjustments between science and religion, but to flood and transfuse the new and vaster conceptions of the universe and man's place in it ... with the old Scriptural sense of unity, rationality, and love beneath and above all, with all its wide consequences.[13]

Hall believed that psychology was giving modern people a radically new vocabulary for understanding their relationship to God. In many ways Hall's views prefigured those of the Swiss psychologist Carl Jung's concerning the connection between our personal unconscious mind and the collective unconscious (i.e., God). Hall maintained that each of us is unconsciously connected with a life force, *elan vital*, through which God sustains the progressive evolution of nature. Through the unconscious we come into contact with

> mighty soul powers not our own, but which are so wise, benignant, and energetic ... and come from the larger self ... with which we are continuous. It is beneath, and not above us, immanent and not transcendent.[14]

Psychology enabled Hall to understand how he was inwardly connected to a "wise, benignant, and energetic" spiritual power. He no longer had faith in the Bible, ritual, or formal religious institutions, but he now affirmed the unconscious mind as an infallible source of inspiration and guidance. The unconscious, Hall wrote, provides mental life with a "wisdom beneath us we cannot escape if we would, and on which, when conscious purpose and endeavor droop, we can rest back, with trust, as on 'everlasting arms.'"[15]

Hall's contributions to the emerging field of academic psychology were impressive. He is usually credited with establishing the first research laboratory. He also developed one of the nation's first doctoral programs in psychology and encouraged many of the era's finest minds to pursue a Ph.D. in this modern social science. More than anything, however, Hall helped turn the concepts of "development" and "the unconscious" into symbols befitting an unchurched spirituality. His research and writings emboldened fellow psychologists to pursue their new academic enterprise confident that they were redirecting—not repudiating—their spiritual impulses. Empirical studies of the lawful stages of individual development could be embraced as shedding light on humanity's role in the larger sweep of cosmic evolution. Psychology thus offered Hall and other early American psychologists a satisfactory compromise between their head and their heart, between their desire for progressive knowledge and their irrepressible religious intuitions.

The Triumph of Psychological Spirituality: William James

William James (1842–1910) is arguably the most gifted thinker in American history. A member of the Harvard University faculty, James wrote the most influential textbook ever written in the history of academic psychology.[16] In mid-career he turned his attention from psychology to philosophy. As a philosopher he became the premier exponent of pragmatism, America's major contribution to philosophical thought. Yet pervading both his psychological and philosophical writings was an abiding interest in religious matters. In his later career James developed a new philosophical perspective known as radical empiricism. By "radical" empiricism James meant an empiricism that acknowledges "inner" as well as "outer" facts. Foremost among the inner facts that James had in mind as important to an empirical understanding of the universe are religious or mystical experiences. He argued that these, too, must be included in any comprehensive interpretation of reality. Applying his radical empiricism, James produced the most important study of religious experience ever written, *The Varieties of Religious Experience*.[17] The book forcefully argues that the root and center of religion is personal mystical experience. Theology, doctrines, rituals—in fact, all the things we associate with formal religious institutions—are peripheral to authentic spirituality. James proposed that we have outgrown our inherited religious traditions and must now develop a "science of religion." A science of religion would replace theology and instead explain religion on the basis of a fully developed psychology of the unconscious mind.

If any one individual has ever personified what it means to be "spiritual, but not religious," it was William James. Unlike other pioneering psychologists such as Coe, Hall, Baldwin, Leuba, or Starbuck, James did not grow up in a religiously conventional family. James's father was something of a religious maverick. Henry James Sr. invited metaphysicians of every stripe into his home to discuss matters of religious philosophy. Bored by the teachings of existing churches, Henry instead found inspiration in the teachings of Emanuel Swedenborg as well as in the views of his friend, Ralph Waldo Emerson. William thus grew up in a household that encouraged speculation about the existence of higher metaphysical levels of reality and about the possibility of an "influx" of spiritual energy into our physical world.

Henry James Sr. urged his eldest son to devote himself to the era's most prestigious intellectual endeavor—science.[18] The advice was, however, in conflict with Henry's own conviction that metaphysics is the highest and most sublime realm of human thought. William understandably had difficulty deciding whether to pursue the study of physics or metaphysics. He initially found little comfort in his father's speculative philosophies, and failed to seize on one grand metaphysical scheme as the pattern around which to organize his life. He developed nervous disorders, which were to plague him for the rest of his life. Chronic insomnia, eye trouble, digestive problems, and back pains were cruel reminders that his metaphysical upbringing hadn't helped him get a handle on life. He was haunted by an all-encompassing sense of despair, futility, and worthlessness. He described his condition as that of acedia, the feeling "that everything is hollow, unreal, dead ... [when] nothing is believed in ... all sense of reality is fled from life."[19]

James suffered from a very modern disease: spiritual malaise. He yearned for a grand spiritual dimension to his life, yet felt alienated from conventional religion. James stands out among modern religious thinkers because—as psychologist Erik Erikson has said of

Martin Luther—he was able "to lift his individual patienthood to the level of a universal one and try to solve for all what he could not solve for himself alone."[20] James felt the absence of God. He finally had no choice but to rely on himself. He bravely tried to grab hold of his life by turning from questions of eternity to those of the present moment; from speculation about metaphysical heavens to an empirical understanding of the here-and-now. He resolved to rely on himself, his own feeling for the truth, and his own willpower. In his words, "If we have to give up all hope of seeing into the purposes of God, or to give up theoretically the idea of final cause, and of God anyhow as vain and leading to nothing for us, then the only thing left to us is will."[21]

His father's faith in higher powers having failed him when he needed guidance most, William now concentrated his energies on improving his own capacity for effective worldly action. His newly found belief in willpower gave William confidence that, on a purely humanistic basis, he could transcend his incapacitation and take control of his life. James's confidence in personal willpower went hand-in-hand with his belief that the salvation of the universe (the achievement of unity and wholeness) is by no means certain. Human action is necessary if the world is to make progress toward greater wholeness. For James, this was one of the main problems he had with conventional religion. By teaching us to rely solely on God's miraculous intervention, churches undermine human resolve. Instead, James developed a metaphysics that celebrated the role of human action in determining the final shape of the universe. He eventually articulated a psychological model describing how each of us is continuous with higher, spiritual powers; by looking within, we, too, can awaken to our own spiritual powers.

James initially decided against a career in either philosophy or psychology. He believed that he was not strong enough for the task of trying to understand the meaning of the whole universe. It was healthier, he thought, to focus on smaller details and only gradually arrange them together to catch a glimpse of the larger puzzle. His first position at Harvard was in the department of physiology. Implicit in this decision was his deep commitment to the inductive or scientific method of seeking truth. James admired the inductive approach to truth partly because of his personal desire for a stable reality to lean on. He had a deep commitment to making personal experience the basis of all beliefs about life. The inductive method of science builds on such personal observation and experience, cautiously formulating hypotheses that are to be held lightly and revised as new facts appear. This inductive approach to truth, James would later proclaim, was as applicable to issues of religious faith as it is to the natural sciences.

After several years teaching general physiology, James turned his attention to the study of the brain. From there, he soon found himself tackling the most difficult issues in the newly created discipline of psychology. The psychological concept that seemed most exciting to him was the recent "discovery" of the unconscious mind (or what he and his collaborator F. W. Myers often called the "subliminal self"):

> The most important step forward that has occurred in psychology since I have been a student of that science is the discovery, first made in 1886, that, ... each of us is in reality an abiding psychical entity far more extensive than he knows—an individuality which can never express itself completely through any corporeal manifestation. The self manifests itself through the organism; but there is always some part of the self unmanifested, and always, as it seems, some power of organic expression in abeyance or reserve.[22]

James had long been fascinated by psychic phenomena. He spent a great deal of his professional life investigating spirit mediums, telepathy, ghost apparitions, and clairvoyance.[23] These phenomena suggested the possibility of interaction between the physical and metaphysical realms of existence, promising to bridge science and religion. The psychology of the unconscious provided James with a theoretical model for including such phenomena in a scientific understanding of the mind. He now had good reason to believe that "the world of our present consciousness is only one out of many worlds of consciousness that exist ... and that although in the main their experiences and those of this world keep discrete, yet the two become continuous at certain points, and higher energies filter in."[24] James had relocated his father's Swedenborgian-inspired belief in "correspondence" and "influx" in a new religious outlook. James was convinced that a truly empirical science must recognize that we inhabit a wider spiritual environment as surely as we do our physical and social environments. Moreover, he believed that there was solid empirical evidence that our highest good lies in adapting to (opening ourselves to the influence of) this spiritual environment:

> The further limits of our being plunge, it seems to me, into an alto-
> gether other dimension of existence from the sensible and merely
> "understandable" world. Name it the mystical region, or the supernat-
> ural region, whichever you choose. ... we belong to it in a more inti-
> mate sense than that in which we belong to the visible world, for we
> belong in the most intimate sense wherever our ideals belong.[25]

This spiritual outlook was important to James because it contained
"a contact with 'science' which the ordinary theologian lacks."[26] Science was at last confirming what the mesmerists and mind curists
had been proclaiming all along: "We inhabit an invisible spiritual environment from which help comes."[27] Adapting to this spiritual envi
ronment does not require us to surrender personal judgment or
pledge faith in ancient creeds. Quite the contrary. Critical thinking
frees us from the narrow ways of thinking that have dominated both
traditional religion and traditional science. Rational thinking alone,
however, will not open us up to the invisible spiritual environment
from which higher energies come. In James's view, "there are resources in us that naturalism with its literal and legal virtues never
recks of, possibilities that take our breath away, of another kind of
happiness and power based upon giving up our own will and letting
something higher work for us."[28] In this psychological adjustment,
"our deepest destiny is fulfilled ... work is actually done upon our finite personality. For we are turned into new men, and consequences
in the way of conduct follow in the natural world upon our regenerative changes."[29]

James was eager to proselytize on behalf of his "spiritual, but not
religious" stance. He wrote a series of popular essays with such titles
as "The Gospel of Relaxation" and "Energies of Men" in which he introduced his audiences to unchurched religious philosophies such as
parapsychology, Yoga, positive thinking, and mind cure. James was
particularly enthusiastic about the mind curists. Alone among the intellectuals of his day, he appreciated the religious importance of their
message. James frequently visited mind curists for help in overcom-
ing his own psychological and spiritual malaise. He knew firsthand
how their ideas had "come as a revelation to many whose hearts the
church-Christianity had left hardened."[30] He called mind cure's
unique combination of metaphysical belief and practical self-help

exercises "the gospel of healthy-mindedness." It was apparent to him that this healthy-minded message was meeting the spiritual needs of those who were dissatisfied with both the religion and science of their day. He predicted that mind cure's "gospel of healthy-mindedness" was destined to have as great an impact upon popular spirituality in the future as Luther's and Calvin's theology had done over the past four hundred years.[31]

James casts a long shadow over American intellectual and religious thought. Academic departments of psychology, philosophy, and religious studies still consider him one of the most influential thinkers in the history of their disciplines. His writings have been required reading for both undergraduate and graduate students for almost four generations. As a "highbrow" intellectual, James gave respectability to the long line of unchurched spiritual traditions he had inherited from the Swedenborgians, Transcendentalists, mesmerists, and mind curists. James's ability to give eloquent expression to these unchurched traditions prompted historian William Clebsch to nominate James as one of the three greatest religious thinkers in American history (alongside the Puritan preacher Jonathan Edwards and Ralph Waldo Emerson). Clebsch remarks that James "drew out the implications of his forerunners' positions. In so doing he set the agenda for American religious thought, now fully distinct from theology, in the twentieth century."[32] James, at least for intellectuals, helped separate religious thinking from biblical theology. The agenda he set for modern religious thought was an essentially psychological one: the personal quest to achieve attitudes and states of consciousness in which we become continuous with an invisible spiritual environment from which higher energies come.

From Emerson to James to Rogers: The American Psychological Tradition

Perry Miller's "From Edwards to Emerson" is perhaps the greatest essay ever written about American intellectual history. In it Miller maintained that "certain basic continuities persist in a culture ... and underlie the succession of ideas."[33] The particular continuity that fascinated Miller was a strain of American spirituality that contained "an indestructible element which was mystical, and a feeling for the universe which was almost pantheistic."[34] He detected hints of this spiritual strain in Jonathan Edwards's writings. Edwards's mystical streak was restrained by the strict Puritan theology that insisted on a great gulf between humans and God. Edwards nonetheless recognized that there are moments in which we seem to receive a "new spiritual sense" through which we can directly receive God's spiritual emanations. This mystical feel for God's indwelling presence became far more pronounced in Ralph Waldo Emerson. Freed from the constraints of biblical theology, Emerson celebrated humanity's capacity to be recipients of inflowing spiritual energies. And, of course, this same strain of mystical spirituality surfaced again in the writings of William James who made it central to both America's psychological and religious heritage.[35]

There are, then, "certain continuities" in American culture that underlie the development of psychological ideas characterized by a "mystical feeling for the universe." Not all psychological theories are covertly religious, however. There are at least three main theoretical orientations in American psychology. The first theoretical model to gain widespread recognition was Freud's system of psychoanalysis. Psychoanalysis is essentially antireligious. Freud put his faith in reason, not supernatural powers. He maintained that humans are primarily driven by instincts (the two most powerful of which are the instincts toward aggression and sexuality). Instincts are antisocial; they drive us to seek immediate, personal pleasure regardless of the social consequences. We can create a more civilized world only by repressing our antisocial instincts and instead trying to organize our lives on the basis of reason. The kind of reason Freud had in mind was a scientific-like approach to the cold, hard facts of life. In Freud's view religion diverted us from the harsh realities of everyday life by conjuring up illusions of supernatural powers that will magically rescue us or help us to enter a heavenly paradise when we die. Freud believed that the first step toward psychological maturity was to renounce the illusions of religion and learn to meet life's challenges in a fully rational manner. Freud's bold secularism attracted a loyal following among a small coterie of American intellectuals; but it fated his views to be rejected by the general public who had come to expect something very different from psychological theories. True, some psychoanalytic terms have filtered into the public's everyday vocabulary (id, ego, superego, Oedipus complex, penis envy, repression, projection), but they have done so in ways unrelated to Freud's own cultural vision. A few popularized versions of psychoanalysis made some inroads into popular American culture, but only to the extent that they first accommodated to the basic continuities that underlie the succession of psychological ideas in America.[36]

The second main theoretical orientation in American psychology is also incompatible with the mystical, pantheistic tendencies of unchurched American spirituality. Behaviorism is generally thought to have originated with John Broadus Watson's 1913 article, "Psychology as the Behaviorist Views It."[37] Watson believed that psychology needed to be established as a thoroughly objective science. He and other academic psychologists seized on the successes achieved in the study of animal behavior and argued that the laboratory methods used in the study of animals should become the foundation of behavioral science. First Watson, then later the Harvard psychologist B. F. Skinner, became proponents of the behaviorist school of psychological thought. They maintained that a properly scientific psychology must focus on topics that can be objectively studied in laboratory experiments. Terms such as "consciousness," "the unconscious," and "inner experience" were to be discarded from the psychological lexicon because they could be neither objectively defined nor measured. Behaviorists were interested solely in understanding and controlling behavior, not sneaking subjectivist philosophy into an experimental science where it did not belong. Behaviorism was more than a social science. It was also a cultural vision. Advocates of behaviorism hoped to reduce the complexities of modern civilization to simple laws that can be studied and manipulated in order to produce a more efficient society.[38] This cultural agenda appealed to a good many secular humanists who had already rejected religion and yearned for a thoroughly rational outlook on life. But it became a bête noire for those who were dissatisfied with both organized religion and materialistic science. They needed a very different psychological vocabulary to describe their deepest beliefs and vision.

Both psychoanalysis and behaviorism have had adherents within the ranks of professional psychologists. Yet neither generated large popular followings. Since the mesmerists and mind curists, popular audiences have expected that psychological theories will address their everyday needs or interests. Many of these needs and interests are broadly spiritual in nature. It was thus all but inevitable that another school of psychological thought would emerge to meet consumer demand. It was also all but inevitable that this new psychological outlook would resonate more clearly with the "certain continuities" that have persisted in America's unchurched spiritual traditions.

In the early 1960s, psychologist Abraham Maslow announced the formation of a third theoretical orientation in American psychology:

> The two comprehensive theories of human nature most influencing psychology until recently have been the Freudian and the experimentalistic-positivistic-behavioristic. All other theories were less comprehensive and their adherents formed many splinter groups. In the last few years, however, these various groups have rapidly been coalescing into a third, increasingly comprehensive theory of human nature, into what might be called a "Third Force."[39]

Maslow joined forces with Anthony Sutich to establish the *Journal of Humanistic Psychology* to accelerate the coalescence of these "various groups." As the journal explains, the third force in psychology is defined by its concern with the study of "human capacities and potentials that have no systematic place either in positivistic or behavioristic theory or in classical psychoanalytic theory, e. g., creativity, love, self, growth, organism, basic need-gratification, self-actualization, higher values, ego-transcendence."[40] Rollo May put it slightly differently when he explained that humanistic psychology sought to "unite science and ontology" and recapture "the American genius for combining thought and action (as shown so beautifully in William James)."[41]

Carl Jung was one of the many psychologists who came to be associated with this third school of thought. Jung was Freud's closest colleague for many years and his psychological theories were first developed as part of the psychoanalytic tradition. In mid-career, however, he parted ways with Freud. During his lifetime, Jung had largely been ignored by American audiences, both academic and popular. By the time of his death in 1961, however, his theories were being rediscovered as an important ally in the fight to reconnect psychology with spiritual philosophy.[42] Jung argued that in addition to the personal unconscious described by Freud, we also have a point of inner connection with the "collective unconscious." This was Jung's way of referring to God in a psychological vocabulary befitting the modern era. By relocating God deep within the human psyche, Jung was able to develop a psychological theory "where the collusion of nature and spirit became a reality."[43] Jung's psychology focused on what he called the individuation process, a lifelong path of self-discovery and self-transformation. According to Jung, the individuation process is guided not by environmental forces but rather by the collective unconscious. There is thus no line separating psychology and spirituality. The goal of each is to help us gain awareness of the deeper levels of our psyche, a process of self-discovery that brings us face-to-face with the kinds of symbolic and mythic truths contained in the world's great wisdom traditions. Jung's spiritually charged writings succeeded in making the concept of God (the collective unconscious) relevant to a class of educated persons who would be repelled by religious language. His influence reached far and wide. His theories gave a vocabulary for expressing the spiritual significance that many find in the study of altered states of consciousness such as dreaming, out-of-the-body experiences, and drug-induced mysticism. Jung's methods for deciphering the symbolic nature of the mind can also be linked with Joseph Campbell's enormously popular writings on mythology and Thomas Moore's bestselling work on finding spirituality in everyday life, The Care of the Soul.[44]

Any number of writers contributed to the emerging "third force." Viktor Frankl, Ken Wilber, Stansilav Grof, Ira Progoff, Roberto Assagioli, and Rollo May were all leading voices in this recasting of psychological thought. The two principal leaders of the movement, however, were Abraham Maslow and Carl Rogers. Maslow is best known for his theory of the hierarchy of human needs. His basic hypothesis was that humans are motivated to meet their most pressing needs. The most potent of these are for food and shelter. If these basic needs are met, we will then be motivated to meet needs that are largely social in nature such as peer acceptance and self-esteem. Assuming these social needs are also satisfied, we are then motivated to pursue the "highest" needs that, according to Maslow, are for self-actualization. Self-actualization represents humanity's drive to transcend biological and social determinisms and express ourselves in free and creative ways. Maslow's studies of self-actualizing people led him to conclude that "man has a higher and transcendent nature, and that is part of his essence."[45]

> We have seen that there is not an absolute chasm between man and the reality which is beyond him. He can identify with this reality, incorpo-

rate it into his own definition of his self, be loyal to it as to his self. He then becomes part of it and it becomes part of him. He and it overlap.[46]

This point of overlap, which Maslow often called "the farther reaches of human nature," made it possible to argue that the transcendent part of human nature falls within the domain of psychology (rather than theology). Maslow found that when humans have satisfied their basic physiological and social needs, they frequently have "peak experiences." These experiences are especially intense moments in which individuals are overwhelmed by the sensations of ecstasy, wonder, and awe. Peak experiences take us beyond our accustomed way of viewing life and impart a vivid perception "of the whole cosmos or at least the unity and integration of it and of everything in it, including his Self."[47]

Maslow believed that peak experiences are the cornerstone of genuine religion. Peak experiences afford persons "practically everything that Rudolf Otto defines as characteristic of the religious experience—the holy; the sacred, creature feeling, humility; gratitude and oblation; thanksgiving; awe before the *mysterium tremendum*; the sense of the divine, the ineffable."[48] According to Maslow, organized religions are merely an attempt to communicate the experiential features of a peak experience to non-peakers (those who have never had a peak experience). Maslow warned his readers that for most people religion is little more than

> A set of habits, behaviors, dogmas, forms, which at the extreme becomes entirely legalistic and bureaucratic, conventional, empty, and in the truest meaning of the word, anti-religious. ... Organized Religion, the churches, finally may become the major enemies of the religious experience and the religious experiencer.[49]

Maslow frequently pointed to the similarities between his views about personal spirituality and those of such writers as William James, Ralph Waldo Emerson, Walt Whitman, and the Zen philosopher D. T. Suzuki. Maslow believed that his studies of peak experiences supported these writers' view that spirituality has to do with adding a new zest to this life, not procuring an afterlife. He found that peak experiences bring with them the life-altering insight that "religion's Heaven is actually available in principle all through life. It is available to us now, and is all around us."[50] Put differently, they permit us to "see the universal in and through the particular and the eternal in and through the temporal and momentary."[51]

Maslow believed that his work was bridging the gap between traditional religion and traditional science. After all, "If, as actually happened on one platform, Paul Tillich defined religion as 'concern with ultimate concerns' and I then defined humanistic psychology in the same way, then what is the difference between a supranaturalist and a humanist?"[52] Humanistic psychologists were pursuing lines of investigation that brought them onto intellectual ground very similar to that staked out by liberal theologians. Both groups, Maslow noted, had come to define God "not as a person, but as a force, a principle, a gestalt-quality of the whole of Being, an integrating power that expresses the unity and therefore the meaningfulness of the cosmos, the 'dimension of depth.'"[53] Maslow's not so subtle implication was that psychology is further removed from the corruptions of organized religion and is therefore a more reliable path to mature spiritual understanding.

The connection between psychology and unchurched American spirituality is poignantly illustrated in the life and career of humanistic psychology's most influential theorist, Carl Rogers.[54] Like many of the pioneering figures of American psychology, Rogers was raised in a very conservative Protestant family. His indoctrination into biblical theology had a twofold impact on his subsequent intellectual development. On the one hand, he understood how a religious outlook gives meaning to life. Yet, he finally rebelled against the narrowness of his parents' religious beliefs. Throughout his young adulthood Rogers became increasingly hostile toward biblical fundamentalism and the rigid personality traits he associated with it. In later life he remembered the tremendous impact that the writings of Ralph Waldo Emerson had on him, confirming in him the possibility of a nature-oriented spirituality and the need for genuine self-reliance. By the time he entered college he could no longer profess his family's religious faith. In a term paper titled "The Source of Authority in Martin Luther," he adduced historical evidence in support of the view that "man's ultimate reliance is upon his own experience." A few years later he made the more radical break from his childhood religion when he suggested that "perhaps Jesus was a man like other men— not divine."[55]

By the end of his college years, Rogers had gradually come to believe that it was possible to speak about humanity's "highest nature" without any reference to the Bible or to a Supreme Being. He was convinced that we must look for meaning within human experience, not outside it. He still, however, yearned for a life that was in some way spiritual. He finally decided to enter Union Theological Seminary with the intention of pursuing a career in religious leadership. At that time Union was already known for its liberal leanings, and many of its faculty tended to equate religious commitment with involvement in progressive social causes. Rogers had thus chosen an ideal environment within which to pursue his abiding interest in "the meaning of life and the possibility of the constructive improvement of life for individuals."[56]

His studies at Union brought Rogers to a personal, theological, and professional crossroads. He came to the realization that his belief in personal freedom and his confidence in human reason made it impossible for him to continue in seminary education. He decided that "it was a horrible thing to have to profess a set of beliefs in order to remain in one's profession." By this time he had already taken a few courses in psychological counseling at Columbia University, which was right across the street from Union. He decided to quit his studies at Union and instead enter "a field in which I could be sure my freedom of thought would not be limited."[57] At Columbia he was at last able to free himself from the confines of biblical theology and redirect his idealistic impulses to the field of counseling psychology. Within just a few more years he would earn both national and international renown for his newly developed "client-centered" approach to psychotherapy.

The basic premise of client-centered therapy is that everyone possesses the resources for self-integration and growth within him- or herself. Successful therapy does not depend on the active intervention of the therapist. Therapists can only enable personality growth in other persons, they cannot cause it. Instead, therapists—like everyone who aspires to promote growth in others—must provide a supportive environment in which individuals can get in touch with their own "organismic valuing process." Rogers believed that every person has an innate, biologically grounded impulse toward wholeness and self-actualization. This actualizing tendency is guided by an innate valuing process that steers individuals toward growth-enhancing experiences. Rogers realized that individuals often rely on the dictates of society rather than their innate valuing process. A successful therapist must provide a warm, accepting environment. Clients respond to this safety and acceptance by dropping the defensive masks with which they have been facing life and instead learning to explore the full range of their own experience. The "client-centered" relationship frees individuals from values acquired from external sources so that they can trust their own inner feelings and view their lives as a fluid, ongoing process. Rogers found that those who had been provided such growth-enhancing environments tended to replace the values that society had programmed into them with a new value system grounded in their own innate valuing process.[58]

To call Rogers's psychology "humanistic" is ultimately misleading. His entire career was dedicated to fighting the strictest forms of humanism found in psychoanalysis and behaviorism. Rogers's humanism was almost an exact replica of Emerson's "romantic individualism."[59] Rogers believed that humanity's growth-oriented potentials originate outside the psychological realm. He asserted that "our organisms as a whole have a wisdom and purpose which goes well beyond our conscious thought."[60] Rogers's "client-centered" theory presupposed the existence of a causal power that transcends all the instinctual or environmental forces ordinarily described by academic psychologists. His brand of humanism places primary emphasis on "a flood of experiencing at a level far beyond that of everyday life."[61]

Rogers was well aware that the idea of a preconscious, "organismic" actualizing tendency had ontological and metaphysical implications. His theoretical outlook envisioned the

> human organism as a pyramid of organic functioning, partly suffused by an unconscious knowing, with only the tip of the pyramid being fleetingly illuminated by the flickering light of fully conscious awareness ... some of my colleagues have said that organismic choice—the nonverbal, subconscious choice of being—is *guided by the evolutionary flow.* I would agree and go one step further. I would point out that in psychotherapy we have learned something about the psychological conditions which are most conducive to self-awareness. With greater self-awareness a more informed choice is possible, a choice freer from introjects, a conscious choice which is even *more in tune with the evolutionary flow.* There is (to use Claude Naranjo's term) an *organismic convergence with that directional evolutionary process.*[62]

In all of this, Rogers recapitulates, chapter and verse, the harmonial worldview behind American philosophies of self-reliance. Like Jonathan Edwards, Ralph Waldo Emerson, and William James, Rogers holds that authentic human action is a direct function of an inward identification with Being itself. According to the Rogerian notion of optimal human living—no less than the Emersonian or Jamesian—by opening ourselves to the raw impressions of nature we also take hold of the spiritual principle of things. Thus "psychological congruence" is to Rogers what "consent to Being in general" was to Edwards, "divine influx" to Emerson, and "incursions from the subliminal self" to James. All point to a psychological process whereby individuals can apprehend, and become inwardly connected to, an immanent divinity.

Rogers represents the furthest point in the gradual psychologizing of this enduring brand of American spirituality. The shifts from Edwards to Emerson, Emerson to James, and finally James to Rogers all take us progressively further from the conceptual categories of traditional Western theology. This is not, however, to say that Rogers is any less metaphysical than his predecessors. He firmly believed that the orderly laws governing psychological growth are "aspects of the same order we find in the universe as a whole."[63] Paralleling Emerson's view of "correspondence" between various dimensions of the universe, Rogers established his humanistic psychology on the thesis that "there appears to be a formative tendency at work in the universe, which can be observed at every level."[64]

> Thus, when we provide a psychological climate that permits persons to be ... we are tapping into a tendency which permeates all of organic life as a tendency to become all the complexity of which the organism is capable. And on an even larger scale, I believe *we are tuning in to a potent creative tendency which has formed the universe* ... and perhaps we are touching the cutting edge of our ability to transcend ourselves, to create new and more spiritual directions in human evolution.[65]

Rogers's desire to learn more about how we might "tune in" to the creative energies of the universe prompted him to delve into all kinds of metaphysical topics. He was fascinated by such phenomena as precognition, telepathy, psychic healing, out-of-the-body experiences, and the mystical experiences triggered by psychedelic drugs. The fact that people were trying to investigate these subjects in a scientific way suggested to him that we were "on the verge of discovering a new type of lawful order."[66] It was Rogers's hope that by learning more about this lawful order we could move beyond the narrow confines of conventional science and conventional religion and at last truly understand the art of spiritual living. Of one thing he was quite certain. He had seen with his own eyes that the ideas and practices associated with humanistic psychology promoted personal growth far more effectively than the theology associated with his religious upbringing. He had, moreover, witnessed how this innovative approach to spiritual living could help individuals "feel they are in touch with, and grasp the meaning of, this evolutionary flow."[67]

Popular Psychology and the Quest for the Hidden Self

Americans' interest in popular psychology goes back at least to the 1840s. One reason for this is the continuing influence of the Protestant ethic. The Puritan settlers who put such an indelible mark on American life were heirs to a strict, Calvinist theology that included belief in predestination. According to this theology, humans can do nothing to procure their own salvation. The power of salvation is in God's hands alone. Because God is both all-knowing and all-powerful, our eternal future has already been decided. This doctrine understandably caused many Protestants to become anxious about the fate of their souls. When they consulted their ministers about this anxiety, they were often told that a possible indication of God's disposition toward them was the degree of their worldly success. It seemed safe to assume that anyone in whom God's saving spirit was present would be prosperous in this world, too.

According to Max Weber's famous thesis, people in Protestant countries were motivated to become successful as a way of assuaging their anxiety about salvation.[68] Weber argued that those raised in this cultural heritage are anxious to acquire personality traits conducive to worldly success. They are, for example, eager to be efficient, conscientious, and frugal. To the extent that Weber was right, we would also expect people in Protestant-dominated cultures to be naturally attracted to "self-help psychologies." The writings of Benjamin Franklin are often held up as an example of how the Protestant ethic made Americans eager to consume self-help advice. Franklin's writings make for an especially interesting example of the Protestant ethic because he personally rejected the theological basis of Puritanism. Although Franklin doubted most Bible-based beliefs, he subscribed to Puritanism's cultural program. His pithy maxims laid out a strategy for inculcating habits necessary for success in ways that appealed to the religious and nonreligious alike—making him one of the fore-fathers of the American self-help tradition.[69]

Puritanism, and the Protestant ethic with which it is associated, has surely been influential in predisposing Americans to self-help philos-ophies. We might think of this as the "ascetic" side of American cul-ture in that it counsels self-discipline and self-denial as the principal route to oneness with God. There is, of course, also an "aesthetic" side to American spiritual life.[70] Aesthetic spirituality contrasts sharply with the ascetic posture commonly found in conservative Protestant-ism. It involves neither doctrinal creeds nor biblical morality, but in-stead emphasizes the experience of beholding God as present within the natural universe. This aesthetic approach to spirituality is associ-ated with the harmonial spirituality we have traced through the his-tory of unchurched American religious life. Its message is that spiritual composure, physical health, and even economic well-being follow automatically once we establish an inner rapport with the cos-mos. The aesthetic approach to spiritual life is likely to express itself in philosophies intended to help individuals adjust themselves in ways that will lead to a new, more functional relationship with God (conceived as an immanent spiritual power continuously available to those with proper metaphysical awareness).

Popular psychologies have been prime carriers of this aesthetic spiritual outlook. The term *popular psychology* is intended to draw at-tention to psychological writings directed toward the general reading public. Popular psychologies attract a following only to the degree that they offer ideas or strategies that can help persons deal with the problems of everyday life. What distinguishes a psychology as "popu-lar" is not the academic credentials of the author but the way it is in-tended to be consumed. Any psychology can be considered popular when its main purpose is to help general reading audiences symbol-ize and resolve problems that confront them in the course of daily liv-ing. And while some psychological ideas have attracted a popular following by promising solutions to specific problems such as smok-ing or overeating, most are concerned with regenerating the whole person. Most, therefore, become carriers of unchurched spirituality.

Emerson's essay on "Self-Reliance" might be considered one of the first religiously-charged popular psychologies. The mesmerists, mind curists, and New Thought writers went further than Emerson in translating metaphysical ideas into psychological language. First published in 1897, Ralph Waldo Trine's *In Tune with the Infinite* has sold more than four million copies. Other early authors such as Elizabeth Towne, Orison Swett Marsden, and Frank Haddock also proved that there was a huge commercial market for books on spiritual shortcuts to worldly prosperity.[71] Nor did these early installments in the genre come solely from the ranks of "middlebrow" writers. No less a recognized authority than William James also addressed his own psychologized spiritualilty to the general reading public. His essays on "The Gospel of Relaxation" and "The Energies of Men" assured readers that their unconscious minds contained deep reservoirs of creative energy.[72] James's practical suggestions concerning how to tap into the creative energies hidden deep within ourselves articulated what was to become one of the most persistent agendas in twentieth-century American spiritual life.

It was, however, the Reverend Norman Vincent Peale who successfully converted Americans to the gospel of the unconscious. Peale was an ordained minister who served a number of Methodist churches before finally assuming duties as pastor of Marble Collegiate Church in New York City—a church belonging to the staunchly conservative Dutch Reformed Church in America.[73] Marble Collegiate was one of the most prominent churches in the nation. Its members tended to be well-educated, wealthy, and apace of cultural developments. Peale's special genius had nothing to do with his grasp of Reformed theology. It was rather that he intuitively understood his parishioners and their spiritual restlessness. Most members of his church cared even less than he did about the intricacies of Dutch Reformed theology. They wanted a religious message that would make a practical difference in their lives. And this is precisely what Peale gave them.

In 1952, Peale published *The Power of Positive Thinking*. It was destined to become one of the most influential books in American religious history. Peale aimed to help his readers think of God as a power available to them as they went about their daily lives. God, he told them, can be thought of as a loving energy that flows into us, enhancing our own power so that we might attain success in all that we do. *The Power of Positive Thinking* introduced millions of middle-class readers to the harmonial belief that "by channeling spiritual power through your thoughts. ... you can have peace of mind, improved health, and a never-ceasing flow of energy."[74] In articulating this psychological gospel, Peale never turned to the likes of Calvin or other renowned theologians in his church's tradition. Instead, he cited Emerson and James to make a case for the religious, even Christian, character of his belief that our unconscious minds have continual access to the spiritual power that flows throughout the universe:

> Years ago Emerson said there are unexplored chambers of the human mind which some day will be opened to release unrealized spiritual powers. A French psychiatrist says that there is another element present in the mind beyond the conscious and subconscious. This element he terms "the superconscious." The characterization is interesting. Perhaps it was to this "superconscious" that Christ referred when He said, "If you have faith ... nothing shall be impossible unto you."[75]

Peale suggested that his readers envision God as an "electrical energy" invisibly surrounding the material universe. Once we understand this, we are then in a position to understand that the Kingdom of God is truly within us. To avail ourselves of this kingdom, we need only learn to "picturize, prayerize, and actualize." This was Peale's self-help formula for initiating the flow of divine energy into our lives. He carefully explained how we should first visualize the desired outcome, then set aside regular periods of time for quiet prayer or meditation, and finally act in the assurance that God will provide us with all the power needed to achieve our desired goals. Most important, Peale proclaimed, the formula works: "There is a higher Power, and that ... power is constantly available. If you open to It, it will rush in like a mighty tide."[76]

Peale's "psychological spirituality" completely inverted traditional Christian teachings about the relationship between humans and God. Orthodox Christian theology teaches that God is our Lord and Master; we should worship and adore Him in His own right. Roy Anker points out that for Peale, however, "faith assumes value primarily because it constitutes the means by which the believer taps into the flow of divine power. ... In Peale's scheme, human desire, not divine grace, predominates. The result is that God becomes servant instead of loving and righteous Master or Lord. Within positive thinking, faith becomes quasi-magical, wherein one invokes its power to elicit God's power."[77] Peale would likely have strenuously objected to the charge that his system renders God "a servant." He would, however, have taken great satisfaction in the fact that he helped hundreds of thousands—perhaps millions—to think their way past viewing God as a sin-hating master. He found it far more important for modern persons to understand God as "the recreative power that flows constantly through the universe" and to awaken to the very real fact that "all around you at this moment is divine healing energy ... [which is] available to you if you will believe."[78] This understanding, Peale believed, was the foundation of an exciting spirituality, a spirituality that could make a practical difference in our lives. And it is this understanding that, as Anker further observes, makes it impossible to overestimate "the role that Peale and especially *The Power of Positive Thinking* played in inserting New Thought theology into the mainstream of American religion and thereby reshaping the core, mood, and configurations of American religious life."[79]

In recent years M. Scott Peck has similarly affected the mood of American religious life. He, too, uses a "psychology of the unconscious" to help people in their quest for love, traditional values, and spiritual growth. In his bestseller, *The Road Less Traveled* (with well over five million copies in print), Peck warns his readers that they tend to define religion too narrowly. Most of us, he argues, "operate from a narrower frame of reference than that of which we are capable, failing to transcend the influence of our particular culture, our particular set of parents and our particular childhood experience."[80] Peck urges us to move beyond equating religion with belief in God or membership in a worshipping group. If we are to grow, then we must expand our worldview to include new knowledge of the larger world. The "new knowledge" that he refers to is linked to the "fact" that most of us use a mere 5 percent of our minds. By exploring the other 95 percent "you will come to discover that this vast part of your mind, of which you now have little awareness, contains riches beyond imagination." The most precious of all the inner riches awaiting our discovery is what Peck calls "the God within us." The road less taken, the road leading to full spiritual growth, begins with the discovery that "our unconscious is God. God within us. We were part of God all the time."[81]

Books extolling the powers of the hidden self have become a staple of the consumer book trade. As influential sources of contemporary thought, they have successfully inserted the major themes of un-churched spirituality into the stock of ideas with which the American reading public takes its bearings on life. Their influence has, of course, by no means been limited to the unchurched. They have also appealed to church members who seek to supplement their churches' teachings with the views of psychological experts. It is thus inevitable that the influence of these popular psychologies in "reshaping the core, mood, and configurations of American religious life" reaches straight into some of our churches, too.

Co-opting the Churches

Popular psychology is perhaps the best example of how unchurched sources of spirituality might gradually come to reshape the inner meaning of churched religion as well. Many church leaders in the early twentieth century were eager to adopt these progressive-sounding ideas in their ministry. The first ministerial activity to in-corporate psychological insight was pastoral counseling. Beginning with the Reverend Elwood Worcester's Emmanuel Movement in Boston, Protestant ministers began studying the latest psychological theories, hoping to make their counseling ministries more relevant to the people they served.[82] By the mid-twentieth century, virtually every seminary in the nation offered courses in pastoral counseling that surveyed the era's current psychological theories. Progressive minis-ters, many buoyed by Peale's popularity and renowned theologian Paul Tillich's interest in cultural symbols of "ultimate concern," picked up on current psychological buzzwords and worked them into their weekly sermons. By the late 1960s, mainline denomina-tions began responding to the growing interest in Eastern religions, meditation, and various "spiritual disciplines" by offering special workshops in Christian spirituality. Much of the churches' under-standing of what such spirituality is all about came from the writings of such eclectic thinkers as Thomas Merton, Joseph Campbell, Henri Nouwen, and Morton Kelsey. Virtually all these authors shared Kelsey's belief "that there is a depth in humankind called the uncon-scious through which one experiences the spiritual world."[83]

Western religious traditions have continually changed over time. Much of this change began with the incursion of popular religion into the laity's understanding of faith (for example the conflation of pagan fertility rituals with Christian Christmas and Easter). This is particularly true in the churches' programs for offering care and guidance where the ministry has traditionally adopted each new era's psychological concepts.[84] What has been happening over the past few decades, then, is hardly new. But it has had important consequences in redefining people's affiliation with Christian organizations. It is easy to understand why so many church leaders attacked the views of Norman Vincent Peale. Peale was undermining the doctrinal positions that distinguish Christianity. Peale ignored biblical understandings of God and instead invited his readership to think of God as an ever-present spiritual power. Peale was even less respectful of traditional understandings of original sin and the depravity of the human condition. He preached instead a gospel of renewal that had nothing to do with asking people to seek forgiveness. Instead, he asked only that we set about correcting those personality traits that prevent us from connecting with the power of God. To most church leaders, Peale had fallen captive to the idols and values of a non-Christian culture. In opening the door to popular psychology, Peale had invited his parishioners and readers to embrace the very mix of ideas that the churches feared would be their undoing. And, worst of all, Peale's message proved contagious.

It is hard to escape the impression that those who attacked Peale—and, by inference, all forms of psychological spirituality—begrudged Peale his success. Peale's critics, as Roy Anker summarizes, displayed a "characteristic high-culture disdain, a kind of intellectual phariseeism, … [resenting] the success of the popular but in their criticism failed to recognize the extent to which their own views are historically conditioned by the winds of taste, class, gender, race, self-interest, and intellectual faddishness."[85] The real point is not that Peale embraced the spiritual importance of ideas that originated outside the churches. His parishioners and readers were already familiar with most of these ideas. What Peale did was to encourage them to forge ahead, unshackled by the guilt that often attends a break from tradition. He gave his approval to attempts to supplement traditional church teachings with new ideas that might make a practical difference in people's lives. In short, he implicitly endorsed the seeker-style of modern spirituality.

With or without the likes of Norman Vincent Peale, educated Americans are going to avail themselves of a wide range of views and insights that bear on their religious understanding of the world. Whether such spiritual exploration is to be encouraged—for un-churched or churched seekers—is a question too important to leave to the partisans on either side of the issue.

6

Barnes & Noble as Synagogue
The New Eclecticism in American Religion

Americans are among the most religious people on earth. More than 90 percent tell pollsters that they believe in a Supreme Being. Church membership and attendance at weekly worship services are near an all-time high. Yet it is also clear that profound changes are taking place in the way Americans understand their personal faith. Sociologist Robert Wuthnow's study of spirituality in America since the 1950s indicates that "a traditional spirituality of inhabiting sacred places has given way to a new spirituality of seeking."[1] By "habitation spirituality" Wuthnow means the spirituality associated with formal religious institutions. Habitation spirituality is what goes on in churches and synagogues: formal worship, instruction in traditional creeds, emphasis on loyalty to a particular religious heritage. Organized religions are mindful of the boundaries that demarcate their special habitat. These boundaries consist of the rituals and doctrines that separate them from other religious groups as well as from the nonreligious. Habitation spirituality offers security, stability, and certainty to those who stay inside these boundaries. It appears, however, that these boundaries have become more permeable. Influences from the outside have been seeping in. And many have found it exciting to travel into new spiritual territory.

In contrast, seeker spirituality represents the spiritual style of an explorer or sojourner, not a settler. Seekers forego the security and certainty of habitation spirituality in exchange for more personal freedom. They rarely expect to find absolute truths, but instead seek provisional truths; that is, wisdom that is practical in the sense of meeting everyday needs. It appears that seeker spirituality is gradually altering the American religious landscape. As Wuthnow explains, "despite evidence that churches and synagogues are, on the surface, faring well, the deeper meaning of spirituality seems to be moving in a new direction in response to changes in U.S. culture ... [leaving] many Americans struggling to invent new languages to describe their faith."[2]

The goal of this book has been to show that "seeker spirituality" is hardly new. Even in the colonial era, many Americans looked beyond the nation's churches to find a language suitable for describing their encounters with the sacred. There is, however, a change in the relative cultural influence of these two modes of spirituality. Prior to the 1960s, people who thought of themselves as spiritual, but not religious, were aware that they didn't quite fit the expected pattern. And, unlike church members, they had few opportunities to interact with others who shared their spiritual interests. Slowly but surely, seeker spirituality began to coalesce into a network of like-minded souls. The process began back in the nineteenth century. Proponents of various metaphysical "isms" (Transcendentalism, Swedenborgianism, mesmerism, spiritualism) forged pathways that gradually connected seekers who were otherwise separated by geography. They traveled lecture circuits, published journals, and established small organizations both on the local and national level. By the early twentieth century, there were even some New Thought churches such as Divine Science and Unity in which fellow seekers could gather for inspirational talks and seminars. Some Unitarian churches also attracted those who wished to combine independent thinking with mystical interests.

As the twentieth century progressed, centers offering instruction in Eastern religions or Jungian psychology emerged in larger metropolitan areas. Health food stores, science fiction clubs, and alternative healing centers also became gathering spots for those attracted to alternative worldviews. Interest in exotic spiritual philosophies grew at a record pace as the Baby Boomer generation entered young adulthood. Predictably, supply grew to match demand. America's spiritual marketplace burgeoned as dozens of new magazines, journals, and newsletters appeared. Many of these were pioneers in using the communication technologies of the worldwide web.

Over the past decade, bookstores have emerged as the most important centers of unchurched spirituality. Ranging from small local stores specializing in metaphysical literature to the large national chains such as Borders and Barnes & Noble, bookstores function as the virtual synagogues of spiritual instruction. These stores have large sections labeled Bible, Christianity, and Judaica that offer publications on habitation spirituality. Alongside them now are even larger sections devoted to books on Eastern religions, New Age religion, and self-help philosophies (often extending over into either the management or leadership sections). These section headings overlap considerably. Any of them might contain books on angels, astrology, tarot cards, the *I Ching*, holistic healing, ecospirituality, feminist theology, yoga, transpersonal psychology, flying saucers, Atlantis, trance channeling, near-death experiences, modern pagan philosophies, or any of dozens of Asian spiritual traditions. Wade Clark Roof, who has studied the shifting patterns in Baby Boomer religion, notes that "words like *soul*, *sacred*, and *spiritual* resonate to a curious public. The discourse on spiritual 'journeys' and 'growth' is now a province not just of theologians and journalists, but of ordinary people in cafes, coffee bars, and bookstores around the country."[3]

The boundaries of American religion are clearly being redrawn. The suppliers of unchurched spirituality are no longer seen as addressing a small group of "kooks" who just don't fit into respectable American society. A full 20 percent of the population aspire to be "spiritual, but not religious"—eschewing the one-size-fits-all faith of established churches to piece together only those beliefs that meet their personal needs or interests. Moreover, this new eclecticism also shapes the personal piety of many who attend our nation's established churches.

In a Different Voice

The freedom to choose is one of the hallmarks of American culture. Yet, until recently, this freedom had only a limited application to the world of religion. Americans were free to choose whether they wanted to join a church and, if so, which church. But then their choice becomes more restricted. Churches promote loyalty to specific creeds; a person is free to choose different creeds only at the peril of risking the rewards of church membership. Not everyone can feel comfortable with a spiritual style that limits his or her freedom to choose. Indeed, many believe that it is not only the right, but even the duty, of every person to establish her or his own criteria for religious belief. They consider that wholesale acceptance of any church's teachings somehow lacks the integrity of "owning" one's own faith. And, too, some of these individuals have experienced nothing but frustration in existing churches. They may have come to resent the authoritarian structure of churched religion. Some who value curiosity and intellectual development find church teachings stifling. Others may resent the sexism that has historically defined most religious institutions. Still others may simply have become bored. Weekly worship services seem to them to lack spontaneity or genuine spiritual feeling.

Our unchurched traditions speak in a different voice, a voice that often seems inspiring to the spiritually restless. First and foremost, they offer the exciting possibility that we—even now—participate in a wider spiritual universe. Newcomers discover that they are surrounded by higher energies and powers. This discovery sparks their metaphysical imaginations. It prompts them to embark on a spiritual journey aimed at establishing a deeply personal relationship with these higher levels of existence. This journey promises to be one of ecstatic adventure. America's unchurched traditions offer vivid descriptions of the steps one must take to achieve mystical communion with life-transforming powers. Their teachings and practices heighten expectation of personal spiritual discovery with a sense of excitement that churches may find hard to match.

Metaphysical excitement can create a new zest for living. Seekers often say that "being religious" is for people who are worried about death, while "being spiritual" is for those who want to get the most out of life. Unchurched systems teach us that it is our spiritual responsibility to promote the full expression of life here on earth. Once we have learned to connect with metaphysical energies and powers, we must utilize them to enrich our own and others' lives. Healing, growth, and development are proclaimed as the goals of spiritual living, not humility or self-abnegation. As William James put it,

> Not God but life, more life, a larger, richer more satisfying life, is in the last analysis the end of religion. The love of life, at any and every level of development, is the religious impulse.[4]

James's reference to "the love of life, at any and every level of development" echoes our unchurched traditions' emphasis on the spiritual significance of growth and development. Seeker spirituality embraces cosmic evolution as the meaning of existence.[5] Understood metaphysically, development "at any and every level" contributes to the gradual unfolding of a mighty cosmic process. Our personal lives are part of this grander metaphysical scheme. Each step that we take toward greater complexity and consciousness in our own lives contributes to the progressive evolution of the universe. Faith in the cosmic patterns of growth and evolution makes these spiritualities decidedly melioristic. They affirm that every situation we encounter contains possibilities for progress or improvement. The universe is seen to be warm and welcoming, responsive to our desires for growth and development. By controlling our attitudes toward outer circumstances, we can take control of our own spiritual destinies.

Our alternative spiritual philosophies have developed new images of God. These images are, for the most part, pantheistic. They point to the presence of God within all living things. New images of God bring with them new ideas about moral duty. Biblical religion defines morality in terms of obedience to the commands of a Heavenly Father who watches over us from above. Our unchurched traditions, on the other hand, teach the ethical importance of recognizing the presence of God within ourselves and each other. They stress the holistic, interdependent nature of our evolving universe. Because everything in life is interconnected, we have a moral responsibility to promote "life, at any and every level of development." This makes every form of exploitation a sin against the "god within." Sexism, racism, and insensitivity to ecological issues prevent individuals or organisms from expressing their full divine potentials and thus reveal a total lack of spiritual understanding.

Unchurched religious thought speaks to us in a different voice regarding the nature of religious truth. America's alternative spiritual systems rarely insist on uniformity or teach infallible doctrines. Religious truth, they argue, is symbolic in nature. Humans can point to higher realities, but they cannot possess them in the form of tidy dogmas. Persons who identify themselves as seekers insist on the pluralistic nature of religious insight. They do this, however, not because it is currently fashionable, but because it is rooted in their metaphysical systems. This is why seekers are characteristically tolerant of other religious viewpoints. Their tolerance doesn't reflect some conscious effort to be politically correct; it stems from the belief that insights about God are as infinite as there are people. Because God's being is expressed through every individual's life, we can always learn from others' experiences.

| Religious Objections

This "different voice" understandably grates on those rooted in the religions of our churches. There are, of course, substantive theological disagreements between these two modes of spirituality. Our established religious institutions accept the special authority of the Bible. For Christian Churches, this includes belief in the unique divinity of Jesus. And, in Jewish congregations, members are expected to adhere (some more strictly than others) to the inherited traditions of Talmudic law. Furthermore, both Jews and Christians believe that humans are in some way fallen or in rebellion against God. They consequently proclaim that the path leading to the atonement for our sins is a narrow one; one we stray from at the risk of eternal estrangement from God. Our unchurched traditions, meanwhile, have long ago turned their backs on these concerns. Not only are their religious "answers" tantamount to heresy, even their questions run counter to Western religious orthodoxy.

Objections to unchurched spirituality are probably more about style than substance. On these points, secularists often join with church leaders in their criticism of efforts to be spiritual, but not religious. Secularists aren't concerned with doctrinal issues, but they agree with those churched individuals who find these alternative systems superficial and faddish. It is, for example, often said that our unchurched religions are utterly narcissistic. They entice people to equate self-growth and self-discovery with the path to knowledge of

God. They direct our attention inward, getting us to focus on our own private thoughts, diverting our attention from the political, economic, and social forces that have such a profound influence on human well-being. In this way they sever us from the nitty-gritty of interpersonal relationships and true community. While they might help us feel good about ourselves, they do little to help build a world that can sustain such feelings of well-being over time.

Those who indict our unchurched traditions for fostering excessive self-absorption often employ the term "Sheilaism." In the mid-1980s, a group of scholars studied how various forms of individualism affected American life. They interviewed a young nurse by the name of Sheila Larson who told them "I believe in God. I'm not a religious fanatic. I can't remember the last time I went to church. My faith has carried me a long way. It's Sheilaism. Just my own little voice."[6] The danger of Sheilaism, according to these scholars, is that it fails to connect the individual with any particular community or to any particular religious practice. In the long run, Sheilaism deprives us of a language genuinely able to mediate among self, society, the natural world, and ultimate reality. Such spiritual philosophies tend to

> fall back on abstractions when talking about the most important things. They stress "communication" as essential to relationships without adequately considering what is to be communicated. They talk about "relationships" but cannot point to the personal virtues and cultural norms that give relationships meaning and value.[7]

Others note the relatively facile nature of the mystical spirituality these systems promote. Newcomers are encouraged to dabble in spiritual practices without the rigorous discipline associated with the mystical traditions of the world's major religions. Classical mystical texts depict a path requiring years of sustained asceticism, including disciplined prayer and exercises aimed at cultivating humility and the submission of one's personal will to religious authority. American spiritual systems are considerably less demanding. Those attracted to these systems appear to seek out mystical experiences to reassure themselves of the existence of a supernatural realm. It seems, however, that they are content to leave this "higher dimension" at the periphery of their lives, not really wanting it to alter their previously defined interests and values. Sociologist Robert Wuthnow suggests that these forms of mysticism are therefore shallow and inauthentic. He claims that they typically portray the supernatural as mysterious, ineffable, or unknowable. An influx of the supernatural into our lives can reassure us of the existence of a "more" without requiring us to rearrange our priorities. Paranormal events "not only reinforce belief that the supernatural exists but also persuade people that the supernatural cannot in any way be understood and, therefore, it need not take much of their time. The supernatural remains a mysterious force, not something that is revealed in an authoritative text or institution."[8]

America's unchurched traditions are also accused of overlooking the tragic dimension of life. From Transcendentalism on, most unchurched spiritual systems invoke a Neoplatonic view of evil. That is, they view evil as the absence of good rather than an independent reality. Evil is thought to be nothing more than the chaos out of which evolutionary forces gradually build into greater consciousness and love. This is in sharp contrast to Christianity which has historically emphasized both the fallen nature of our creaturely existence and the existence of a malevolent devil. Secular critics as well find fault with unchurched religion's deliberate refusal to admit the existence of genuine tragedy or evil. Even William James chided his fellow advocates of harmonial spirituality for not taking this issue seriously enough. His own personal bouts with melancholy prompted him to write that

> The method of averting one's attention from evil, and living simply in the light of good is splendid as long as it will work. It will work with many persons; it will work far more generally than most of us are ready to suppose, and within the sphere of its successful operation there is nothing to be said against it as a religious solution. But it breaks down impotently as soon as melancholy comes; . . . the evil facts which it refuses positively to account for are a genuine portion of reality; and they may after all be the best key to life's significance, and possibly the only openers of our eyes to the deepest levels of truth.[9]

Critics argue that this failure to acknowledge evil is closely connected with a tendency to underestimate life's complexity. Spiritual thinking often has a magical element. Being spiritual entails faith that higher powers can enter into and exert causal influence in our world. Such faith leads us to pay a great deal of attention to the beliefs and practices that can coax higher powers into working on our behalf.

Those who don't share this harmonial faith are understandably quick to denounce it as naïve. Spiritual thinking flies in the face of good common sense. It ignores all of our accumulated knowledge concerning the effects of biological, psychological, economic, and social factors on the quality of human life. It thus predisposes us to magical thinking and to stubborn anti-intellectualism. It can also prevent us from adopting what might be called a "moral realism" that leads us to acknowledge the structural impediments to human progress and seek to improve them through carefully calculated programs of action.

There is, finally, a general disdain for the lowbrow character of many of the books and lectures that promulgate alternative spiritualities. Few proponents of these systems have anywhere near the formal theological education of their churched counterparts. Their writings consequently lack the polish and sophistication that are found in those of professional theologians. There are, for example, often inconsistencies in what they say about the nature of God or God's relationship to natural processes. Most of these spiritual philosophies aren't very systematic, but instead appear as a patchwork of ideas eclectically assembled from a variety of disparate sources. Whereas most religious writings utilize vocabulary created by centuries of shared theological tradition, unchurched traditions are more idiosyncratic and tend to imitate faddish trends in popular culture.

Objections Overruled

These objections are hardly new. From the time that Puritan ministers denounced their era's folk traditions to contemporary lampooning of New Age religion, alternative worldviews have been subjected to relentless criticism. There has, however, been an obvious lack of evenhandedness in these criticisms. Purely secular criticisms have probably been the most fair. Those who are committed to a purely rational approach to life typically oppose any and all religious thinking. Assuming these standards are applied equally to churched and unchurched religion, their negative assessment of the naïve and magical elements of unchurched spirituality deserve a fair hearing. The case is quite different with objections raised concerning the apparent religious shortcomings of our unchurched traditions. We might, for example, examine the charge that our unchurched spiritual traditions foster narcissism. This is an especially curious accusation given the fact that evangelical Christians boldly proclaim that "Jesus loves me." Most people convert to Christianity in hope of procuring individual salvation. And, too, most believe in the power of prayer to coax God into intervening on their behalf. Perhaps the question should be narcissistic compared to whom? Furthermore, the objection ignores what psychologists tell us about narcissism. Most psychologists, particularly those affiliated with the object relations and self-theory schools of psychoanalytic thought, believe that psychological health requires a certain kind of narcissism. They have a great deal of clinical evidence to suggest that full psychological health requires a healthy self-love. What they call "healthy narcissism" comes from knowing ourselves to be loved and prized by a "higher Other." The alternative spiritualities we have covered understand this very well. They offer both beliefs and practices that enable individuals to feel connected with, and empowered by, such a "higher Other" and in so doing promote psychological health.[10] It is even possible that they promote such psychological health more readily than established religions, particularly for those who find it difficult to relate to more traditional understandings of God.

The phenomenon of Sheilaism may be discomforting to many church leaders, but it is hardly a sign of religious immaturity. On the contrary, Sheila had managed to find—and listen to—her own voice. This young woman gradually accepted responsibility for owning her own system of beliefs. She matured to the point where she could differentiate between religious concepts and identify those concepts that most closely connected with her life. She developed a sense of personal relationship to God and translated the love and power she gained from this relationship into concrete acts of caring for others. Sheila learned to listen to her own inner voice and to be her own authority in spiritual matters. The fact that many Baby Boomers are following paths similar to Sheila's should be taken as a sign of maturity and authenticity, even if it does result in fewer traditional believers.

Robert Bellah and his colleagues were probably right that Sheilaism is often associated with difficulty in identifying a coherent cultural vision. They argued that many who fall into the category of being spiritual, but not religious stress communication without adequately considering what is worth communicating and stress relationships without adequately considering what personal virtues and cultural norms give relationships meaning. This objection has some merit. But, again, compared to whom? Fair play requires us to apply evaluative criteria evenly. How many of those who belong to a Protestant, Catholic, or Jewish congregation would have anything more profound to offer on these topics? One might, in fact, argue that our unchurched spiritual systems approach these topics with more adequate consideration than their churched counterparts. Contemporary seekers are typically aware of our era's philosophical and religious dilemmas and would be uncomfortable simply reiterating traditional views of what is worth communicating or what cultural norms give relationships meaning. They are skeptical of easy answers, especially those that ask for unswerving allegiance. They may not have a polished cultural vision, but they have identified some of the perspectives that they believe any such vision must include. They have affirmed the relevance of scientific, racial, gender, and ecological points of view and are unwilling to settle for cultural visions that omit them.

It is probably true that some people explore novel spiritual systems in a superficial way. Others, however, become paragons of spiritual intensity. Wade Clark Roof's study of Baby Boomer religiosity found that a full 9 percent of the population can be classified as "highly active seekers," individuals whom he found to be deeply involved in their own personal quests.[11] This raises the question about what it means to be "superficial" in one's commitment to a religious system. Many Catholics today identify themselves as "cafeteria Catholics," openly admitting that they pick and choose from church teachings as they see fit. Are they more superficial than other Catholics, especially if their reason for picking and choosing is that they have more thoroughly considered the philosophical complexities of belief? The question, again, becomes superficial—compared to whom?

We might consider the related criticism that curiosity about the existence of paranormal events doesn't seem to alter seekers' everyday commitments or priorities. Again, compared to whom? We know, of course, that many evangelicals are very comfortable with middle-class American culture. Historically, being blessed by Jesus doesn't guarantee any significant change in born-again Christians' lives. Those who pursue their spiritual journeys outside established churches are probably no better on this score. This should not, however, prevent us from acknowledging that their fascination with supernatural phenomena performs a vital function in preventing their capitulation to a wholly secular way of viewing the world. Those attracted to our unchurched traditions are not deciding between biblical and metaphysical approaches to religion. They are instead debating whether in good personal conscience they can claim to believe in any kind of religion at all. Most realize that secular understandings of the world have a certain intellectual authority and cannot easily be ignored. If they are to embrace any religious views, these views must strike them as somehow more than science and philosophy—not less. They require some kind of evidence indicating that our universe cannot be exhaustively explained by science. They, like William James before them, are in search of white crows. They are seeking a single event that proves that—at least occasionally—our world receives an influx from a spiritual "more." Our unchurched spiritualities respond to this modern spiritual need. Their testimonies concerning paranormal phenomena help prevent some people from forever shutting the door to religious ways of thinking about their lives. I believe that anything that helps hold this door open is of spiritual value, even if many people understandably play it safe and linger near the entranceway.

It is also difficult to justify the accusation that unchurched traditions tend to minimize the presence of tragedy or evil in life. First, few completely deny evil. However, many of these traditions suggest that we have the resources within ourselves to overcome the challenges that confront us in life. A common belief among those who are spiritual, but not religious is that we have the power to create our own reality. In some instances this devolves into sheer credulity. Beginning with the New Thought movement in the late 1800s, some have argued that thoughts are themselves the most potent forces in the world, capable of invisibly going out into the material universe and magically altering reality in conformity with our personal desires. Unfortunately, experience shows that thoughts do not wield an omnipotent power and cannot in and of themselves alter the vast web of biological, economic, and political forces that exert causal influence on our lives. To this extent the cult of the power of positive thinking belies a magical understanding of the universe. Yet, given churched religion's belief in the efficacy of ritual and prayer, it would be unfair to accuse only unchurched philosophies of lacking "realistic" approaches to life's problems. Belief in the power of positive thinking also draws people's attention to one of our most important freedoms. We do not always have the freedom to control outer circumstances, but we do always have the freedom to construct our attitude toward these circumstances. These traditions show us how we might construct our attitudes in spiritually significant ways. They alert us to how we might participate in God's ongoing creation of the universe. They typically urge us to consider ourselves co-creators of this evolving universe and to use our thoughts and actions to steer the world toward greater levels of wholeness and love. These philosophies thus blend their belief in metaphysical meliorism with their confidence in psychological meliorism (that is the power of beliefs to become self-fulfilling prophecies). As William James wrote, "the systematic cultivation of healthy-mindedness as a religious attitude is therefore consonant with important currents in human nature and is anything but absurd."[12]

The Test of Maturity

It is often insinuated that unchurched spiritualities are somehow less mature than their churched counterparts. Judgments about the relative maturity of one form of spirituality in comparison with another are tricky. They depend entirely on the criteria being used. Secularists might propose criteria that make it difficult for any kind of spirituality to be considered mature. For example, Sigmund Freud argued that religion necessarily thwarts the full use of human reason and therefore always stands in the way of full psychological maturity. Religionists, on the other hand, might propose biblical criteria or a particular tradition's understanding of saintliness. In this case all forms of spirituality other than their own will be found wanting.

There is, however, a possible middle ground. Academic scholars and theologians have for several decades acknowledged the possibility of using modern psychology to define the distinguishing characteristics of a mature religious faith.[13] Fields of ministry such as pastoral counseling have developed models that combine religious and psychological insights about the nature of "healthy personality." Two models that have garnered widespread acceptance are those proposed by Gordon Allport and James Fowler. Allport was a professor of personality theory at Yale University. He agreed with Freud that many persons are religious in ways that foster psychological immaturity. Allport added, however, that it was also possible to be religious in ways that are congruent with the highest levels of personality development. He used criteria drawn from his psychological research to argue that a religious faith can be consistent with psychological health to the degree that it is (1) well differentiated, (2) dynamic, (3) productive of a consistent morality, (4) both comprehensive and integral, and (5) heuristic.[14] By well differentiated Allport means that a mature religious outlook is one in which reason plays a strong role. A differentiated religious outlook emphasizes some ideas while regarding others as less important. This is in contrast to the all-or-nothing character of an immature religious outlook based on blind acceptance. Because many persons accept their religious beliefs without much personal reflection, they aren't capable of revising them in the light of new experience and their faith is consequently rigid, defensive, and intolerant. A differentiated faith, on the other hand, can either acquire or abandon beliefs in the light of ongoing personal experience. It would seem that the 20 percent of the population who can be considered "spiritual, but not religious" are likely to score high marks on this important measure of spiritual and psychological maturity. Seekers, by definition, have abandoned a "one-size-fits all" set of religious doctrines and have assumed responsibility for making their own choices concerning religious belief.

The second and third criteria—being dynamic and productive of a consistent morality—point to the most vulnerable parts of almost all religious orientations to life. This was, in fact, the principal reason Karl Marx believed religions serve as the opiate of the people. Religions often stifle human initiative. They teach us to have faith in, and rely on, supernatural powers. As a consequence, religion has an inherent danger of functioning more like a sedative than a stimulant. This is true for both churched and unchurched religious outlooks. Neither score consistently high marks on these scales of religious maturity. Take, for example, the books on angels or guardian spirits that counsel readers to rely on their supernatural helpers. To the very extent people trust their guardian helpers they fail to become dynamic agents in their own right. This, of course, is no less true of churched believers who are taught that God, saints, or Jesus have the power to work on their behalf. What makes a set of beliefs distinctively religious is this conviction that there are higher powers that can exert causal influence in our world. Many unchurched spiritual systems have developed images of God that promote a dynamic and ethically consistent orientation to life. By thinking of God as a "power from within" rather than a "power over" us, they stress the role of human agency in the ongoing creation of our universe. Their view that God works in and through our natural universe is reminiscent of Benjamin Franklin's counsel that "God helps those who help themselves." But, on average, it must be admitted that neither our churched nor unchurched spiritualities have supported ethical thinking that is as comprehensive as their secular critics would require of them.

Allport's fourth criterion stipulates that a mature religious outlook be integral and comprehensive. All too often people compartmentalize their religious faith. A compartmentalized faith is one in which religious beliefs and practices are clearly set off from the rest of our ideas about what makes something good, true, or meaningful. Religion can thus be thought of as involving only beliefs about the afterlife, church attendance, participating in weekly rituals, and so forth. This allows people to hold rigidly to a specific set of religious beliefs while nonetheless going about the rest of their lives utilizing an entirely different set of beliefs and reasoning processes. In Allport's view, faith must be consistent with what scientific reason has already helped us comprehend about the way the universe functions—anything less could not be truly comprehensive. Comprehensiveness, furthermore, brings us to the recognition that no one person's or even one culture's knowledge of how God relates to our world can be fully adequate. The quest for comprehensiveness entails humility and tolerance. For nearly two centuries, our unchurched traditions have tried to unite science and religion. They have also drawn on the insights of many world religions. The fact that most proponents of these traditions lack some of the intellectual polish that we find in "highbrow" academic circles should not diminish our appreciation of their exemplary quest to be both integral and comprehensive.

Allport's final criterion of spiritual maturity is that a religious outlook have a heuristic or open-ended quality to it. Psychological health requires mental and emotional flexibility. A mature faith consequently can't be built on a closed system of doctrines. It must, instead, view the spiritual life as a journey or quest. A heuristic faith is open, eager, and fresh—always hoping to gain new insights. Those who are spiritual, but not religious typically pursue insights from al-

most any philosophical, scientific, or religious source. They describe
their spiritual quest as a journey. Many, even after years of exploring
alternative systems, still see themselves as "just beginning to grow."
Not only does this image of the spiritual quest as a journey seem to
comport well with Allport's criteria for spiritual maturity, it embraces the realities of modern society with its high degree of pluralism, mobility, and temporally limited social ties.[15]

Our unchurched traditions thus fare very well when held up to the
scrutiny of Allport's criteria of mature religious faith. This is a sufficiently important issue to warrant at least one more look. James
Fowler's research while serving as director of the Center for Faith Development at Emory University provides another helpful way to assess religious maturity. Fowler drew on respected theories in
developmental psychology to examine the process through which
people acquire religious belief systems.[16] Fowler discovered that individuals progress through a series of stages in the course of their faith
development. Most people follow the same sequence of development, although some individuals pass through a given stage more
rapidly than others (and many find no reason to move past the fourth
stage). The first three stages correspond to the early stages in our cognitive development. Stage One, primal faith, represents a young
child's earliest relationships with the world. It therefore mostly consists of prelinguistic dispositions toward trust or anxiety. About the
age of four, children enter into Stage Two in which they begin to acquire religious ideas by observing and learning from their parents.
Stage Three begins as children gradually adopt the attitudes and
moral rules of their community. Religious ideas in this stage are one-
dimensional and literal, largely acquired from the stories and rituals
they have been taught. By early adulthood, they enter into Stage Four,
the stage of conventional faith. Adopting their community's religious
heritage provides mental and emotional stability. And, by accepting
their community's shared faith, they benefit from a sense of solidar-
ity or communal belonging.

Many remain in Stage Four for the rest of their lives. But, according
to Fowler, it is inevitable that some individuals will question the authority behind their community's conventional beliefs. Stage Five begins the moment people begin to accept responsibility for thinking
through religious and moral issues on their own. Fowler calls this the
"individuating process" whereby people tailor a religious outlook to

fit their personal intellectual standards. This stage requires a qualitatively new awareness of oneself as responsible for making personal decisions about what one truly does—or does not—believe. Whereas Stage Four consists largely of submission to authority, Stage Five entails active attempts to arrive at personal opinions concerning the tensions in religious faith: the relative versus the absolute, the individual versus the community, self-fulfillment versus service to others, the demands of reason versus the need for emotional security Many of the choices made in Stage Five are ideological, meaning that they embrace only one side of each pair at the expense of acknowledging the important truths expressed in the other. Fowler's Stage Six moves beyond polarities and recognizes the truth in positions other than one's own. This stage, which Fowler terms the "paradoxical-consolidative" stage, recognizes that life itself contains polarities. It is alert to paradox and the need for multiple interpretations of reality. Symbols, myths, scientific method, logical analysis, and scriptural stories—some of which were repudiated in Stage Five—are newly appropriated as complementary vehicles for grasping truth. Stage Six is also ready for community beyond that of tribal, class, or ideological boundaries. To be genuine, this readiness must acknowledge the self-sacrificing cost of true community and be prepared to translate values and beliefs into risk and action.[17]

Fowler's model of faith development provides a second measuring stick against which to assess unchurched spirituality. It is obviously difficult to make sweeping generalizations about how those who consider themselves "spiritual, but not religious" compare to their churched counterparts in terms of progression toward fully mature faith. Yet seekers, by definition, have made a conscious decision to move beyond conventional faith. They have decided to question authority and to begin taking responsibility for "owning" their own faith. Our unchurched traditions introduce them to a number of ideas that would seemingly facilitate movement through the successive stages of spiritual development (belief in the symbolic nature of religious language, the importance of religious pluralism, the spiritual value of identifying with the whole community of life on this planet, and the possibility of mystical connection with the Ultimate).

It is hard to estimate just how many of those who consider themselves "spiritual, but not religious" successfully work through the fifth or sixth stages in Fowler's model of faith development. Many probably do. The literature written by and for highly active seekers at least appears to embrace the universality and commitment that Fowler associates with highly advanced forms of religious faith. A larger number, however, probably don't quite reach this degree of spiritual attainment. In truth, many seekers remain too uncertain about the value of a spiritual—as opposed to secular—orientation to life to commit fully to any one religious path. This causes them to fixate on the fifth or individuating stage, often being more certain about what it is they reject about religion than about what they accept. It also fates them to continuous experimentation rather than coming to a new sense of closure. Their perpetual spiritual journey nonetheless reveals many of the characteristics that Fowler believes are essential to ongoing faith development. Those who insist on individuating their faith at least have the consolation of knowing that their journey requires a great deal of emotional courage and intellectual effort. Their spiritual journey thus has an intrinsic value to them regardless of just how far they decide to travel. Most, after all, believe that humans should never expect to arrive at a final destination or to possess absolute truth. But, as Wade Clark Roof has noted of this growing cohort of Baby Boomers, "if metaphysical certainty is not possible, there are provisional approximations to hold on to even if they are no more than just that."[18] Their faith is an open-ended one, affirming that our perceptions of truth—like the universe itself—are forever evolving. Many never finally achieve the mystical insights for which they quest. Some probably never intended to do much more than dabble in these metaphysical beliefs and practices. But in the meantime these unchurched traditions keep religious wonder alive in those who have rejected both scientific materialism and conventional religion. And thus the many Americans who find themselves with no option other than "being spiritual, but not religious" seem to have achieved as high a level of spiritual maturity as might reasonably be expected in our modern era.

A Glimpse into the Future

Predicting future trends in American religion is far from an exact science. We can't even be very sure about current trends. Surveys indicate, for example, that a higher percentage of people are affiliated with a church today than at any time in American history.[19] Yet, Wade

Clark Roof notes that there may be "a gap—perhaps an increasing gap—between what people 'say' about religious attendance and what they actually 'do,' but we have no firm basis on which to draw any conclusions."[20] Understanding what people are really "doing" religiously is a guessing game. For example, some evidence suggests that there is an increase of serious churchgoers. At the same time, there is an increase in those who report being wholly uninvolved with a church. The two ends of the spectrum are moving apart. In this sense "the cleavage between the so-called churched and unchurched sectors has widened for this generation."[21]

It would be easy to misinterpret the widening gap between churched and unchurched. In Europe, this gap separates the relatively small number of religious persons from the nonreligious majority. In the United States, however, only a small percentage of the population can be considered wholly without spiritual interests. The rest of the unchurched are, in varying degrees, spiritual but not religious. What is unique about American culture is that the gap separating churched and unchurched has to do with how people are religious, not whether they are religious. Furthermore, many casual church attenders are aware that this gap runs right through them, too. Many casual churchgoers seek a more relevant spirituality by actively supplementing church teachings with ideas and practices drawn from the nation's unchurched traditions. This mingling of churched and unchurched spirituality has been going on for some time. It is likely to continue and probably accelerate in the near future. Studies of Baby Boomers indicate that many have been attending a church largely because they thought that it would provide them with assistance in raising their children. Now that many of the Boomers' families are grown up, they feel less need for the services that churches provide. They are consequently becoming more infrequent in their church attendance (but ostensibly fulfilling their spiritual needs in other ways). Still other Baby Boomers continue casual attendance, but actively supplement their church's teachings with whatever other ideas come their way. And, too, many mainstream denominations consciously adopt some of the vocabulary of unchurched spiritualities as a way of making their message seem more relevant to contemporary audiences. The hard-core constituences of churched and unchurched spiritualities may be drifting further apart, but there is still lots of room in the middle.

Back in the 1960s, many social theorists predicted that Americans would soon follow the pattern of Europe and steadily abandon church affiliation in favor of secular attitudes. The gradual secularization of Western cultures, they argued, is an inevitable process. Even though the United States was lagging behind, it was destined to witness the same demise of religious belief. This has not really happened. Even the unchurched haven't abandoned their religious interests. Yet the secularization theory was probably not altogether wrong. It correctly understood that we are all products of socialization. It also understood that modern socialization processes would have a significant impact on our ability to affirm the "absolute truths" of any one religious tradition. The technologies of global communication have made it increasingly difficult to socialize contemporary Americans in a tribal or parochial cultural heritage. Science has provided a universal language for pursuing reliable knowledge that competes quite favorably with religious faith. Increased social mobility also makes us less vulnerable to any one subculture's attempts to pressure us into conforming to a narrow worldview. Secularization theories correctly understood these changes and their inevitable impact on how we are socialized into a belief system. It turned out, however, that instead of leading to the eradication of spiritual interests, these changes have prompted Americans (especially those with the greatest exposure to these modern trends) to explore different avenues in pursuit of these interests. It is difficult to think that this pattern won't continue into the foreseeable future—creating a favorable environment for unchurched traditions, but probably at the expense of churches' ability to sustain the loyalty of casual attenders.

What will America's religious landscape look like in the future if the churches lose some of their current market share? First, there is no evidence that our current church structure is going to change any time soon. Our churches will continue to inform the religious thinking of strong and loyal constituencies. What is being suggested here is that churches will have less influence over casual attenders, and that many who would formerly have sustained these weak ties to churches will instead drift completely away. This is not necessarily reason for concern. It is never comforting to see important social institutions weaken, but this shouldn't cause us to overestimate how well they have been performing cultural tasks or conclude that other institutions aren't capable of performing these tasks even better. There are many sources of community besides the church. Most people establish their strongest communal bonds at work, in their schools or neighborhoods, or through association with other people in a recreational context. And while churches have historically sought to teach moral values, it is not at all clear that these values are in any way superior to those acquired through other social institutions or cultural activities.

Most of us are too quick to equate religion with the activities of churches. Perhaps a part of the problem of American culture is that we haven't been helped to see the spiritual importance of everyday activities. This was, in fact, the message of the most famous Protestant theologian of the twentieth century, Paul Tillich.[22] Tillich urged us to stop thinking of religion as a separate compartment of life. It is better, he argued, to view religion as the dimension of depth in all compartments or functions of life. Tillich believed that the essence of religion was to be grasped by the ultimate power or meaning of being. Genuine religion is a state of ultimate concern. It prompts us to rearrange all our interests or concerns in an effort to align our lives with this "power of being." Tillich recognized two related implications of his religious vision. First, he wanted us to see that much of what happens in a church isn't distinctively spiritual. Second, he wanted us to realize that religion is not a separate compartment of life. Instead, genuine religion has to do with the underlying sense of depth or ultimacy that underlies all life-affirming activities. We are thus just as likely to find genuinely spiritual activity in science, social work, education, counseling, ecology, or progressive social causes as we are in church activities. Many unchurched traditions have been delivering a message similar to Tillich's. They have encouraged individuals to transform their spiritual convictions into a cohesive way of life, discovering how harmony with the "power of being" can empower them to participate in the progressive growth and unfolding of our universe. They have, in other words, helped many Americans redirect—not repudiate—their spiritual impulses.

Being "spiritual, but not religious" will likely continue to be the only viable option for a growing sector of the American population. Whether this is good or bad for American culture depends largely on what we expect religion to provide. It is improbable that unchurched religion will soon give rise to the kinds of comprehensive systems of doctrine, ritual, and congregational activity that we have long associated with our nation's churches. Yet those who choose to be spiritual, but not religious do not consider these to be the most important functions of religion. Their greatest spiritual need is to view life with a sense of wonder, to feel connected with the sacred meanings and powers that permeate everyday life. They hope for beliefs and practices that might help them sustain such a state of wonder and thus make spirituality possible in an otherwise secular world. This may not be everything we have traditionally expected of religion. But, as we look to the intellectual and cultural complexities that will confront citizens of the twenty-first century, it would be a shame to hope for less.

Appendix
Unchurched Religion: A Scholarly Agenda

Several of my previous books have made contributions to the scholarly study of unchurched American religion.[1] This book, however, was written for a general readership. Its goal was to provide an historical and thematic overview of some important traditions in American religious life. My narrative was synthetic in nature, emphasizing continuities and similarities that help make the case for the existence and importance of these unchurched traditions. This was its strength, but also its weakness. My narrative inadvertently diverted attention away from more subtle differences and discontinuities in the way that unchurched Americans—both past and present—have constructed their religious views of the world. Obviously, a great deal more needs to be known about the way that individuals who are "spiritual, but not religious" utilize both churched and unchurched religious traditions in their personal lives.

Scholars wanting to investigate this field further should begin by consulting Wade Clark Roof's *Spiritual Marketplace: Baby Boomers and the Remaking of American Religion* (Princeton, NJ: Princeton University Press, 1999) and Robert Wuthnow's *After Heaven: Spirituality in America Since the 1950s* (Berkeley: University of California Press, 1998). Both these works are sociological in nature and could be supplemented with Meredith B. McGuire's "Mapping Contemporary American Spirituality: A Sociological Perspective," *Christian Spirituality Bulletin* 5 (Spring, 1997): 1–8. Other sociological studies of trends in contemporary American spirituality are referenced in the notes to the introduction of this book.

Helpful background information on spiritual trends in the late twentieth century can be found in Robert Ellwood's *The Fifties Spiritual Marketplace: American Religion in a Decade of Conflict* (New Brunswick, NJ: Rutgers University Press, 1997) and *The Sixties Spiritual Awakening* (New Brunswick, NJ: Rutgers University Press, 1994). A relatively new journal, *Nova Religio: The Journal of Alternative and Emergent Religions*, is dedicated to the study of new religious movements, many of which might be considered examples of unchurched American spirituality.

I might suggest a few of the steps that need to be taken if we are to further our understanding of unchurched America. We need a more thorough demographic and subjective mapping of unchurched Americans as a contemporary population—who they are and what they are seeking as they sort through the various "sources" outlined in this book. Wuthnow and Roof have provided a start. So, too, have Brian Zinnbauer and Kenneth Pargament in their article on "Religiousness and Spirituality: Unfuzzying the Fuzzy" in the *Journal for the Scientific Study of Religion* 36 (December, 1997): 549–64. This is difficult information to obtain, perhaps even more difficult to interpret. Consider, for example, the complexities in understanding the spirituality of the thirty-eight-year-old teacher interviewed by sociologist Meredith McGuire. This woman, raised a Roman Catholic, now attends Mass only about every other month, usually to please her mother. Yet, despite her lack of religious commitment, she considers herself very spiritual and on her home altar she has placed "amethyst crystals used in healing meditations, oriental incense and Tibetan prayer bell, a large colorful triptych of Frida Kahlo, and a modern representation of the Virgin of Guadalupe as a young Chicana in running shoes."[2] McGuire suggests that for this middle-class woman Christianity has been reduced to one "cultural resource" alongside others, which she selectively employs with relative autonomy. Yet we may never fully understand just what this woman seeks and how these "cultural resources" fit together in her search.

We need to be alert to subtle differences in the way that different people utilize both churched and unchurched religious traditions in their individual quests. One way of doing this is to create several categories according to which we might compare people's spiritual styles. For example, we might begin by comparing the degree to which different persons "mingle" unchurched with churched beliefs or practices. Among other things, this would allow us to distinguish between efforts to use unchurched religious traditions as a way of complementing as opposed to replacing the practices of established religious institutions.

A second category we might use is one that would distinguish between people's quests for prosperity and their quests for purity. When all is said and done, these are two of the most powerful motivations to think or act religiously. A great deal of religious beliefs and practices are connected with people's search for enhanced worldly prosperity (e.g., more worldly affluence, better health for oneself or loved ones, good fortune, protection while traveling, assistance at critical moments, improving one's personal afterlife, etc.) and their search for inner purity (e.g. forgiveness, atonement, renewal, alignment with the sacred). The quest for prosperity seemingly aligns religion with the instrumental pursuit of this-worldly goals, while the quest for purity emphasizes restoring ontological relationships for their intrinsic value. And the quest for prosperity generally entails coaxing higher powers into serving the needs of the self, while the quest for purity emphasizes the self's need for surrender or capitulation to higher powers. In practice, however, these distinctions are often blurred. Nonetheless, attention to the relative preponderance of these alternating motivations might alert us to important differences in the underlying dynamics of contemporary unchurched spirituality.

Closely related to the distinction between quests for prosperity and purity are two additional issues. The first concerns whether persons understand sacred power as existing within the human self or outside the self. As we saw in the matter of New Age healing theories, the vocabularies used by many of our unchurched traditions make it difficult to make a clear-cut distinction between these two understandings of the self's relationship to the sacred—again suggesting the need for some kind of scale measuring relative emphasis. This distinction can potentially help us better understand what people hope to accomplish through various spiritual practices ranging from techniques for self-alteration to supplication. A second issue involves the relative emphasis placed on free will and determinism. Unchurched religions, much like their churched counterparts, often give conflicting messages about the extent to which our lives are connected with a web of metaphysical influences. How individuals interpret and act on these messages greatly affect the overall tone of their personal spirituality.

Other scholars will surely nominate other categories for distinguishing between spiritual styles. I might, however, suggest one final issue that strikes me as important for further scholarship in the field of unchurched religion. The study of those who are spiritual, but not religious presents a new opportunity to investigate the connection between personality structures and religious belief. Wade Clark Roof, for example, noted that seekers are more likely to be social isolates or to have fewer strong social relationships than their churched counterparts. Roof writes that "they have broken away from the churches and synagogues, an indication that they are not perhaps as socially anchored in their communities as are most other Americans. Conventional believers have their faiths reinforced through association with others of a similar outlook; but the lack of strong social ties is functional for [seekers], freeing them to pursue their own personal spiritual journeys uninhibited by conventional sanctions."[3] Assuming that he is correct in this observation, the issue of cause and effect would be a fascinating research agenda. Are some of us psychologically predisposed to take the road less traveled? Or do our unchurched religions foster any of a variety of antisocial attitudes ranging from elitism to a desire for prolonged periods of introspection requiring privacy? Continued study of seekers (and their friends or family members) has the potential to disclose a great deal about the connection between personality traits and religious style.

Notes

Introduction

1. Roger Finke and Rodney Stark, *The Churching of America* (New Brunswick, NJ: Rutgers University Press, 1992), 16. This figure represents their estimate of the unchurched population in 1980. Assuming that this was a reasonably accurate calculation, it would still not be clear whether this would be a reliable estimate of the number of persons who are currently unchurched. On the one hand, Finke and Stark observed that the number of "unaffiliated" had been declining in the twentieth century. On the other hand, scholars such as Wade Clark Roof have accumulated data to suggest that the percentage of "unaffiliated" is higher among the Baby Boomer generation (and that even those who are religiously affiliated have weak connections with churches and might well be expected to cease attending when their families have been raised). See Wade Clark Roof, *Spiritual Marketplace: Baby Boomers and the Remaking of American Religion* (Princeton, NJ: Princeton University Press, 1999).

Several different studies seem to confirm the estimate that between 38 and 40 percent of the population is unchurched. Dean R. Hoge, Benton Johnson, and Donald A. Luidens conducted an intensive study of the patterns of religious affiliation among Baby Boomers who had been born into families affiliated with the Presbyterian denomination. Their sample population was probably biased in favor of persons who are fairly conservative in their lifestyle and have less-than-average conflict with churches. Nonetheless, their study suggests that precisely 38 percent of the population is unchurched (with an additional 10 percent who do attend a church at least six times per year, but are not members—making the total as high as 48 percent, depending on the precise definition of "unchurched"). See *Vanishing Boundaries: The Religion of Mainline Protestant Baby Boomers* (Louisville, KY: Westminster/John Knox, 1994). Of additional interest are the findings that appear in Warren Wolfe and Martha Sawyer Allen, "Minnesotans Overwhelmingly Believe There Is a Watchful God," *Minneapolis Star and Tribune* (August 30, 1987), 1A, 4A. Wolfe and Allen's survey of Minnesotans suggests that up to 54 percent of the population are not active members of a church. Because their survey did not separate out varying degrees of "active involvement," it includes those who retain marginal affiliation and is thus consistent with an estimate in the 38 to 40 percent range.

2. Meredith McGuire, "Mapping Contemporary American Spirituality," *Christian Spirituality Bulletin* 5 (Spring 1997): 3–8.

3. Hoge, Johnson, and Luidens provide a fascinating discussion of various types of unchurched persons. See *Vanishing Boundaries*, 129–62. Their study found that 48 percent of the people they interviewed could be considered unchurched (yet, because this figure included those who actually did belong to a church even though they rarely attended, it tends to confirm my estimate of 38 to 40 percent).

4. Wade Clark Roof's studies of the religious patterns of the Baby Boomer generation indicate that 15 percent of Boomers are secularists. See *Spiritual Marketplace*, 212.

5. If we include all of these individuals in the unchurched category, then it is possible that we are referring to at least 48 percent of the population (and perhaps even higher depending on an accurate estimate of the percentage of wholly nonreligious persons in the total population). Yet common sense tells us that many of these persons (i.e., those who either still belong to a church but rarely attend or those who sometimes attend a church, but do not belong) deserve to be considered churched in some sense. We might, therefore, suggest a common-sense solution to this problem and simply divide these two groups in half, counting half of these people as churched (though only marginally affiliated) and half as unchurched (though not fully representative of the larger category). Dividing these groups in half accords with our earlier estimate that between 38 to 40 percent of the population should be considered unchurched.

6. Wade Clark Roof, *A Generation of Seekers: The Spiritual Journeys of the Baby Boom Generation* (San Francisco: HarperSanFrancisco, 1993), 79.

7. Abraham Maslow, *Religions, Values, and Peak Experiences* (New York: Viking, 1970), viii. Cited in Roof, *A Generation of Seekers*, 79–80.

8. Roof, *Spiritual Marketplace*, 85.

9. In his *Spiritual Marketplace*, Roof describes a category called "metaphysical believers and spiritual seekers" that is seemingly broader than, but includes, individuals he had described as "highly active seekers" in his *A Generation of Seekers*. He estimates that about 14 percent of Baby Boomers fall into this category. My own category, that of being "spiritual, but not religious," would be broader yet. My estimate that 20 percent of Americans can be characterized by the "spiritual, but not religious" label approximates the 21 percent of Baby Boomers who Hoge, Johnson, and Luidens placed in their "uninvolved, but religious" category and the 19 percent who were defined as "mystical believers" in the 1987 Minnesota survey. See note 2.

10. Brian Zinnbauer, Kenneth Pargament, et al., "Religion and Spirituality: Unfuzzying the Fuzzy," *Journal for the Scientific Study of Religion* 36 (December, 1997): 549–64.

11. Ibid., 561.

12. McGuire, "Mapping Contemporary American Spirituality," 5.

13. Discussions of the demographic traits associated with interest in unchurched spirituality can be found in Wade Clark Roof's *A Generation of Seekers*, 79–88; Brian Zinnbauer, Kenneth Pargament, et al., "Religion and Spirituality: Unfuzzying the Fuzzy," and Hoge, Johnson, and Luidens, *Vanishing Boundaries*, 129–62. See also the Princeton Religious Research Center and the Gallup Organization, Inc., *The Unchurched American* (Princeton, NJ: Princeton Religious Research Center for the National Council of Churches, 1978).

14. Although the best studies of popular religion are probably those that study specific instances of nontheological religiosity such as Robert Orsi's *The Madonna of 115th Street: Faith and community in Italian Harlem, 1880–1950* (New

Haven, CT: Yale University Press, 1985); Peter Williams's *Popular Religion in America: Symbolic Change and the Modernization Process in Historical Perspective* (Englewood Cliffs, NJ: Prentice-Hall, 1980); and Charles H. Lippy, *Being Religious American Style: A History of Popular Religiosity in the United States* (Westport, CT: Greenwood Press, 1994) are excellent scholarly overviews of the topic. See also Charles Lippy's *Modern American Popular Religion: A Critical Assessment and Annotated Bibliography* (Westport, CT: Greenwood Press, 1996).

15. William James, *The Varieties of Religious Experience* (Cambridge, MA: Harvard University Press, 1985), 382.

16. See the discussion of the similarities between "lay liberals" and "uninvolved but religious persons" in Hoge, Johnson, and Luidens, *Vanishing Boundaries*, 138–44.

17. Lippy, *Being Religious American Style*, 230.

18. Robert Wuthnow, *After Heaven: Spirituality in America Since the 1950s* (Berkeley: University of California Press, 1998), 136.

Chapter One

1. Perhaps the best recent study of the historical vicissitudes of church membership in the United States is Roger Finke and Rodney Stark, *The Churching of America, 1776–1990: Winners and Losers in Our Religious Economy* (New Brunswick, NJ: Rutgers University Press, 1992). See also Edwin Gaustad, *Historical Atlas of Religion in America* (New York: Harper & Row, 1976).

2. Hector St. John de Crevecoeur, *Letters from an American Farmer and Sketches of Eighteenth-Century America*, ed. Albert E. Stone (New York: Penguin, 1981), 76.

3. Excellent studies of the role that magical and occult practices played in colonial America include Jon Butler's *Awash in a Sea of Faith* (Cambridge, MA: Harvard University Press, 1990); Richard Weisman's *Witchraft, Magic, and Religion in 17th-Century Massachusetts* (Amherst: University of Massachusetts Press, 1984); and Richard Godbeer's *The Devil's Dominion: Magic and Religion in Early New England* (Cambridge: Cambridge University Press, 1992).

4. Jon Butler, "Magic, Astrology, and the Early American Religious Heritage, 1600–1760," *American Historical Review* 84 (1979). 317–46. Readers might also wish to consult Butler's article "The Dark Ages of American Occultism, 1760–1848" in Howard Kerr and Charles Crow, eds., *The Occult in America: New Historical Perspectives* (Urbana: University of Illinois Press, 1983), 58–78.

5. An especially helpful discussion of astrological discourse in early New England can be found in Richard Godbeer, *The Devil's Dominion*, 122–52. See also Herbert Leventhal, *In the Shadow of the Enlightenment: Occultism and Renaissance Science in Eighteenth-Century America* (New York: New York University Press, 1976).

6. There are many scholarly studies of witchcraft in colonial America. Readers might begin with the accounts offered by Jon Butler in "Magic, Astrology, and the Early American Religious Heritage, 1600–1760"; Richard Godbeer's *The Devil's Dominion*; and Richard Weisman's *Witchraft, Magic, and Religion in 17th-Century*

Massachusetts. Perhaps the best overall account of the events surrounding the Salem witchcraft episode is Paul Boyer and Stephen Nissenbaum's *Salem Possessed: The Social Origins of Witchcraft* (Cambridge, MA: Harvard University Press, 1974). A discussion of the Andover and Salem witchcraft trials can be found in Chadwick Hansen, "Andover Witchcraft and the Causes of the Salem Witchcraft Trials," in Howard Kerr and Charles Crow, eds., *The Occult in America*, 38–57.

7. A discussion of the fusion of European, Caribbean, and African elements in colonial African-American religion can be found in George Eaton Simpson, *Black Religions in the New World* (New York: Columbia University Press, 1978) and Albert Raboteau, *Slave Religion: The "Invisible Institution" in the Antebellum South* (New York: Oxford University Press, 1978).

8. Butler, "Magic, Astrology, and the Early American Religious Heritage, 1600–1760," 326–30.

9. Bronislaw Malinowski, *Magic, Science and Religion* (Garden City, NY: Doubleday, 1954).

10. Godbeer, *The Devil's Dominion*, 9.

11. Butler, "Magic, Astrology, and the Early American Religious Heritage, 1600–1760," 319.

12. There is considerable scholarly debate about the exact relationship between the churched and unchurched elements of colonial religiosity. Richard Weisman (*Witchcraft, Magic, and Religion in 17th-Century Massachusetts*) argues that they presented two "competing cosmologies" and that the proponents of each cosmology considered themselves in direct opposition to one another. David Hall, on the other hand, maintains that the two were perceived as complementary and readily blended together in everyday life. Hall further contends that the clergy were almost as likely as the laity to meld magical and Christian belief systems. See David Hall, *Worlds of Wonder, Days of Judgment: Popular Religious Belief in Early New England* (New York: Alfred A. Knopf, 1989). Both Jon Butler ("Magic, Astrology, and the Early American Religious Heritage, 1600–1760") and Richard Godbeer (*The Devil's Dominion*) are probably more accurate when they mediate between these two positions and argue that most people differentiated between magic and Christianity, but nonetheless saw fit to draw on each as needs merited.

13. Godbeer, *The Devil's Dominion*, 17. See Godbeer's succinct summary of competing interpretations of the relationship between magic and Christianity, 14–18.

14. Benjamin Franklin, cited in *Benjamin Franklin: Representative Selections*, Frank L. Mott and Chester E. Jorgenson, eds. (New York: American Book Co., 1936), 69–70.

15. Thomas Jefferson, *The Writings of Thomas Jefferson*, Andrew A. Lipscomb, ed. (Washington, DC: The Thomas Jefferson Memorial Association, 1903), 15:492.

16. See Jefferson's *The Life and Morals of Jesus of Nazareth, Extracted Textually from the Gospels of Matthew, Mark, Luke, and John* (Boston: Beacon Press, 1951).

17. Cited in Daniel Boorstin, *The Lost World of Thomas Jefferson* (Boston: Beacon Press, 1960), 706–07.

18. Reliable overviews of Freemasonry can be found in William Stemper's "Freemasons" in Mircea Eliade, ed., *Encyclopedia of Religion*, 16 vols. (New York: Macmillan Publishing Co., 1987), 5: 416–19, and Catherine Albanese, *America: Religions and Religion* (Belmont, CA: Wadsworth Publishing Co., 1992), 440–42. More extensive discussions of Freemasonry can be found in Edmond Mazet, "Feemasonry and Esotericism" in Antonie Faivre and Jacob Needleman, eds., *Modern Esoteric Spirituality* (New York: Crossroad, 1992), 248–76; and Lynn Dumenil, *Freemasonry and American Culture, 1880–1930* (Princeton, NJ: Princeton University Press, 1984).

19. Albanese, *America: Religions and Religion*, 441.

20. Mazet, "Freemasonry and Esotericism," 249.

21. Helpful accounts of revivalism and the role that the major awakenings have had in American religious life can be found in standard surveys such as Sydney Ahlstrom, *A Religious History of the American People* (New Haven, CT: Yale University Press, 1972); William McLoughlin, *Revivals, Awakenings, and Reform* (Chicago: University of Chicago Press, 1978); or Winthrop Hudson, *Religion in America* (New York: Charles Scribner's Sons, 1965).

22. Whitney Cross, *The Burned-Over District* (Ithaca, NY: Cornell University Press, 1950), 183.

23. Ahlstrom, *A Religious History of the American People*, 483.

24. A concise definition and explanation of key Swedenborgian concepts can be found in Robin Larsen, ed., *Emanuel Swedenborg: A Continuing Vision* (New York: Swedenborg Foundation, 1988). In addition to the helpful essays in Larsen's volume, readers interested in learning more about Swedenborgian teachings might consult Marguerite Beck Block's *The New Church in the New World* (New York: Octagon Books, 1968).

25. John Humphrey Noyes, cited in Whitney Cross, *The Burned-Over District*, 343.

26. Bret Carroll offers an excellent discussion of the connections, and differences, between spiritualism, Transcendentalism, and Swedenborgianism in his *Spiritualism in Antebellum America* (Bloomington: Indiana University Press, 1997). This paragraph draws heavily on Carroll's assessments.

27. Ralph Waldo Emerson, *The Complete Works of Ralph Waldo Emerson*, 12 vols., (New York: AMS Press, 1968), 1: 130.

28. Ibid., 1:10.

29. Ibid., 1:73

30. Ibid., p. 135. William McLoughlin, *Revivals, Awakenings, and Reform*, 103.

31. Eugene Taylor, "Emerson: The Swedenborgian and Transcendentalist Connection," in Robin Larsen, ed., *Emanuel Swedenborg: A Continuing Vision*, 134.

32. Ibid., 135.

33. A more complete account of Poyen's lecture tour can be found in my *Mesmerism and the American Cure of Souls* (Philadelphia: University of Pennsylvania Press, 1982). The citation here comes from Poyen's personal account of his efforts on behalf of mesmerism, titled *Progress of Animal Magnetism in New England* (Boston: Weeks, Jordan, 1837). Other accounts of Mesmer's life and theories can

be found in Henri Ellenberger, *The Discovery of the Unconscious* (New York: Basic Books, 1970); Vincent Buranelli, *Franz Anton Mesmer: The Wizzard from Vienna* (New York: McCann, Cowan, and Geoghegan, 1975); and Frank Podmore, *From Mesmer to Christian Science* (New York: University Books, 1963).

34. Franz Anton Mesmer, quoted in Ellenberger, *The Discovery of the Unconscious*, 62.

35. Poyen, *Progress*, 35.

36. William Stone, *Letter to Dr. A. Brigham on Animal Magnetism* (New York: George Dearborn, 1837), 81.

37. A Practical Magnetizer [pseud.], *The History and Philosophy of Animal Magnetism and Practical Instructions for the Exercise of Its Power* (Boston: 1843), 8.

38. A Gentleman of Philadelphia, *The Philosophy of Animal Magnetism together with the System of Manipulating Adopted to Produce Ecstasy and Somnambulism* (Philadelphia: Merrihew and Dunn, 1837).

39. Chauncy Townhend, *Facts in Mesmerism* (London: Bailliere Press, 1844), 222.

40. LaRoy Sunderland, *"Confessions of a Magnetizer" Exposed* (Boston: Redding, 1845), 22.

41. George Bush, *Mesmer and Swedenborg* (New York: John Allen, 1847), 160.

42. Joseph Buchanan, *Neurological System of Anthropology* (Cincinnati: 1854), 195.

43. Ibid., Appendix I.

44. Ibid.

45. Poyen, *Progress*, 88.

46. Ibid.

47. A Gentleman of Philadelphia, *The Philosophy of Animal Magnetism*, 68.

48. Ibid., 71.

49. A Practical Magnetizer, *The History and Philosophy of Animal Magnetism*, 19.

50. Theodore Leger, *Animal Magnetism, or Psychodynamy* (New York: D. Appleton, 1846), 18.

51. John Dods, *The Philosophy of Mesmerism* (Boston: William Hall, 1843), 137.

52. John Dods, *The Philosophy of Electrical Psychology* (New York: Fowler and Wells, 1850), 22.

53. Ibid., 28.

54. George Bush, *Mesmer and Swedenborg*, 147.

55. Ibid., 137.

56. Cross, *The Burned-Over District*, 342.

57. Andrew Jackson Davis, *The Great Harmonia* (Boston: Mussey and Co., 1852), 26. See also Davis's longer autobiographical reflections in *The Magic Staff* (New York: J. S. Brown, 1857).

58. Ibid., 31.

59. Ibid., 45. In his *The Discovery of the Unconscious*, historian Henri Ellen-

berger has advanced a hypothesis concerning the instrumental role of what he calls "creative illness" in the discovery of psychological insights. It is interesting in this light to note that, just prior to his "breakthrough," Davis underwent a severe emotional breakdown. Although the details are unclear, he is believed to have been unconscious for well over a day. He later claimed to have been "living wholly in the interior world." It was from this point onward that his journeys into the mesmeric state would be imbued with great spiritual significance.

60. An excellent discussion of spiritualism's complex relationships with both Swedenborgianism and Transcendentalism can be found in Bret Carroll's *Spiritualism in Antebellum America*, 18–27.

61. Ibid.,17.

62. For an excellent scholarly overview of the feminist aspects of spiritualism, see Ann Braude, *Radical Spirits: Spiritualism and Women's Rights in Nineteenth-Century America* (Boston: Beacon Press, 1989).

63. R. Laurence Moore provides an extended analysis of spiritualism's unique place in American intellectual history in his *In Search of White Crows: Spiritualism Parapsychology, and American Culture* (New York: Oxford University Press, 1977).

64. Cited in Bret Carroll, *Spiritualism in Antebellum America*, 39.

65. Ibid.

66. Ibid., 40.

67. Cross, *The Burned-Over District*, 342.

Chapter Two

1. Phineas P. Quimby, *The Quimby Manuscripts* (New York: Thomas Crowell, 1921), 180. More extensive descriptions of Quimby's life and thought can be found in my *Mesmerism and the American Cure of Soul* (Philadelphia: University of Pennsylvania Press, 1982) and *Americans and the Unconscious* (New York: Oxford University Press, 1986).

2. Quimby, *The Quimby Manuscripts*, 243.

3. The best descriptive history of the New Thought movement is Charles Braden's *Spirits in Rebellion: The Rise and Development of New Thought* (Dallas, TX: Southern Methodist University Press, 1963). Braden provides an overview of the Metaphysical Club's statement of purpose in his introductory paragraph, 9–18.

4. Walter Felt Evans, *Mental Medicine: A Treatise on Medical Psychology* (Boston: H. H. Carter, 1886),104.

5. Ralph Waldo Trine, *In Tune with the Infinite* (New York: Crowell, 1897), 16.

6. Ibid., from the preface.

7. Walter Felt Evans, *The Primitive Cure: The Nature and Power of Faith, or Elementary Lessons in Christian Philosophy and Transcendental Medicine* (Boston: H. H. Carter, 1885), 125.

8. Henry Wood, *Ideal Suggestions Through Mental Photography* (Boston: Lee and Shepard, 1893), 41 and 97.

9. Sydney Ahlstrom, *A Religious History of the American People* (New Haven,

CT: Yale University Press, 1972), 1019.

10. Discussions of New Thought's demographic appeal can be found in Charles Braden's *Spirits in Rebellion*; Donald Meyer's *The Positive Thinkers* (New York: Doubleday and Co, 1965); Gail Thain Parker's *The History of Mind Cure in New England* (Hanover, NH: University Press of New England, 1973); and (assuming a certain affinity between New Thought and Christian Science); David Moberg's *The Church as a Social Institution* (Englewood Cliffs, NJ: Prentice-Hall, 1960). Summarizing these discussions we might note that over 95 percent of New Thought's adherents lived in cities. Many of them had only recently arrived from smaller towns and were still seeking ways to adjust to an urban environment. Their names reflect little ethnic diversity, with most suggesting white, Anglo-Saxon, Protestant descent. It also seems safe to infer that the majority were drawn from the middle or even upper middle classes, since New Thought concepts were disseminated through lectures, pamphlets, and books that would appeal only to those inclined to set aside large blocks of time for thought or reading. Middle-class women in the late nineteenth century had much more leisure time and far fewer constructive outlets for their energies than did their male counterparts. The only role open to them, that of the housewife, was being further diminished by the forces of modernization. The family unit was gradually losing its economic and emotional cohesiveness—a process they were powerless to arrest. Many, quite understandably, found themselves incapacitated by psychosomatic ailments. New Thought provided a new outlet for their otherwise involuted energies. It got them out of their homes and in touch with people who would listen sympathetically and then coax them into discovering interesting new things about themselves. Many saw the opportunity for assuming leadership positions and soon became teachers, lecturers, authors, and administrators of local, state, or national organizations.

11. Readers interested in the historical background of esoteric spirituality in America might consult Robert Ellwood, *Religious and Spiritual Groups in Modern America* (Englewood Cliffs, NJ: Prentice-Hall, 1973) and Antoine Faivre and Jacob Needleman, eds., *Modern Esoteric Spirituality* (New York: Crossroad, 1992).

12. Bruce F. Campbell's *Ancient Wisdom Revived: A History of the Theosophical Movement* (Berkeley: University of California Press, 1980) is the most complete account of the origins and teachings of Theosophy.

13. Ibid., 35.

14. See Mary Farrell Bednarowksi's discussion of how new religions' claims concerning ancient origins enhances their ability to generate utopian enthusiasm in *New Religions and the Theological Imagination in America* (Bloomington: Indiana University Press, 1989).

15. Catherine Albanese, *America: Religions and Religion* (Belmont, CA: Wadsworth Publishing Co., 1992), 268.

16. In his highly regarded *American Religious Thought* (Chicago: University of Chicago Press, 1973), William Clebsch identifies Jonathan Edwards, Ralph Waldo Emerson, and William James as the three principal spokespersons for the "aesthetic spirituality" that he deems best characterizes the distinctively American

mode of religious thinking. Of these three, only Edwards maintained any connection with institutional religion.

17. Among the helpful biographies of William James are Ralph Barton Perry's *The Life and Character of William James*, 2 vols. (Boston: Little, Brown, 1935); Gerald Myers, *William James: His Life and Thought* (New Haven, CT: Yale University Press, 1986), Howard Feinstein, *Becoming William James* (Ithaca, NY: Cornell University Press, 1984); Gay Wilson Allen, *William James* (New York: Viking Press, 1967); and Linda Simon, *Genuine Reality: A Life of William James* (New York: Harcourt, Brace & Co., 1998).

18. A more detailed discussion of the role of James's nitrous oxide intoxication and its role in the development of American metaphysical thought can be found in both my "Drugs and the Baby Boomers' Quest for Metaphysical Illumination," *Nova Religio* (Fall, 1999) and *Stairways to Heaven: Drugs and American Religion* (Boulder, CO: Westview Press, 2000).

19. William James, *The Varieties of Religious Experience* (Cambridge, MA: Harvard University Press, 1985), 307.

20. Ibid., 408.

21. An excellent introduction to James's interest in psychical research is Robert McDermott's preface to William James's *Essays in Psychical Research* (Cambridge, MA: Harvard University Press, 1986). Readers also might wish to consult Gardner Murphy and Robert O. Ballou, eds., *William James on Psychical Research* (New York: Viking Press, 1960), and Eugene Taylor, *William James on Consciousness Beyond the Margin* (Princeton, NJ: Princeton University Press, 1996).

22. William James, *Essays in Psychical Research*, 131.

23. William James, *A Pluralistic Universe* (New York: E. P. Dutton, 1971), 259, 267.

24. Expanded discussions of these authors and their metaphysical spirituality can be found in my *Stairways to Heaven*.

25. Expanded discussions of these authors and their metaphysical spirituality can be found in the final chapter of my *Americans and the Unconscious*.

26. A brief overview of the "I AM" movement can be found in Robert Ellwood's *Religious and Spiritual Groups in America*, 121–25.

27. Helpful descriptions of Edgar Cayce's life and thought can be found in Thomas Sugrue, *There Is a River: The Story of Edgar Cayce* (New York: Henry Holt, 1945); Jess Stearn's *Edgar Cayce: The Sleeping Prophet* (New York: Doubleday, 1967); and J. Gordon Melton, ed., *New Age Encyclopedia* (Detroit: Gale Research, 1990), 89–91.

28. The most important of the books recording Seth's teachings is Jane Roberts, *Seth Speaks: The Eternal Validity of the Soul* (Englewood Cliffs, NJ: Prentice-Hall, 1972). Since Jane Roberts' death, other channelers have also claimed to be conduits for Seth's messages, resulting in some intriguing metaphysical and legal issues about the validity of copywriting books authored by spirits.

29. Michael F. Brown provides a convenient overview of J. Z. Knight's career in his extraordinarily helpful examination of contemporary trance channeling, *The Channeling Zone: American Spirituality in an Anxious Age* (Cambridge, MA: Har-

vard University Press, 1997).

30. See Marianne Williamson, *A Return to Love: Reflections on the Principles of a Course in Miracles* (New York: HarperCollins, 1992), 66.

31. Ibid.

32. Brown, *The Channeling Zone*, 54–57. The following account is a slightly edited version of Brown's fine study of the personal meanings of involvement with trance channeling.

33. Brown provides a helpful overview of channeling's principal beliefs, 47–49.

34. See the section on "Angel Awakenings" in Robert Wuthnow, *After Heaven: Spirituality in America Since the 1950s* (Berkeley: University of California Press, 1998). These studies are cited on 122.

35. Ibid., 121.

36. Billy Graham, *Angels: God's Secret Agents* (Garden City, NY: Doubleday, 1975), 15.

37. Linda Georgian, *Your Guardian Angels* (New York: Fireside Books, 1994).

38. Betty Eadie, *Embraced by the Light* (New York: Bantam Books, 1994), xv.

39. Raymond Moody, *Life After Life* (New York: Bantam Books, 1976).

40. Michael Sabom, *Recollections of Death: A Medical Investigation* (New York: Harper & Row, 1982).

41. See Kenneth Ring, *Life at Death: A Scientific Investigation of the Near-Death Experience* (New York: Coward, McCann & Geoghegan, 1980). In a paper titled "Paranormal Aspects of Near-Death Experiences: Implications for a New Paradigm" delivered to the American Academy of Religion in November 1980, Dr. Ring wrote:

> If our consciousness actually operates through *three* bodies—rather than just "in" the physical part of our being—then obviously the death of the physical body, rather than annihilating consciousness, *frees* it. Following [this] formulation, the out-of-body experience which occurs near death is actually a state of affairs where one's consciousness is functioning fully in the astral body. ... The encounter with a "presence" or a "being of light" and the entrance into a "higher world" also are facts of the [near-death experience] which are easy to account for within [this] framework. Each of the three bodies is said to be sensitive to a different energy domain. The physical body is of course responsive to the physical world to which its sensory systems are "naturally" suited. The astral body (and similarly the causal body) is attuned to another (but penetrating) energy domain, usually said to be of "higher frequencies." When one is functioning in one's astral body, therefore, one becomes sensitive to the things of that world (or domain).

42. Robert Wuthnow, *After Heaven: Spirituality in America Since the 1950s* (Berkeley: University of California Press, 1998), 134.

43. The most widely cited theory of faith development is James Fowler's model of the six basic stages leading to spiritual maturity. Importantly, Fowler identifies "conventional faith" as the fourth of these six stages. Conventional faith, after all, is largely arrived at secondhand, accepted as a "one-size-fits-all" commodity. Conventional faith is based on loyalty and obedience rather than carefully rea-

soned responses to the critical issues about religion raised by modern science, biblical scholarship, psychological and sociological understandings of social conditioning, or philosophical critique of the truth claims posed by religion. For this reason Fowler identifies Stage Five as that next stage of mature faith that builds on critical reflection of the very human, fallible bases of theological doctrines. According to Fowler, this fifth stage toward mature spirituality requires taking responsibility for one's own beliefs—including self-consciously rejecting any beliefs that cannot be squared with one's overall scientific and philosophical understanding of the world. It would seem that almost everyone attracted to articulate forms of unchurched spirituality have entered this stage. In Fowler's view, they are almost always at a higher stage of faith development than the more conventional of their churched counterparts. See James Fowler, *Stages of Faith* (San Francisio: Harper & Row, 1981).

44. Wuthnow, *After Heaven*, 139.

45. Ibid.,137.

46. R. Laurence Moore, "The Occult Connection? Mormonism, Christian Science, and Spiritualism" in Howard Kerr and Charles Crow, eds., *The Occult in America: New Historical Perspectives* (Urbana: University of Illinois Press, 1983), 156.

47. James Redfield, *The Celestine Prophecy* (New York: Warner Books, 1993). In addition to various websites that discuss topics related to Redfield's work, readers might wish to consult Redfield's monthly newsletter *The Celestine Journal* or *The Tenth Insight: Holding the Vision* (New York: Warner Books, 1996).

48. This biographical information comes from *The Celestine Prophecy* website, www.celestinevision.com.

Chapter Three

1. Much of this section on Americans' appropriation of Eastern religious ideas is indebted to the editorial summaries provided by Thomas Tweed and Stephen Prothero in their *Asian Religions in America: A Documentary History* (New York: Oxford University Press, 1999). Also of great assistance is Carl T. Jackson, *The Oriental Religions and American Thought: Nineteenth-Century Explorations* (Westport, CT: Greenwood Press, 1981).

2. Tweed and Prothero, *Asian Religions in America*, 26.

3. An excellent overview of this debate as well as Emerson's "discovery of the East" can be found in Carl T. Jackson, *The Oriental Religions and American Thought*, 45–62.

4. It is interesting to note that Vivekananda had no interest in promoting the occult conceptions that most Americans associated with the "mystic East." Noting that Theosophy and other metaphysical movements had predisposed American audiences to expect tales of paranormal and magical powers, Vivekananda worked hard to stress the more serious philosophical side of Hindu religious thought. In his private papers, he dismissed Theosophy as an "Indian grafting of American Spiritualism—with only a few Sanskrit words taking the place of spiritualistic jargon—Mahatama missiles taking the place of ghostly raps

and taps, and Mahatmic inspiration that of obsession by ghosts." Yet, for all this, Vivekananda did indeed believe in, and publicly speak about, the occult phenomena and powers traditionally associated with advanced training in Yoga. Occult or psychic phenomena were valuable, he taught, insofar as they point toward the attainment of a higher state of consciousness. See Steven Walker, "Vivekananda and American Occultism" in Howard Kerr and Charles Crow, *The Occult in America: New Historical Perspectives* (Urbana: University of Illinois Press, 1983), 162–75.

5. Sister Christine, "Memories of Swami Vivekananda," in Thomas Tweed and Stephen Prothero, eds., *Asian Religions in America*, 146.

6. Paramahansa Yogananda, *Autobiography of a Yogi* (Los Angeles: Self-Realization Fellowship, 1969), 574.

7. The "Aims and Ideals" of the Self-Realization Fellowship are included as an appendix to Yogananda's *Autobiography of a Yogi* (Los Angeles: Self-Realization Fellowship, 1969).

8. Representative selections from the works of most of these popularizers of Asian religious thought can be found in Tweed's and Prothero's *Asian Religions in America*.

9. This list comes from Alan Watt's autobiography, *In My Own Way* (New York: Pantheon Books, 1972), 169 and 237.

10. Alan Watts, *This Is It: and Other Essays on Zen and Spiritual Experience* (New York: Vintage Books, 1973), 90.

11. Ibid., p. 79. In *Beyond Theology: The Art of Godmanship* (New York: Vintage Books, 1973), Watts wrote that "any attempt to marry Vedanta to Christianity must take full account of the fact that Christianity is a contentious faith which requires an all-or-nothing commitment to Jesus as the one and only incarnation of the Son of God" (xii).

12. See Thick Nhat Hanh, *The Miracle of Mindfulness* (Boston: Beacon Press, 1987). A Zen monk since the age of sixteen, Thick Nhat Hanh as become especially influential in teaching both "mindfulness" meditation practices and the ethical imperative of nonviolence.

13. Thomas Tweed estimates that there are 1,515 Buddhist centers in America. See Thomas Tweed, "Asian Religions in the United States: Reflections on an Emerging Subfield" in Walter H. Cosner and Sumner B. Twiss, eds., *Religious Diversity and American Religious History* (Athens: The University of Georgia Press, 1997), 25. In *The Complete Guide to Buddhist America* (Boulder, CO: Shambhala, 1998), Don Morreale lists 1,062 Buddhist meditation centers in North America. Buddhist monasteries focused on Tibetan meditational practices can be found in Berkeley, Boulder, and New Jersey. Theravadin centers stretch from Massachusetts to California, while Zen centers dot the country from Providence to San Francisco and Los Angeles. See Tweed's and Prothero's brief summary of the growth of meditation centers in *Asian Religions in America*, 224–26, 251, 254, 261, and 285.

14. Fritjof Capra, *The Tao of Physics* (Boulder, CO: Shambhala, 1975), 25. See also Gary Zukav's *The Dancing Wu Li Masters: An Overview of the New Physics* (New York: Wiliam Morrow and Co., 1979) and Bruce Holbrook's *The Stone*

Monkey: An Alternative Chinese-Scientific Reality (New York: William Morrow and Co., 1981.

15. Capra, *The Tao of Physics*.

16. See Tweed and Prothero, *Asian Religions in America*, 7.

17. Martin Baumann, "The Dharma Has Come West: A Survey of Recent Studies and Sources," *Journal of Buddhist Ethics*, vol. 4 (1997): 198.

18. See James William Coleman, "The New Buddhism: Some Empirical Findings" in Duncan R. Williams and Christopher S. Queen, eds., *American Buddhism: Methods and Findings in Recent Scholarship* (Richmond, England: Curzon Press, 1999), 91–99.

19. This material, almost verbatim, comes from Peter Gregory's excellent article "Describing the Elephant," *Religion and American Culture* 11 (Summer 2001): 14. Gregory's article thoughtfully reviews recent scholarship on American Buddhism and this entire paragraph relies heavily on his synthesis.

20. Rick Fields, "Divided Dharma: White Buddhists, Ethnic Buddhists, and Racism," in Charles S. Prebish and Kenneth K. Tanaka, eds., *The Faces of Buddhism in America* (Berkeley: University of California Press, 1998), 202.

21. Gregory, "Describing the Elephant," 20.

22. A good point of introduction to feminist religious thought is Carol Christ and Judith Plaskow, eds., *Womanspirit Rising: A Feminist Reader in Religion* (San Francisco: Harper & Row, 1979). Although the selections are now somewhat dated, they provide a concise overview of the major ideas that underlie feminist spiritualities. Early classics in the field include Rosemary Reuther's *Liberation Theology* (New York: Paulist Press, 1972) and *New Woman/New Earth* (New York: Seabury Press, 1975) as well as Mary Daly's *The Church and the Second Sex* (New York: Harper & Row, 1968) and *Beyond God the Father* (Boston: Beacon Press, 1973).

23. Catherine Albanese, *Nature Religion in America: From the Algonkian Indians to the New Age* (Chicago: University of Chicago Press, 1990).

24. See Stephen Fox, *John Muir and His Legacy: The American Conservation Movement* (Boston: Little, Brown, 1981), 53.

25. John Muir, "Anthropocentrism and Predation," cited in Lois K. Daly, "Ecological Activism," in Peter H. Van Ness, ed., *Spirituality and the Secular Quest* (New York: Crossroad, 1996), 448. Daly's essay is an excellent introduction to ecological spiritualities, with special focus on the spiritual dimension of three environmental activists: John Muir, Rachel Carson, and Dave Foreman.

26. Wendell Berry, *A Continuous Harmony* (New York: Harcourt Brace Jovanovich, 1972), 6.

27. Ibid., 7.

28. See Bill Devall and George Sessions, *Deep Ecology* (Salt Lake City: Peregrine Smith Books, 1985).

29. Charlene Spretnak, *The Spiritual Dimension of Green Politics* (Santa Fe, NM: Bear, 1986), 41. An excellent overview of Spretnak's discussion of the spiritual dimensions of commitment to Green causes can be found in Catherine Albanese's *Nature Religion in America*, 173–76. My summary of Spretnak's views

and the quotations I cite come from Albanese's discussion of how Spretnak and other environmental activists factor into the ongoing transmission of "nature religion" in America.

30. Spretak, *The Spiritual Dimensions of Green Politics*, 42.

31. Ibid., 71.

32. Stephan Bodian and Florence Windfall, "Seeing Green," *Yoga Journal* (March/April 1988): 78.

33. See James Lovelock, *Gaia: A New Look at Life on Earth* (New York: Oxford University Press, 1979).

34. Bodian and Windfall, "Seeing Green," 77.

35. See the many essays contained in Jace Weaver, ed., *Defending Mother Earth: Native American Perspectives on Environmental Justice* (New York: Orbis Books, 1996). The quotation comes from the back cover. For an example of recent scholarship arguing that some of the pro-environmental beliefs attributed to traditional Native American societies is a product of recent times, see Sam Gill, *Mother Earth: An American Story* (Chicago: University of Chicago Press, 1987).

36. Vine Deloria, Jr., *God Is Red* (New York: Dell Publishing, 1973).

37. See Catherine Albanese, *America: Religions and Religion* (Belmont, CA: Wadsworth Publishing, 1992), 493.

38. Ibid., 495.

39. Ibid.

40. Helpful introductions to the history and basic teachings of both Neo-Paganism and modern American witchcraft can be found in both J. Gordon Melton's chapter on the "Magick Family" in *Encyclopedia of American Religions*, 5th ed. (Detroit, MI: Gale Research, 1996), 163–70 and Margo Adler's *Drawing Down the Moon: Witches, Druids, Goddess-worshippers and other Pagans in America Today* (New York: Penguin, 1986).

41. See Margaret Murray, *The Witch-Cult in Western Europe* (London, 1931; republished by Oxford University Press, 1962) and Gerald Gardner, *Witchcraft Today* (London: Rider, 1954).

42. Wicca is not a monolithic tradition. Readers might wish to consult "The Wiccan Revival" and "The Craft Today" in Margo Adler's *Drawing Down the Moon* for a succinct overview of the major Wiccan traditions (e.g., Traditionalist, Garderian, Alexandrian, Georgian, NROOGD, Dianic, or the School of Wicca) found in contemporary Britain and America.

43. See Danny Jorgensen and Scott Russell, "American Neopaganism: The Participants' Social Identities," *Journal for the Scientific Study of Religion* 38 (September 1999): 325–38. Jorgensen's and Russell's study includes succinct summaries of previous scholarship on American Neo-Paganism, including a detailed bibliography.

44. Jorgensen and Russell estimate that there are at least 200,000 American Neo-Pagans. In his introduction to *Magical Religion and Modern Witchcraft* (Albany: State University of New York Press, 1996), James R. Lewis estimates that there are about 300,000 serious participants in the Neo-Pagan movement. In an article titled "The Contemporary Neo-Pagan Revival" included in this same vol-

ume, Judy Harrow estimates that there are over 250,000 goddess worshippers in the United States (9).

45. Jorgensen and Russell, "American Neopaganism."

46. Adler, *Drawing Down the Moon*, 22.

47. One of the most influential of all spokespersons for the Neo-Pagan movement, Starhawk, writes that "people tell me over and over again [that the term witch] has negative connotations. It is a word that scares people, word that shocks or elicits nervous, stupid laughter. . . .Yet I prefer the word Witch to prettier words, because the concept of a Witch goes against the grain of the culture of estrangement. It should rub us the wrong way. If it arouses fear or negative assumptions, then those thought-forms can be openly challenged and transformed, instead of molding us unseen from within our minds." See Starhawk, *Dreaming the Dark: Magic, Sex and Politics* (Boston: Beacon Press, 1982), 25.

48. Starhawk, *Dreaming the Dark*, 4.

49. Adler, *Drawing Down the Moon*, viii.

50. Starhawk, *Dreaming the Dark*, 71.

51. See Starhawk, *The Spiral Dance: A Rebirth of the Ancient Religion of the Great Goddess* (San Francisco: HarperSanFrancisco, 1989), 10–11.

52. See Margo Adler, *Drawing Down the Moon*, 415.

53. Ibid., 430–31.

54. Wade Clark Roof, *Spiritual Marketplace: Baby Boomers and the Remaking of American Religion* (Princeton, NJ: Princeton University Press, 1999), 203–12. Roof found that about 15 percent of all Baby Boomers can be considered "dogmatists"; 33 percent are born-again Christians; 25 percent are mainstream believers; and 12 percent are nonreligious secularists.

55. Gallup survey, cited in Robert Wuthnow, *After Heaven: Spirituality in America Since the 1950s* (Berkeley: University of California Press, 1998), 137.

56. Wade Clark Roof, *A Generation of Seekers: The Spiritual Journeys of the Baby Boom Generation* (San Francisco: HarperSanFrancisco, 1993), 9. Roof found, for example, that 47 percent of Boomers believe that "all religions are equal" and that while only 28 percent would prefer to stick to a single faith, 60 percent stated that they would prefer to explore the teachings of other religions. It would seem plausible to conclude that a full 60 percent of the Baby Boomer generation is self-consciously open to the validity of unchurched sources of spiritual understanding and, in this sense, could to some degree or another be described as "spiritual, but not religious."

Chapter Four

1. Claudia Wallis, "Why New Age Medicine is Catching On," *Time* (November 4, 1991): 68–76.

2. David Eisenberg et al., "Unconventional Medicine in the United States: Prevalence, Costs, and Patterns of Use," *New England Journal of Medicine* 328 (28 January 1993): 246–52.

3. A more detailed study of the religious dimensions of alternative medicine can be found in my earlier book, *Alternative Medicine and American Religious Life*

(New York: Oxford University Press, 1989).

4. See the discussion of healing in Gerald Kittel, *Theological Dictionary of the New Testament* (Grand Rapids, MI: Eerdmans, 1978), 3:194–215; Ronald Numbers and Darrel Amundsen, eds., *Caring and Curing: Health and Medicine in the Western Religious Traditions* (New York: Macmillan Publishing Co., 1986); and William Clebsch and Charles Jaekle, *Pastoral Care in Historical Perspective* (New York: Aronson, 1975).

5. Many massage and breathing systems, although emphasizing their known physiological properties, nonetheless frequently make oblique references to metaphysical energies. It is common for massage and breathing therapies to utilize Eastern notions of a subtle body energy such as *ch'i* or *prana* and thus implicitly invoke worldviews in which physical life is seen to be ontologically dependent on sustaining continuous harmony with, or periodically receiving "influxes" from, an ultimate metaphysical reality such as Brahman, the Dao, the Great Ultimate, the Cosmic Body of the Buddha, and so on.

6. D. D. Palmer, *The Chiropractor's Adjuster* (Portland, OR: Portland Printing House, 1910), 35.

7. Ibid., 491.

8. *The Chiropractor* 5 (1909): inside front cover.

9. B. J. Palmer, *Do Chiropractors Pray?* (Davenport, IA: Palmer School of Chiropractic, 1911), 27.

10. Eugene Linden, "My Excellent Alternative Adventure," *Time* (November 4, 1991): 76.

11. G. F. Riekman, "Chiropractic," in *The Holistic Health Handbook* (Berkeley, CA: And/Or Press, 1978), 174.

12. Mary Belknap, Robert Blau, and Rosaline Grossman, eds., *Case Studies and Methods in Humanistic Medicine* (San Francisco: Institute for the Study of Humanistic Medicine, 1975), 18.

13. Herbert A. Otto and James W. Knight, eds., *Dimensions in Wholistic Healing: New Frontiers in the Treatment of the Whole Person* (Chicago: Nelson-Hall, 1979), 3.

14. Ibid.,10.

15. Kenneth Pelletier, *Holistic Medicine* (New York: Delacorte Press, 1979), 93.

16. Norman Cousins, *Anatomy of an Illness* (New York: Norton, 1979).

17. Norman Cousins, *Human Options* (New York: Norton, 1981), 167.

18. "Interview with Bernard Siegel," *ReVision* 7 (Spring 1984): 92.

19. Shirley MacLaine, *Dancing in the Light* (New York: Bantam Books, 1985), 8.

20. Ibid., 37.

21. Ibid., 111.

22. Dolores Krieger, *The Therapeutic Touch* (Englewood Cliffs, NJ: Prentice-Hall, 1979), 13.

23. Ibid., 77.

24. Cited in Ernest Kurtz's history of the movement, *Not-God: A History of Alcoholics Anonymous* (Center City, MN: Hazelden Press, 1979), 19–20. See also Er-

nest Kurtz, "Twelve Step Programs," in Peter H. Van Ness, ed., *Spirituality and the Secular Quest* (New York: Crossroad, 1996), 277–304.

25. *Alcoholics Anonymous*, 2d ed. (New York: Alcoholics Anonymous, 1955), 569.

26. Alcoholics Anonymous, like evangelical Protestantism, believes that recovering personal wholeness requires that we first recognize that we are not in control of our lives. Wholeness is understood to be something that is received, not commanded. Improvement of any kind can proceed only with our prior recognition that we are not-God, but are rather limited in both power and significance. Yet it is this very acknowledgment of our limitation as not-God that makes possible our connection with the Fulfilling Other. Bill W. also paralleled evangelical religion when he organized A.A. into small groups who bring new converts together for weekly rituals at which they describe their previous unworthiness and their subsequent discovery of a higher power.

27. Bill W., cited in Kurtz, *Not-God*, 177.

28. Ibid.

29. Ibid., 178.

30. See *Twelve Steps and Twelve Traditions* (New York: Alcoholics Anonymous, 1952), 63.

31. Ibid., 37.

32. See Deepak Chopra's *Quantam Healing* (New York: Bantam Books, 1990), *Ageless Body, Timeless Mind* (New York: Crown Books, 1994), or *Perfect Weight: The Complete Mind/Body Program for Achieving and Maintaining Your Ideal Weight* (New York: Crown Books, 1996). Chopra's website provides information about his lecture tours, workshops, and seminars. People are also invited to spend time at the spa located at the Chopra Center for Well Being in La Jolla, California. The website includes several testimonials from persons who had stayed at the center:

> I found the 7-day stay to be a significant event in my life. Dr. Chopra's vision, viewpoint, and teachings spurred me to reawaken a dormant spiritual side of myself. I highly recommend the 7-day program for any person, young or old, who is ready to fully and deeply observe and cleanse themselves from top to bottom.—F. Borray

> My week at The Chopra Center for Well Being was magical and miraculous. Healing occurred at all levels of my being through the experience of the program and the unconditional love and support I received.—L. Hanniford

> The mental tools and concepts I learned at the Chopra Center for Well Being have opened up a whole New World for me that I never knew existed. My perspective on life and career has taken a 180-degree turn for the better. The changes in my life as a result of the meditation program have been nothing short of profound. One indication that showed me things were really on track is my golf game. This past Saturday, I shot the best 18 hole round of my life.—T. O'Brien

33. See Deepak Chopra, *The Seven Spiritual Laws of Success: A Practical Guide*

to the Fulfillment of Your Dreams (San Rafael, CA: Amber-Allen, 1994) and *The Way of the Wizard: Twenty Spiritual Lessons for Creating the Life You Want* (New York: Crown Books, 1995).

34. From Deepak Chopra's website: www.chopra.com.

35. Daya Sarai Chocron, *Healing with Crystals and Gemstones* (York Beach, ME: Weiser, 1983), 4.

36. Korra Deaver, *Rock Crystal: The Magic Stone* (York Beach, ME: Weiser, 1985), 40.

37. Ibid., 16.

38. Katrina Raphael, *Crystal Healing: The Therapeutic Application of Crystals and Stones* (New York: Aurora, 1987), 20–21.

39. Deaver, *Rock Crystal*, 7.

40. Mircea Eliade, *Rites and Symbols of Initiation* (New York: Harper & Row, 1965), 3.

41. See Richard Katz, *Boiling Energy: Community Healing among the Kalahari Kung* (Cambridge, MA: Harvard University Press, 1982). This is an excellent study of the role that belief in a subtle energy (which the Kung call *num*) plays in healing individuals and in strengthening commitment to communally held beliefs. Whether called *num*, *kundalini*, *ch'i*, animal magnetism, or *prana*, it would seem that belief in the possibility of experiencing a metaphysical energy is a common feature of initiation into many mystical belief systems. Readers might also wish to consult Catherine Albanese's fine article on the role of belief in subtle energies in American metaphysical religion, "The Subtle Energies of Spirit: Explorations in Metaphysical and New Age Spirituality," *Journal of the American Academy of Religion* 67 (June, 1999): 305–26.

42. *Holistic Health Handbook*, 13.

43. Joy Lubove, "Dual Evolution," *Chiropractor* 5 (1909): 74.

44. Shirley MacLaine, *Dancing in the Light* (New York: Bantam Books, 1985), 110.

45. Cited in Krieger, *Therapeutic Touch*, 108.

46. Janet Quinn, "Therapeutic Touch: One Nurse's Evolution as a Healer," in *Therapeutic Touch: A Book of Readings*, ed. Marianne Borelli and Patricia Heidt (New York: Springer, 1981), 62. See in the same book: Patricia Heidt, "Scientific Research and Therapeutic Touch"; Marianne Borelli, "Meditation and Therapeutic Touch"; Janet Macrae, "Therapeutic Touch: A Way of Life"; and Honore Fontes, "Self-Healing: Getting in Touch with Self to Promote Healing."

47. William James, "The Will to Believe," in *The Will to Believe* (New York: Dover, 1956), 3.

Chapter Five

1. Martin Gross, *The Psychological Society* (New York: Basic Books, 1978), 8, 4. A more penetrating critique of the cultural consequences of psychological thought can be found in Philip Rieff, *The Triumph of the Therapeutic* (New York: Harper & Row, 1966).

2. Christopher Lasch, *The Culture of Narcissism* (New York: Warner, 1979), 33.

3. My earlier work, *Americans and the Unconscious* (New York: Oxford University Press, 1986), provides an extended analysis of the religious origins of academic psychology.

4. Baldwin, Hall, Starbuck, Leuba, and Coe all at one time anticipated a career in the ministry before redirecting their energies to a more scientifically based means of studying and nourishing human nature. All specifically attributed their career shift to the inability of their conversion experiences to hold up under the pluralizing forces of modern life. With the possible exception of James Leuba, who was more interested in refuting than refurbishing religious thought, all were trying to develop new ways of thinking religiously. See their respective autobiographies in Vergilius Ferm's *Religion in Transition* (New York: Macmillan Publishing Co., 1937) and E. G. Boring and G. Lindzey, *A History of Psychology in Autobiography* (New York: Appleton-Century-Crofts, 1967).

5. An excellent discussion of how psychological theories emerged to (1) "explain away" competing religious models and (2) advance new, liberal religious models can be found in Ann Taves, *Fits, Trances, & Visions* (Princeton, NJ: Princeton University Press, 1999). Other helpful studies of religious factors in the rise of modern psychology are Peter Homans, "A Personal Struggle with Religion: Significant Fact in the Lives and Work of the First Psychologists," *Journal of Religion* 62 (1982): 128–44, and Peter Homans, *Jung in Context* (Chicago: University of Chicago Press, 1980).

6. Edwin Starbuck, *The Psychology of Religion* (New York: Charles Scribner's Sons, 1901), 108.

7. Ibid., 105. Emphasis mine.

8. Ibid., 146.

9. Edwin Starbuck, "Religion's Use of Me," in Vergilius Ferm, *Religion in Transition*, 204.

10. Ibid., 202.

11. Dorothy Ross, *G. Stanley Hall: The Psychologist as Prophet* (Chicago: University of Chicago Press, 1972), 45.

12. G. S. Hall, *Life and Confessions of a Psychologist* (New York: D. Appleton, 1923), 359.

13. G. S. Hall, "The New Psychology," pt. 2, *Andover Review* 3 (March, 1885): 248.

14. G. S. Hall, *Adolescence*, 2 vols. (New York: D. Appleton, 1904), 2:342.

15. Hall, "The New Psychology," 126.

16. Two helpful starting points for assessing William James's influence on the history of American psychology would be the introductory essay by Gerald Meyers and Rand Evans in William James, *The Principles of Psychology*, 3 vols. (Cambridge, MA: Harvard University Press, 1983) and Joseph Adelson, "Still Vital After All These Years," *Psychology Today* 16 (April, 1982): 52–59.

17. Three helpful starting points for assessing the influence of *The Varieties of Religious Experience* would be the introductory essay by John E. Smith in William James, *The Varieties of Religious Experience* (Cambridge, MA: Harvard University Press, 1985), Donald Capps and Janet Jacobs, ed., *The Struggle for Life: A Com-*

panion to William James's The Varieties of Religious Life (Society for the Scientific Study of Religion, 1995), and Robert C. Fuller, "Fresh Takes on a Classic: William James's Varieties Approaches its Centennial," *Religious Studies Review* 26 (April 2000): 151–55.

18. Henry James once confided to his close friend Ralph Waldo Emerson that he ought to "learn science and bring myself first into men's respect, that thus I may better speak to them." Quoted in Ralph Barton Perry, *The Thought and Character of William James*, 2 vols. (Boston: Little, Brown, 1935), 1: 30. This assumption that metaphysics can, and should, be rooted in sound empirical knowledge prefigured the course of William's own transition from physiology to psychology, and finally to philosophy and religious reflection.

19. William James, *Principles of Psychology*, quoted in Clebsch, 145.

20. Erik Erikson, *Young Man Luther* (New York: W. W. Norton, 1962), 67.

21. Henry James, Jr., ed., *Letters of William James* (Boston: Kraus Reprint Co., 1969), 1: 130.

22. William James, *The Varieties of Religious Experience*, 190, 403.

23. See Robert A. McDermott's introduction to William James, *Essays in Psychical Research* (Cambridge, MA: Harvard University Press, 1986). Other discussions of James's interest in psychical research can be found in Gardner Murphy and Robert O. Ballou, eds., *William James on Psychical Research* (New York: Viking Press, 1960) and R. Laurence Moore, *In Search of White Crows: Spiritualism, Parapsychology, and American Culture* (New York: Oxford University Press, 1977).

24. James, *Varieties*, 408.

25. Ibid., 406.

26. Ibid., 403.

27. James, *A Pluralistic Universe* (New York: E. P. Dutton, 1971), 267.

28. Ibid., 266.

29. James, *Varieties*, 406.

30. Ibid., 98.

31. Ibid., 94.

32. William Clebsch, *American Religious Thought* (Chicago: University of Chicago Press, 1973), 171.

33. Perry Miller, *Errand into the Wilderness* (Cambridge: Belknap Press, 1975), 185.

34. Ibid., 192.

35. William Clebsch's *American Religious Thought* is an extended argument for including William James in the "From Edwards to Emerson" tradition of what he calls aesthetic spirituality. See also the chapter titled "The Psyche as Symbol" in my *Americans and the Unconscious* for a discussion of how Perry Miller's "From Edwards to Emerson" also illuminates the American psychological tradition.

36. For a more extensive account of the patterns by which psychoanalysis was assimilated into American psychological thought, see Chapter 5 of my *Americans and the Unconscious*; Nathan Hale's *Freud and the Americans: The Beginning of Psychoanalysis in the United States, 1876–1907* (New York: Oxford University Press, 1977); David Shakow and David Rapaport, *The Influence of Freud on Amer-*

ican Psychology (New York: International Universities Press, 1964); Joseph Adelson, "Freud in America: Some Observations," *American Psychologist* (1956): 467–70; and F. H. Matthews, "The Americanization of Sigmund Freud: Adaptations of Psychoanalysis Before 1917," *Journal of American Studies* 1 (1967): 39–62.

37. John B. Watson, "Psychology as the Behaviorist Views It," *Psychological Review* 20 (1913): 158–77.

38. For a more thorough examination of the symbolic and cultural dimensions of behaviorism, see Chapter 6 of my *Americans and the Unconscious;* Don Browning's *Pluralism and Personality* (Lewisburg, PA: Bucknell University Press, 1980); David Bakan, "Behaviorism and American Urbanization," *Journal of the History of the Behavioral Sciences* 2 (1966): 5–28; and Paul Creelan., "Watsonian Behaviorism and the Calvinist Conscience," *Journal of the History of the Behavioral Sciences* 10 (1974): 95–118.

39. Abraham Maslow, *Toward a Psychology of Being* (Princeton, NJ: D. Van Nostrand Co., 1962), ix.

40. *Journal of Humanistic Psychology* 1 (1961): vii.

41. Rollo May, *Existence* (New York: Simon and Schuster, 1958), 10.

42. See, for example, Robert E. Valelt, "Carl Gustav Jung (1875–1961): Some Contributions to Modern Psychology," *Journal of Humanistic Psychology* 2 (1962): 23–34, and John Levy, "Transpersonal Psychology and Jungian Psychology," *Journal of Humanistic Psychology* 23 (1983): 42–51.

43. See Carl Jung, *Memories, Dreams, and Reflections* (New York: Random House, 1961), 109.

44. See Joseph Campbell, *The Hero with a Thousand Faces* (Princeton, NJ: Princeton University Press, 1972) and Thomas Moore, *The Care of the Soul* (New York: HarperCollins, 1992).

45. Abraham Maslow, *Religions, Values, and Peak Experiences* (New York: Viking Press, 1970), xvi.

46. Maslow, *Toward a Psychology of Being,* 333.

47. Ibid., 277.

48. Maslow, *Religions, Values, and Peak Experiences,* 54.

49. Ibid., viii.

50. Maslow, *The Farther Reaches of Human Nature* (New York: Viking Press, 1972), 112.

51. Ibid., 115.

52. Maslow, *Religions, Values, and Peak Experiences,* 45.

53. Ibid., 55.

54. I have previously written two articles that explore the religious and cultural significance of Carl Rogers's psychology: "Carl Rogers, Religion, and the Role of Psychology in American Culture," *Journal of Humanistic Psychology* 22 (1982): 21–32, and "Rogers' Impact on Pastoral Counseling and Contemporary Religious Reflection," in Ronald Levant and John Shlien, eds., *Client-Centered Therapy and the Person-Centered Approach: New Directions in Theory, Research and Practice* (New York: Praeger, 1984).

55. Carl Rogers, autobiographical essay in E. G. Boring and G. Lindzey, eds., *A*

History of Psychology in Autobiography, 5: 351. Readers might also wish to read the autobiographical essay, "This Is Me" included in his *On Becoming a Person* (Boston: Houghton Mifflin, 1961).

56. Boring and Lindzey, *A History of Psychology in Autobiography,* 354.

57. Ibid., 355.

58. Carl Rogers, *Client-Centered Therapy* (Boston: Houghton Mifflin, 1965), 522.

59. In a personal communication dated March 21, 1981, Dr. Rogers responded to this point by informing me:

> You have rather shrewdly picked out Emerson. I did a great deal of personal reading during my adolescence (that is, reading not required by school or college), and Emerson was one of my favorites. ... The notion that a divine force might be a struggling force, struggling to express itself through my life and yours, as well as through the physical universe, has always appealed to me.

60. Carl Rogers, *A Way of Being* (Boston: Houghton Mifflin, 1980), 106.

61. Ibid., 122.

62. Carl Rogers, "The Formative Tendency," *Journal of Humanistic Psychology* 18 (1978): 25. Emphasis mine.

63. Rogers, *A Way of Being,* 8.

64. Ibid., 124.

65. Ibid., 137.

66. Ibid., 88.

67. Ibid., 228.

68. See Max Weber, *The Protestant Ethic and the Spirit of Capitalism* (New York: Charles Scribner's and Sons, 1958). A discussion of the scholarly influence of, and debates over, Weber's thesis can be found in Roy Anker's *Self-Help and Popular Religion in Early American Culture* (Westport, CT: Greenwood Press, 1999).

69. Roy Anker's *Self-Help and Popular Religion in Early American Culture* includes a lengthy discussion (including helpful bibliographical information) of Franklin's role in the origins of the American self-help tradition.

70. William Clebsch uses the category of "aesthetic spirituality" to show the continuities that persist in the "from Edwards to Emerson to James" tradition in American religious life. See his *American Religious Thought.*

71. Among Elizabeth Towne's books were *Joy Philosophy* (Chicago: Psychic Research Co., 1903), *Making Money: How to Grow Success* (Holyoke, MA: E. Towne Co., 1929), and *Practical Methods for Self-Development* (Holyoke, MA: E. Towne Co., 1904). Frank Haddock authored a multivolume Power Book Library with such titles as *Power for Success through Culture of Vibrant Magnetism* (Auburndale, MA: Powerbook Library, 2nd. ed., 1910) and *The Power of Will: A Practical Companion-book for Unfoldment of Selfhood through Direct Personal Culture* (Auburndale, MA: Powerbook Library, 2nd ed., 1907). Orison Swett Marden's books include *The Miracle of Right Thought* (New York: Thomas Y. Crowell Co., 1917), *Peace, Power and Plenty* (New York: Thomas Crowell Co., 1909), and

He Who Thinks He Can (New York: Thomas Crowell Co., 1908). Brief descriptions of their careers can be found in Charles Braden, *Spirits in Rebellion: The Rise and Development of New Thought* (Dallas, TX: Southern Methodist University Press, 1977). Scholarly critiques of this genre of popular psychology can be found in Gail Thain Parker's *The History of Mind Cure in New England* (Hanover, NH: University Press of New England, 1973) and Donald Meyer, *The Positive Thinkers* (New York: Doubleday and Co., 1965).

72. William James, "The Gospel of Relaxation" in *Talks to Teachers* (New York: W. W. Norton, 1958) and "The Energies of Men" in *Essays on Faith and Morals* (New York: Meridian, 1962).

73. Carol George has written an excellent biography of Peale: *God's Salesman: Norman Vincent Peale and the Power of Positive Thinking* (New York: Oxford University Press, 1993). See also the extended discussion of Peale's life and thought in Roy Anker's *Self-Help and Popular Religion in Modern American Culture* (Westport, CT: Greenwood Press, 1999).

74. Norman Vincent Peale, *A Guide to Confident Living* (New York: Prentice-Hall, 1948), 154.

75. Norman Vincent Peale, *The Power of Positive Thinking* (New York: Prentice-Hall, 1952), 55.

76. Ibid., 267.

77. Anker, *Self-Help and Popular Religion in Modern American Culture*, 119. Anker's overview of the criticisms leveled against Peale's views is well-balanced and thorough.

78. Peale, *A Guide to Confident Living*, 11 and 161.

79. Anker, *Self-Help and Popular Religion in Modern American Culture*, 119.

80. M. Scott Peck, *The Road Less Traveled* (New York: Touchstone, 1978), 192.

81. Ibid., 243.

82. For a helpful overview of Rev. Elwood Worcester's ministry and a history of the Emanuel movement see Sanford Gifford's *The Emmanuel Movement* (Boston: Francis Countway Library of Medicine, 1996). Readers might also wish to consult E. Brooks Holifield's excellent *A History of Pastoral Care in America* (Nashville, TN: Abingdon, 1983).

83. William Clebsch and Charles Jaekle, *Pastoral Care in Historical Perspective* (New York: Prentice-Hall, 1964).

84. One of the first to notice this shift was Karl Menninger in his *Whatever Became of Sin?* (New York: Hawthorn Books, 1973). Menninger's main thesis was that in unquestioningly adopting psychological theories, Christian ministers simultaneously strayed from their biblical foundations. Another look at the cultural effects of modern psychological understandings is Paul Vitz's *Psychology as Religion: The Cult of Self-Worship* (Grand Rapids, MI: Eerdmans, 1977).

85. Roy Anker, *Self-Help and Popular Religion in Modern American Culture*, 123.

Chapter Six

1. Robert Wuthnow, *After Heaven: Spirituality in America Since the 1950s*

(Berkeley: University of California Press, 1998), 3.

2. Ibid., 1.

3. Wade Clark Roof, *Spiritual Marketplace: Baby Boomers and the Remaking of American Religion* (Princeton, NJ: Princeton University Press, 1999), 7.

4. William James, *The Varieties of Religious Experience* (Cambridge, MA: Harvard University Press, 1985), 399.

5. When describing the mind-cure movement, William James observed that "The idea of a universal evolution lends itself to a doctrine of general meliorism and progress which fits the religious needs of the healthy-minded so well that it seems almost as if it might have been created for their use. Accordingly we find 'evolutionism' interpreted thus optimistically and embraced as a substitute for the religion they were born in, by a multitude of our contemporaries who have either been trained scientifically, or been fond of reading popular science, and who had already begun to be inwardly dissatisfied with what seemed to them the harshness and irrationality of the orthodox Christian scheme." Ibid., 81.

6. Robert Bellah, Richard Madsen, William Sullivan, Ann Swidler, and Steven Tipton, *Habits of the Heart* (Berkeley: University of California Press, 1985), 221.

7. Ibid., 237.

8. Wuthnow, 134.

9. William James, *The Varieties of Religious Experience*, 136.

10. I have presented a detailed argument concerning how alternative medical systems promote "healthy narcissism" in my *Alternative Medicine and American Religious Life* (New York: Oxford University Press, 1989), 129–36.

11. Wade Clark Roof, *A Generation of Seekers: The Spiritual Journeys of the Baby Boom Generation* (San Francisco: HarperSanFrancisco, 1993), 79–83.

12. James, *Varieties*, 80.

13. I might refer readers to my earlier discussion of the use of psychological models to differentiate between mature and immature spirituality in *Religion and the Life Cycle* (Philadelphia: Fortress Press, 1988).

14. Gordon Allport, *The Individual and His Religion* (New York: Macmillan Publishing Co., 1950).

15. See Meredith McGuire, "Mapping Contemporary Spirituality: A Sociological Perspective," *Christian Spirituality Bulletin* 5 (Spring, 1997): 5.

16. James Fowler, *Stages of Faith* (San Francisco: Harper & Row, 1981).

17. Fowler also acknowledges a Stage Seven, what he terms the stage of "universalizing faith." Stage Seven is rare. It is to be found in the religious orientation of those few individuals who develop a selfless identification with all that lives. While these persons surely live *in* the world in that they are agents of caring action, they are in other ways not *of* this world at all. They experience the Ultimate as a live, felt reality. They consider themselves to be members of a cosmic community (frequently referred to with symbols such as the Kingdom of God, Nirvana, Cosmic Consciousness). These rare individuals respond to this awareness by helping to overcome oppression, brutality, and divisions of all kinds. They seem instinctively to know how to relate to others affirmingly, forming deep bonds with persons at other stages of faith development and from other faith traditions.

18. Roof, *Spiritual Marketplace*, 314.

19. See Roger Finke and Rodney Stark, *The Churching of America, 1776–1990* (New Brunswick, NJ: Rutgers University Press, 1992), 16.

20. Roof, *Spiritual Marketplace*, 121.

21. Ibid.

22. A more complete discussion of how Paul Tillich's work helps us understand unchurched spirituality can be found in my essay "Holistic Health Practices" included in Peter Van Ness, ed., *Spirituality and the Secular Quest* (New York: Crossroad, 1996), 227–50.

Appendix

1. My first book, *Mesmerism and the American Cure of Souls* (Philadelphia: University of Pennsylvania Press, 1982) charted the course of the first psychological theory to attract American audiences who were eager to develop a new, psychologically phrased theory of the self and the self's relationship to immanent divine forces. I extended this study with two subsequent books: *Americans and the Unconscious* (New York: Oxford University Press, 1986) traced the spiritual importance of psychological theories of the unconscious from the time of Emerson to the late twentieth century while *Alternative Medicine and American Religious Life* (New York: Oxford University Press, 1989) explored the various ways in which alternative healing systems have simultaneously promulgated alternative metaphysical worldviews. Finally, *Stairways to Heaven: Drugs and American Religious History* (Boulder, CO: Westview Press, 1999) traces the role that mood-altering substances have played in Americans' pursuit of both spiritual ecstasy and religious community.

2. Meredith McGuire, "Mapping Contemporary American Spirituality: A Sociological Perspective," *Christian Spirituality Bulletin* 5 (Spring, 1997): 4.

3. Wade Clark Roof, *A Generation of Seekers: The Spiritual Journeys of the Baby Boom Generation* (San Francisco: HarperSanFrancisco, 1994), 82.

Index